CHELSEA HOUSE PUBLISHERS

Modern Critical Views

Further titles in preparation.

Modern Critical Views

SAUL BELLOW

Modern Critical Views

SAUL BELLOW

Edited with an introduction by

Harold Bloom

Sterling Professor of the Humanities
Yale University

CHELSEA HOUSE PUBLISHERS
New York
Philadelphia

813
SAU

THE COVER:
Saul Bellow is depicted in the desolate urban context of his *The Dean's December,* which ambiguously compounds the darker aspects of Chicago and of Eastern European urban blight.—H.B.

PROJECT EDITORS: Emily Bestler, James Uebbing
ASSOCIATE EDITOR: Maria Behan
EDITORIAL COORDINATORS: Karyn Gullen Browne
EDITORIAL STAFF: Laura Ludwig, Joy Johannessen, Linda Grossman, Peter Childers
DESIGN: Susan Lusk

Cover illustration by Robin Peterson. Photos courtesy of AP/Wide World and UPI/Bettmann.

Printed and bound in the United States of America

10   9   8   7   6   5   4   3   2

Library of Congress Cataloging in Publication Data

Saul Bellow.
  (Modern critical views)
  Bibliography: p.
  Includes index.
  1. Bellow, Saul—Criticism and interpretation—
Addresses, essays, lecutures.   I. Bloom, Harold,   II. Series.
PS3503.E4488Z845   1986   813'.52   85-5964
ISBN 0-87754-622-3

Contents

Editor's Note

This volume gathers together more than three decades of criticism devoted to the fiction of Saul Bellow. Because much of the best of that criticism has been in the form of book reviews, there are relatively brief reviews here by Robert Penn Warren, Irving Howe, John Bayley, John Hollander and Cynthia Ozick. There are also critical essays, or chapters of longer studies, by Richard Chase, Daniel Hughes, Tony Tanner, John Jacob Clayton, Earl Rovit, Gilead Morahg, David Kerner, Alvin B. Kernan, Jeanne Braham and Daniel Fuchs. I have also included excerpts from longer pieces by Frank McConnell and Malcolm Bradbury. Together with my "Introduction," they provide eighteen very varied perspectives upon the American novelist of most significance in the period between Faulkner and Pynchon.

This book is arranged chronologically, and thereby demonstrates something of the evolving shape of Bellow criticism, from early emphases upon the ideological stances of Bellow and the central figures of his novels, through an increasing preoccupation with his and their inner conflicts and dilemmas, on to a more recent series of attempts to contextualize his work in the traditions of nineteenth- and twentieth-century literature. Though no broad agreements have emerged in critical judgment, there does seem to be a common awareness both of Bellow's essential and possibly permanent place in those traditions, and of limitations in his work that make ultimate judgments problematic. What seems clearest is his achievement in comic invention and narrative force. What seems unsettled may have as much to do with his cultural polemics as with the aesthetic achievement of his fiction. Since he is very much still at work, even thirty years of criticism represents only an introductory exploration of his novels and stories.

Introduction

I

By general critical agreement, Saul Bellow is the strongest American novelist of his generation, presumably with Norman Mailer as his nearest rival. What makes this canonical judgment a touch problematic is that the indisputable achievement does not appear to reside in any single book. Bellow's principal works are: *The Adventures of Augie March*, *Herzog*, *Humboldt's Gift*, and in a briefer compass, *Seize the Day*. The earlier novels, *Dangling Man* and *The Victim*, seem now to be period pieces, while *Henderson the Rain King* and *Mr. Sammler's Planet* share the curious quality of not being quite worthy of two figures so memorable as Henderson and Mr. Sammler. *The Dean's December* is a drab book, its dreariness unredeemed by Bellow's nearly absent comic genius.

Herzog, still possessing the exuberance of *Augie March*, while anticipating the tragi-comic sophistication of *Humboldt's Gift*, as of now seems to be Bellow's best and most representative novel. And yet its central figure remains a wavering representation, compared to some of the subsidiary male characters, and its women seem the wish-fulfillments, negative as well as positive, of Herzog and his creator. This seems true of almost all of Bellow's fiction: a Dickensian gusto animates a fabulous array of secondary and minor personalities, while at the center a colorful but shadowy consciousness is hedged in by women who do not persuade us, though evidently once they persuaded him.

In some sense, the canonical status of Bellow is already assured, even if the indubitable book is still to come. Bellow's strengths may not have come together to form a masterwork, but he is hardly the first novelist of real eminence whose books may be weaker as aggregates than in their component parts or aspects. His stylistic achievement is beyond dispute, as are his humor, his narrative inventiveness, and his astonishing inner ear, whether for monologue or dialogue. Perhaps his greatest gift is for creating subsidiary and minor characters of grotesque splendor, sublime in their vivacity, intensity and capacity to surprise. They may be caricatures, yet their vitality seems permanent: Einhorn, Clem Tembow, Bateshaw, Valentine Gersbach, Sandor Himmelstein, Von Humboldt Fleisher, Cantabile, Alec Szathmar. Alas, compared to them, the narrator-heroes, Augie, Herzog, and Citrine, are diffuse beings, possibly because Bellow cannot disengage from them, despite heroic efforts and revisions. I remember *Augie March* for Einhorn, *Herzog* for Gersbach, *Humboldt's Gift* for Humboldt, and even that last preference tends to throw off-center an apprehension of the novel. Augie March and Herzog narrate and speak with tang and eloquence, yet they themselves are less memorable than what they say. Citrine, more subdued in his language, fades yet more quickly into the continuum of Bellow's urban cosmos. This helps compound the aesthetic mystery of Bellow's achievement. His heroes are superb observers, worthy of their Whitmanian heritage. What they lack is Whitman's Real Me or Me Myself, or else they are blocked from expressing it.

II

Few novelists have ever surpassed Bellow at openings and closings:

> I am an American, Chicago born—Chicago, that somber city—and go at things as I have taught myself, free-style, and will make the record in my own way: first to knock, first admitted; sometimes an innocent knock, sometimes a not so innocent. But a man's character is his fate, says Heraclitus, and in the end there isn't any way to disguise the nature of the knocks by acoustical work on the door or gloving the knuckles.

> . . . Look at me, going everywhere! Why, I am a sort of Columbus of those near-at-hand and believe you come to them in this immediate *terra incognita* that spreads out in every gaze. I may well be a flop at this line of endeavor. Columbus too thought he was a flop, probably, when they sent him back in chains. Which didn't prove there was no America.

The end and the start cunningly interlace, very much in the mode of *Song of Myself*, or of the first and last chapters of Emerson's *Nature*. Augie too is an American Transcendentalist, a picaresque quester for the god within the self. *Ethos* is the *Daimon*, both passages say, with Augie as ethos and Columbus as the daimon. One remembers the aged Whitman's self-identification in his "Prayer of Columbus," and it seems right to rejoice, as Whitman would have rejoiced, when Augie comes full circle from going at things, self-taught and free-style, to discovering those near-at-hand, upon the shores of America. That is Bellow at his most exuberant. When weathered, the exuberance remains, but lies in shadow:

If I am out of my mind, it's all right with me, thought Moses Herzog.

Some people thought he was cracked and for a time he himself had doubted that he was all there. But now, though he still behaved oddly, he felt confident, cheerful, clairvoyant, and strong. He had fallen under a spell and was writing letters to everyone under the sun . . . Hidden in the country, he wrote endlessly, fanatically, to the newspapers, to people in public life, to friends and relatives and at last to the dead, his own obscure dead, and finally the famous dead.

. . . Perhaps he'd stop writing letters. Yes, that was what was coming, in fact. The knowledge that he was done with these letters. Whatever had come over him during these last months, the spell, really seemed to be passing, really going. He set down his hat, with the roses and day lilies, on the half-painted piano, and went into his study, carrying the wine bottles in one hand like a pair of Indian clubs. Walking over notes and papers, he lay down on his Récamier couch. As he stretched out, he took a long breath, and then he lay, looking at the mesh of the screen, pulled loose by vines, and listening to the steady scratching of Mrs. Tuttle's broom. He wanted to tell her to sprinkle the floor. She was raising too much dust. In a few minutes he would call down to her, "Damp it down, Mrs. Tuttle. There's water in the sink." But not just yet. At this time he had no messages for anyone. Nothing. Not a single word.

Another *ritorno*, but this time the cycle has been broken. Augie March, like Emerson and Whitman, knows that there is no history, only biography. Moses Herzog has been a long time discovering this truth, which ends his profession, and Charlie Citrine also goes full-circle:

The book of ballads published by Von Humboldt Fleisher in the Thirties was an immediate hit. Humboldt was just what everyone had been waiting for. Out in the Midwest I had certainly been waiting eagerly, I can tell you that. An avant-garde writer, the first of a new generation, he was handsome, fair, large, serious, witty, he was learned. The guy had it all. All the papers reviewed his book. His picture appeared in *Time* without insult and in *Newsweek* with praise. I read *Harlequin Ballads* enthusiastically. I was a student at the University of Wisconsin and thought about nothing but literature day and night. Humboldt revealed to me new ways of doing things. I was ecstatic. I envied his luck, his talent, and his fame, and I went east in May to have a look at him— perhaps to get next to him. The Greyhound bus, taking the Scranton route, made the trip in about fifty hours. That didn't matter. The bus windows were open. I had never seen real mountains before. Trees were budding. It was like Beethoven's *Pastorale*. I felt showered by the green, within . . . Humboldt was very kind. He introduced me to people in the Village and got me books to review. I always loved him.

. . . Within the grave was an open concrete case. The coffins went down and then the yellow machine moved forward and the little crane, making a throaty whir, picked up a concrete slab and laid it atop the concrete case. So the coffin was enclosed and the soil did not come directly upon it. But then, how did one get out? One didn't, didn't, didn't! You stayed, you stayed! There was a dry light grating as of crockery when contact was made, a sort of sugarbowl sound. Thus, the condensation of collective intelligences and combined ingenuities, its cables silently spinning, dealt with the individual poet . . .

Menasha and I went toward the limousine. The side of his foot brushed away some of last autumn's leaves and he said, looking through his goggles, "What this, Charlie, a spring flower?"

"It is. I guess it's going to happen after all. On a warm day like this everything looks ten times deader."

"So it's a little flower," Menasha said. "They used to tell one about a kid asking his grumpy old man when they were walking in the park, 'What's the name of this flower, Papa?' and the old guy is peevish and he yells, 'How should I know? Am I in the millinery business?' Here's another, but what do you suppose they're called, Charlie?"

"Search me," I said. "I'm a city boy myself. They must be crocuses."

The cycle is from Citrine's early: "I felt showered by the green, within" to his late, toneless, "They must be crocuses," removed from all affect not because he has stopped loving Humboldt, but because he is chilled preternaturally by the effective if unfair trope Bellow has found for the workings of canonical criticism: "Thus, the condensation of collective intelligences and combined ingenuities, its cables silently spinning, dealt with the individual poet." There is no history, and now there is also no biography, but only the terrible dehumanizing machine of a technocratic intelligentsia, destroying individuality and poetry, and stealing from the spring of the year the green that no longer is to be internalized.

III

Bellow's endless war against each fresh wave of literary and intellectual modernism is both an aesthetic resource and an aesthetic liability in his fiction. As resource, it becomes a drive for an older freedom, an energy of humane protest against over-determination. As liability, it threatens to become repetition, or a merely personal bitterness, even blending into Bellow's acerbic judgments upon the psychology of women. When it is most adroitly balanced, in *Herzog*, the polemic against modernism embraces the subtle infiltrations of dubious ideologies into the protesting

Moses Herzog himself. When it is least balanced, we receive the narrative rant that intrudes into Mr. Sammler's cosmos, or the dankness that pervades both Chicago and Bucharest in *The Dean's December*. Like Ruskin lamenting that the water in Lake Como was no longer blue, Bellow's Alexander Corde tells us that "Chicago wasn't Chicago anymore." What *The Dean's December* truly tells us is that "Bellow wasn't Bellow anymore," in this book anyway. The creator of Einhorn and Gersbach and Von Humboldt Fleisher gives us no such figure this time around, almost as though momentarily he resents his own genius for the high comedy of the grotesque.

Yet Bellow's lifelong polemic against the aestheticism of Flaubert and his followers is itself the exuberant myth that made *Augie March*, *Herzog* and *Humboldt's Gift* possible. In an act of critical shrewdness, Bellow once associated his mode of anti-modernist comedy with Svevo's *Confessions of Zeno* and Nabokov's *Lolita*, two masterpieces of ironic parody that actually surpass Bellow's *Henderson the Rain King* in portraying the modernist consciousness as stand-up comic. Parody tends to negate outrage, and Bellow is too vigorous to be comfortable at masking his own outrage. When restrained, Bellow is too visibly restrained, unlike the mordant Svevo or the Nabokov who excels at deadpan mockery. Henderson may be more of a self-portrait, but Herzog, scholar of High Romanticism, better conveys Bellow's vitalistic version of an anti-modernistic comic stance. Bellow is closest to Svevo and to Nabokov in the grand parody of Herzog-Hamlet declining to shoot Gersbach-Claudius when he finds the outrageous adulterer scouring the bathtub after bathing Herzog's little daughter. Daniel Fuchs, certainly Bellow's most careful and informed scholar, reads this scene rather too idealistically by evading the parodic implications of "Moses might have killed him now." Bathing a child is our sentimental version of prayer, and poor Herzog, unlike Hamlet, *is* a sentimentalist, rather than a triumphant rejecter of nihilism, as Fuchs insists.

Bellow, though carefully distanced from Herzog, is himself something of a sentimentalist, which in itself need not be an aesthetic disability for a novelist. Witness Samuel Richardson and Dickens, but their sentimentalism is so titanic as to become something different in kind, a sensibility of excess larger than even Bellow can hope to display. In seeking to oppose an earlier Romanticism (Blake, Wordsworth, Whitman) to the belated Romanticism of literary modernism (Gide, Eliot, Hemingway), Bellow had the peculiar difficulty of needing to avoid the heroic vitalism that he regards as an involuntary parody of High Romanticism (Rimbaud, D. H. Lawrence, and in a lesser register, Norman Mailer).

Henderson, Bellow's Gentile surrogate, is representative of just how that difficulty constricts Bellow's imagination. The Blakean dialectic of Innocence and Experience, clearly overt in the scheme of the novel, is at odds with Henderson's characteristically Bellovian need for punishment or unconscious sense of guilt, which prevails in spite of Bellow's attempts to evade Freudian over-determination. Though he wants and indeed needs a psychology of the will, Bellow is much more Freudian than he can bear to know. Henderson is a superbly regressive personality, very much at one with the orphan child he holds at the end of the novel. Dahfu, of whom Norman Mailer strongly approved, is about as persuasive a representation as are his opposites in Bellow, all of those sadistic and compelling fatal ladies, pipe-dreams of a male vision of otherness as a castrating force. Bellow disdains apocalypse as a mode, but perhaps the Bellovian apocalypse would be one in which all of the darkly attractive women of these novels converged upon poor Dahfu, Blakean vitalist, and divested him of the emblem of his therapeutic vitalism.

Without his polemic, Bellow never seems able to get started, even in *Humboldt's Gift*, where the comedy is purest. Unfortunately, Bellow cannot match the modernist masters of the novel. In American fiction, his chronological location between, say, Faulkner and Pynchon exposes him to comparisons he does not seek yet also cannot sustain. Literary polemic within a novel is dangerous because it directs the critical reader into the areas where canonical judgments must be made, as part of the legitimate activity of reading. Bellow's polemic is normative, almost Judaic in its moral emphases, its passions for justice and for more life. The polemic sometimes becomes more attractive than its aesthetic embodiments. Would we be so charmed by Herzog if he did not speak for so many of us? I become wary when someone tells me that she or he "loves" *Gravity's Rainbow*. The grand Pynchonian doctrine of sado-anarchism scarcely should evoke *affection* in anyone, as opposed to the shudder of recognition that the book's extraordinary aesthetic dignity demands from us. It is the *aesthetic* failure of Bellow's polemic, oddly combined with its moral success, that increasingly drives Bellow's central figures into dubious mysticisms. Citrine's devotion to Rudolf Steiner is rather less impressive, intellectually and aesthetically, than the obsessive Kabbalism of *Gravity's Rainbow*. If Steiner is the ultimate answer to literary modernism, then Flaubert may rest easy in his tomb.

IV

And yet Bellow remains a humane comic novelist of superb gifts, almost unique in American fiction since Mark Twain. I give the last words here to what moves me as the most beautiful sequence in Bellow, Herzog's final week of letters, starting with his triumphant overcoming of his obsession with Madeleine and Gersbach. On his betraying wife, Herzog is content to end with a celebration now at last beyond masochism: "To put on lipstick, after dinner in a restaurant, she would look at her reflection in a knife blade. He recalled this with delight." On Gersbach, with his indubitable, latently homosexual need to cuckold his best friend, Herzog is just and definitive: "*Enjoy her—rejoice in her. You will not reach me through her, however. I know you sought me in her flesh. But I am no longer there.*" The unmailed messages go on, generously assuring Nietzsche of Herzog's admiration while telling the philosopher: "*Your immoralists also eat meat. They ride the bus. They are only the most bus-sick travelers.*" The sequence magnificently includes an epistle to Dr. Morgenfruh, doubtless a Yiddish version of the Nietzschean Dawn of Day, of whom Herzog wisely remarks: "He was a splendid old man, only partly fraudulent, and what more can you ask of anyone?" Addressing Dr. Morgenfruh, Herzog speculates darkly "that the territorial instinct is stronger than the sexual." But then, with exquisite grace, Herzog signs off: "*Abide in light, Morgenfruh. I will keep you posted from time to time.*" This benign farewell is made not by an overdetermined bundle of territorial and sexual instincts, but by a persuasive representative of the oldest ongoing Western tradition of moral wisdom and familial compassion.

ROBERT PENN WARREN

The Man with No Commitments

The *Adventures of Augie March* is the
third of Saul Bellow's novels, and by far the best one. It is, in my opinion,
a rich, various, fascinating, and important book, and from now on any
discussion of fiction in America in our time will have to take account of
it. To praise this novel should not, however, be to speak in derogation of
the two earlier ones, *The Dangling Man* and *The Victim*. Both of these
novels clearly indicated Saul Bellow's talent, his sense of character,
structure, and style. Though *The Dangling Man* did lack narrative drive, it
was constantly interesting in other departments, in flashes of characterization, in social and psychological comment. In *The Victim*, however,
Bellow developed a high degree of narrative power and suspense in dealing
with materials that in less skillful hands would have invited an analytic
and static treatment. These were not merely books of promise. They
represented—especially *The Victim*—a solid achievement, a truly distinguished achievement, and should have been enough to win the author a
public far larger than became his. They did win the attention of critics
and of a hard core of discriminating readers, but they were not popular.

The Dangling Man and *The Victim* were finely wrought novels of
what we may, for lack of a more accurate term, call the Flaubert-James
tradition. Especially *The Victim* depended much on intensification of effect
by tightness of structure, by limitations on time, by rigid economy in
structure of scene, by placement and juxtaposition of scenes, by the unsaid
and withheld, by a muting of action, by a scrupulous reserved style. The
novel proved that the author had a masterful control of the method, not

From *The New Republic* 13, vol. 129 (October 26, 1953). Copyright © 1953 by *The
New Republic*.

merely fictional good manners, the meticulous good breeding which we ordinarily damn by the praise "intelligent."

It would be interesting to know what led Saul Bellow to turn suddenly from a method in which he was expert and in which, certainly, he would have scored triumphs. It would be easy to say that it had been from the beginning a mistake for him to cultivate this method, to say that he was a victim of the critical self-consciousness of the novel in our time, to say that in his youthful innocence he had fallen among the thieves of promise, the theorizers. Or it would be easy to say that the method of the earlier books did not accommodate his real self, his deepest inspiration, and that as soon as he liberated himself from the restriction of the method he discovered his own best talent.

These things would be easy to say but hard to prove. It would be equally easy to say that the long self-discipline in the more obviously rigorous method had made it possible for Bellow now to score a triumph in the apparent formlessness of the autobiographical-picaresque novel, and to remember, as a parallel, that almost all the really good writers of free verse had cultivated an ear by practice in formal metrics. I should, as a matter of fact, be inclined to say that *The Adventures of Augie March* may be the profit on the investment of *The Dangling Man* and *The Victim,* and to add that in a novel of the present type we can't live merely in the hand-to-mouth way of incidental interests in scene and character, that if such a novel is to be fully effective the sense of improvisation must be a dramatic illusion, the last sophistication of the writer, and that the improvisation is really a pseudo-improvisation, and that the random scene or casual character that imitates the accidental quality of life must really have a relevance, and that the discovery, usually belated, of this relevance is the characteristic excitement of the genre. That is, in this genre the relevance is deeper and more obscure, and there is, in the finest examples of the genre, a greater tension between the random life force of the materials and the shaping intuition of the writer.

It is the final distinction, I think, of *The Adventures of Augie March* that we do feel this tension, and that it is a meaningful fact. It is meaningful because it dramatizes the very central notion of the novel. The hero Augie March is a very special kind of adventurer, a kind of latter-day example of the Emersonian ideal Yankee who could do a little of this and a little of that, a Chicago pragmatist happily experimenting in all departments of life, work, pleasure, thought, a hero who is the very antithesis of one of the most famous heroes of our time, the Hemingway hero, in that his only code is codelessness and his relish for experience is instinctive and not programmatic. This character is, of course, the character made for the random shocks and aimless corners of experience, but he is not merely irresponsible. If he wants freedom from commitment, he also wants wisdom, and in the end utters a philosophy, the philosophy embodied by the French serving maid Jacqueline, big-legged and red-nosed and ugly, standing in a snowy field in Normandy, hugging still her irrepressibly romantic dream of going to Mexico.

But is this comic and heroic philosophy quite enough, even for Augie? Augie himself, I hazard, scarcely thinks so. He is still a seeker, a hoper, but a seeker and hoper aware of the comedy of seeking and hoping. He is, in fact, a comic inversion of the modern stoic, and the comedy lies in the tautology of his wisdom—our best hope is hope. For there is a deep and undercutting irony in the wisdom and hope, and a sadness even in Augie's high-heartedness, as we leave him standing with Jacqueline in the winter field on the road toward Dunkerque and Ostend. But to return to the proposition with which this discussion opened: if Augie plunges into the aimless ruck of experience, in the end we see that Saul Bellow has led him through experience toward philosophy. That is, the aimless ruck had a shape, after all, and the shape is not that of Augie's life but of Saul Bellow's mind. Without that shape, and the shaping mind, we would have only the limited interest in the random incidents.

The interest in the individual incidents is, however, great. In *The Victim* the interest in any one episode was primarily an interest in the over-all pattern, but here most incidents, and incidental characters, appeal first because of their intrinsic qualities, and, as we have said, our awareness of their place in the overall pattern dawns late on us. In incident after incident, there is brilliant narrative pacing, expert atmospheric effect, a fine sense of structure of the individual scene. In other words, the lessons learned in writing the earlier books are here applied in another context.

As for characterization, we find the same local fascination. The mother, the grandmother, the feeble-minded brother, the brother drunk on success, the whole Einhorn family, Thea, the Greek girl—they are fully realized, they compel our faithful attention and, in the end, our sympathy. As a creator of character, Saul Bellow is in the great tradition of the English and American novel, he has the fine old relish of character for character's sake, and the sort of tolerance which Santayana commented on in Dickens by saying that it was the naturalistic understanding that is the nearest thing to Christian charity.

It is, in a way, a tribute, though a back-handed one, to point out the faults of Saul Bellow's novel, for the faults merely make the virtues more impressive. The novel is uneven. Toward the last third the inspiration seems to flag now and then. Several episodes are not carried off with the characteristic elan, and do not, for me at least, take their place in the thematic pattern. For instance, the Trotsky episode or the whole Stella affair, especially in the earlier stages. And a few of the characters are stereotypes, for example, Stella again. In fact, it is hard to see how she got into the book at all except by auctorial fiat, and I am completely baffled to know what the author thought he was doing with her, a sort of vagrant from some literary province lying north-northeast of the *Cosmopolitan Magazine.* Furthermore, several critics have already said that the character of Augie himself is somewhat shadowy. This, I think, is true, and I think I know the reason: it is hard to give substance to a character who has no commitments, and by definition Augie is the man with no commitments. This fact is a consequence of Bellow's basic conception, but wouldn't the very conception have been stronger if Augie had been given the capacity for deeper commitments, for more joy and sorrow? He might, at least, have tried the adventurer's experiment in those things? That is, the character tends now to be static, and the lesson that Augie has learned in the end is not much different from the intuition with which he started out. He has merely learned to phrase it. There is one important reservation which, however, I should make in my criticism of Augie. His very style is a powerful device of characterization. It does give us a temper, a texture of mind, a perspective of feeling, and it is, by and large, carried off with a grand air. Which leads me to the last observation that the chief release Saul Bellow has found in this book may be the release of a style, for he has found, when he is at his best, humor and eloquence to add to his former virtures.

RICHARD CHASE

The Adventures of Saul Bellow

W̲ith the publication of *Henderson the Rain King*, Saul Bellow confirms one's impression that he is just about the best novelist of his generation. The new book has faults; it is uneven, it is sometimes diffuse. And besides the liability of its real faults, it makes its appeal to literary qualities which, although very much in the American tradition, Serious Readers have learned during the last decades to scorn. For much of its length *Henderson* is a "romance" rather than a "novel." It forfeits some of the virtues of the novel (realism, plausibility, specificity), but gains some of the virtues of romance (abstraction, freedom of movement, extreme expressions of pathos, beauty, and terror). The book is sometimes farcical, melodramatic, zany—qualities that Serious Readers know, know all too well, are inferior to Realism and Tragedy. But *Henderson* has realism and tragedy too, although not so much as some of Bellow's other writings.

Bellow has chosen a fertile subject—a demented American aristocrat at loose ends and in search of his soul. This is a subject which, before *Henderson the Rain King*, few if any American novelists had thought of using, except at the relatively low level of imaginative intensity that characterizes the polite novel of manners. In the brutal, loony, yet finally ennobled Henderson we have a character who for dire realism and significant modernity far surpasses in dramatic intensity the frustrated aristocrats portrayed by writers like Edith Wharton and J. P. Marquand. It is interesting, by the way, that of the few reviewers of *Henderson* I have read, none mentioned the patrician heritage of the hero, although this heritage is of cardinal importance in understanding him. It is as if the reviewers still

From *Commentary* 27 (April 1959). Copyright © 1959 by *Commentary*.

regard "an aristocrat" as nothing but a walking collection of manners and therefore unsuitable for portraiture in anything but a novel of manners. Yet even in democratic America the well-born may receive as part of their birthright a certain dynamism, a distortion of character, a tendency to extreme behavior, or other qualities not easily expressed by a novel of manners.

One praises *Henderson the Rain King* in spite of the fact that in some ways it is not up to the high level Bellow set in *The Adventures of Augie March* and in the short novel *Seize the Day*, the best single piece Bellow has written. It is a thinner brew than *Augie* (but what novel isn't?) and less sustained and concentrated in its impact than *Seize the Day*. After the wonderful first forty pages or so, during which we see Henderson on his home grounds, Connecticut and New York, there is a distinct falling off. We doubt whether Bellow should have sent him off so soon to Africa, where most of his adventures occur. We perceive that the author is not always able to make his highly imaginative Africa into an adequate setting for his hero. We fear that Bellow is in danger of confusing Henderson with another pilgrim to Africa, Hemingway. We feel that the book wanders uncertainly for a bad hour or so in the middle. But then it begins to pull itself together again, overcomes the threadbare plot, and triumphantly concludes in a mad moment of tragi-comedy.

The book's shortcomings, along with certain qualities that strike me as real virtues, have led some Bellow devotees to put *Henderson* down as a failure or at best a misguided lark in a never-never land (if *Augie* is Bellow's *Huck Finn*, is not *Henderson* his *Connecticut Yankee in King Arthur's Court?*). But these adverse judgments are wrong. Bellow still works in a comic tradition that is greater than farce or the comedy of manners. He has not only farce and wit but also humor—a richer thing, being permeated with realism, emotion, and love of human temperament. His imagination is fecund and resourceful. His tradition, at a hazard, includes, besides the naturalistic novel, Mark Twain, Walt Whitman, Joyce, and Yiddish humor.

Over the years Bellow's writing has shown a great deal of flexibility and power of development. He did not start off with the big Thomas Wolfe attempt at an autobiographical first novel. He saved that subject until his third book, *Augie March*, and by doing so possibly avoided the fate of many young writers who have a special story to tell, such as that of being brought up in an immigrant family in an American city, but who find that after the story has been told, they have nothing else to say. True, Bellow's first novel, *Dangling Man*, was ostensibly autobiographical and in some of its passages it caught the experience of a young intellectual in the uncertain days of our involvement in World War II. Yet the story was told with so much reticence as to give a thin, claustral quality to the whole. Bellow's second novel, *The Victim,* was one of those books published in the years just after the war that seemed to promise a resurgence of American writing (and yet how many new writers of those days have failed to fulfill themselves!). As compared with *Dangling Man, The Victim* was notable for its increase in objectivity and drama, and for its picture of the complicated relations between a disorderly, drunken, middle-class Gentile and a hapless but morally self-directing Jew in search of a precarious status. Here Bellow was dealing with what was to be his favorite theme—the impulse of human beings to subject others to their own fate, to enlist others in an allegiance to their own moral view and version of reality. In *The Victim* it is the Jew Leventhal who must resist the attempt of the anti-Semitic Allbee to involve him in his fate. This theme gets its fullest treatment in *Augie March,* but finds its ultimate significance in *Seize the Day.*

The Adventures of Augie March first acquainted us with the formidable music Bellow can make when he pulls out all the stops. Like many other fine American books, it astonishes us first as a piece of language. There are the rather dizzy medleys of colloquial and literary words. For example, Grandma Lausch, the picturesque tyrant of the family in which Augie is brought up, is said to be "mindful always of her duty to wise us up, one more animadversion on the trusting, loving, and simple surrounded by the cunning hearted and the tough." "Not," says Augie, "that I can see my big, gentle, dilapidated, scrubbing, and lugging mother as a fugitive of immense beauty from such classy wrath." There is no doubt that Augie, who tells the whole story in the first-person, is right in describing himself as "gabby." A wayward adolescent, almost a juvenile delinquent, he sometimes seems to resemble Marlon Brando. But he is not sullen and inarticulate in the modern style of American youth—far from it. Like any Rabelais, Whitman, Melville, or Joyce, he loves to catalog things, such as the people in the Chicago City Hall: "bigshots and operators, commissioners, grabbers, heelers, tipsters, hoodlums, wolves, fixers, plaintiffs, flatfeet, men in Western hats and women in lizard shoes and fur coats, hothouse and arctic drafts mixed up, brute things and airs of sex, evidence of heavy feeding and systematic shaving, of calculations, grief, not-caring, and hopes of tremendous millions in concrete to be poured or whole Mississippis of bootleg whisky and beer."

Augie is a real poet and lover of the tongue which his immigrant race has only just learned to speak. He loves to explore its resources. And we don't complain much if he is sometimes a bit on the flashy side, a little pretentious and word-besotted in the language he hurls at our heads. Often he is perfectly simple and as appealing as Huckleberry Finn, whom he sometimes reminds us of, while he is still a boy and beset by odd illusions. If Mark Twain had been willing to use the four-letter word, he might have made Huck say, as Augie does, "I understand that British aristocrats are still legally entitled to piss, if they should care to, on the hind wheels of carriages."

Augie is hard to characterize, and of course that is the point about him. He declines the gambit of the young man in an immigrant family; he does not have the drive to succeed or establish himself in a profession. Believing that to commit oneself to any sort of function in the going concern of society is a form of death, he remains unattached and free, although to what end we never fully learn. He is a little of everything: a student, a petty thief, adopted son, tramp, lover, apprentice to assorted people and trades, a would-be intellectual in the purlieus of the University of Chicago, a supposititious Trotskyite, an eagle tamer, a merchant seaman. He is protean, malleable, "larky and boisterous," vain, strong, vital, and also a bit of a fall-guy, in fact "something of a schlemiel." The plot of *Augie March* is that of Whitman's *Song of Myself*—the eluding of all of the identities proffered to one by the world, by one's past, and by one's friends. Augie calls himself "varietistic," just as Whitman says, "I resist anything better than my own diversity." "What I assume, you shall assume," writes Whitman. And Augie reflects on "what very seldom mattered to me, namely, where I came from, parentage, and other history, things I had never much thought of as difficulties, being democratic in temperament, available to everybody and assuming about others what I assumed about myself." Augie remains elusive and diverse. His fate is not that of any of the memorable people he knows: Grandma Lausch, his brother Simon, Mrs. Renling, Einhorn, Sylvester, Clem Tambow, Mimi, Thea, Stella.

Not that Augie is entirely happy about himself, or sure in his own mind that varietism and freedom from ties will lead him to individual autonomy. Bellow seems to leave him wavering as the novel draws to a close. At one point Augie calls for autonomy, for the unattached individual—"a man who can stand before the terrible appearances" without subjecting himself to any of them. He wants to take the "unsafe" road and be a "personality" rather than take the safe road and be a "type." He resists being "recruited" to other people's versions of reality and significance. And yet Augie strikes us as being puzzled, as we are, by the questions: What *is* his personality, what *is* his version of reality and significance? At any rate we find him wishing that his fate "was more evident, and that I could quit this pilgrimage of mine." At the end he is married and in Paris, "in the bondage of strangeness for a time still," yet oddly wishing that he could return to the States and have children. But even the idea of paternity is not allowed to thwart his desire for unattached selfhood. Where, he asks, is character made? And he answers that "It's internally done . . . in yourself you labor, you wage and combat, settle scores, remember insults, fight, reply, deny, blab, denounce, triumph, outwit, overcome, vindicate, cry, persist, absolve, die and rise again. All by yourself! Where is everybody? Inside your breast and skin, the entire cast." But all this sounds less like an autonomous personality than a man far gone in solipsism and illusion. Augie's concluding words belie the "oath of unsusceptibility" he has taken. At the end he exclaims, "Why, I am a sort of Columbus of those near-at-hand and believe you can come to them in this immediate *terra incognita* that spreads out in every gaze." Augie's wish that people could "come to" each other entirely without any ulterior motive or aggression is praiseworthy, but we share his doubts that they ever can.

"A man's character is his fate," Augie says at the beginning and end of his story. But the question, What is his character? is not answered. The idea of character in *Augie March* is contradictory. Bellow is, from one point of view, in the line of the naturalistic novelists (Norris, Dreiser, and Farrell—who have also written about Chicago), and he therefore conceives of character deterministically as the product of heredity and environment. "All the influences were lined up waiting for me," says Augie. "I was born, and there they were to form me, which is why I tell you more of them than of myself." On the other hand, as I said above, Bellow follows the Whitman tradition, which believes that character is the autonomous self, the given transcendent fact which no amount of natural conditioning can fundamentally change. The naturalistic account is incomplete because it tries to describe only what *produces* character; the transcendentalist account is vague, however liberating and inspiring it may be. A logical difficulty or a moral or metaphysical anomaly doesn't necessarily spoil a fiction. And in fact it strikes me that it is exactly Bellow's mixture of attitudes toward character that makes his novel such a rich experience.

What Augie fears is the death of the self, and his judgment of the contemporary world is that it is terribly resourceful in its stratagems for destroying the self. In *Seize the Day* Tommy Wilhelm comes to understand the death of the self in a harrowing scene in a funeral parlor, a scene more profound and moving than anything the bumptious Augie undergoes. Wilhelm, middleaging, an unemployed salesman, separated from his wife and two children, is on the ebb tide of his fortunes. The scene is in and about a hotel on Broadway and not the least value of the story is the accuracy with which Bellow has reproduced the bleak gerontocracy which has gathered there from all parts of New York and Europe—the "senior citizens," as our culture calls them, the forlorn octogenarians, the wistful widowers, the grimy, furtive old women. One of the aged is Wilhelm's father, a retired doctor with a professional sense of success and rectitude, who regards his hesitant romantic son as "a slob." Malleable like Augie, but less resilient, Wilhelm allows his career to be spoiled at the outset by putting himself under the guidance of Maurice Venice, who promises to get him a job as a movie star but turns out to be a pimp. He has lost, or given up, his job as a salesman of baby furniture, and now is at the mercy of the recriminations directed at him by his father and his wife. Of course, they have their point, but Wilhelm is not entirely wrong in thinking that there is something sinister and inhumanly aggressive in their nagging insistence that (as Augie would say) he allow himself to be recruited to *their* versions of reality.

But in trying to escape from his father and his wife, Wilhelm comes under the influence of Dr. Tamkin, who, whatever else we may think of him, is certainly one of Bellow's most glorious creations. Reminiscing, Augie March had exclaimed, "Why did I always have to fall among theoreticians!" It is a poignant question, suggesting that in a world where no one is certain about truth, everyone is a theoretician. And to the fastest theorizer goes the power; he is the one who can "seize the day." Dr. Tamkin, investor, alleged psychiatrist, poet, philosopher, mystic, confidence man, is one of the fast talkers. He is an adept in the wildly eclectic world of semi-enlightenment and semi-literacy which constitutes the modern mass mind when it expresses itself in ideas, the crazy world of half-knowledge, journalistic clichés, popularized science, and occultism, the rags and tatters of the world's great intellectual and religious heritages. Bellow is a master at describing this state of mind, and a sound moralist in suggesting that a Dr. Tamkin would be less reprehensible if he were merely greedy and materialistic, like the characters in naturalistic novels—but, no, he must also be a mystic, a psychiatrist, and a theoretician. And so Wilhelm, the well meaning, not too bright ordinary man, is all the more bewildered and devastated when the seven hundred dollars he has given Tamkin to invest in lard is lost and he is ruined.

Wandering the streets in search of Tamkin, who seems to appear and disappear in the crowds like a ghost, Wilhelm is jostled by a group of mourners into a funeral parlor where, standing by the coffin of a man he does not know, he weeps uncontrollably for his own symbolic death, the death of the self. In this scene we have in its deepest expression one side of the meaning (as I understand the difficult idea) of Augie's apothegm: "Well, given time, we all catch up with legends, more or less." The same idea is expressed in the odd English of the somewhat incredible King Dahfu in Bellow's new novel: "The career of our specie is evidence that one imagination after another grows literal. . . . Imagination! It converts to actual. It sustains, it alters, it redeems! . . . What Homo sapiens imagines, he may slowly convert himself to." But the human power of actualizing the imaginary is a two-edged sword, which can destroy as well as redeem. We can be destroyed if, as in his moment of final anguish and illumination Wilhelm understands he has done, we allow ourselves to be recruited to, allow ourselves to become actualizations of, other people's versions of reality. Yet catching up with the legend or realizing the imaginary can also be liberating and redemptive. So we gather at the moment when Wilhelm catches up with the legend of his own death—a legend that has been entertained by himself and by those he has known—while he gazes, with the great revelation, at the stranger in the coffin.

Thus it appears that although Bellow's insistence on being free is not a complete view of human destiny, neither is it simply a piece of naivety or moral irresponsibility, as has sometimes been suggested. He believes that if we ever define our character and our fate it will be because we have caught up with our own legend, realized our own imagination. Bellow's fertile sense of the ever-possible conversion of reality and imagination, fact and legend, into each other is the source of the richness and significance of his writing. He differs in this respect from the traditional practice of American prose romance, which forces the real and imaginary far apart and finds that there is no circuit of life between them. (On this point see my book, *The American Novel and Its Tradition.*) Bellow differs, too, from the pure realist, who describes human growth as a simple progress away from legend and toward fact, and from the naturalistic novelist, who conceives of circumstance as always defeating the human impulse of further thrusts toward autonomy. Which is merely to say that Bellow's sense of the conversion of reality and imagination is something he shares with the greatest novelists.

Bellow gives the light treatment to some of his favorite themes in *Henderson the Rain King,* although there are tragi-comic moments which for the extreme expression of degradation and exaltation surpass anything in the previous books. With a fatal predictability, the conventional reviewers, often in the midst of encomia, have reproved Bellow for "descending" to farce, as well as to melodrama and fantasy. It does no good to ask where writers so different as Mark Twain, Dickens, Molière, Joyce, and Aristophanes would be without farce.

This is Bellow's first novel with no Jewish characters (although we hear at the beginning of a soldier named Nicky Goldstein, who told Henderson that after the war he was going to raise mink; with characteristic sensibility, Henderson decides on the spot that he will raise pigs). Perhaps in selecting for his hero a tag-end aristocrat, Bellow is responding in reverse to Henry Adams's statement at the beginning of the *Education* that as a patrician born out of his time he might as well have been born Israel Cohen. At any rate we find Henderson ruefully reflecting that despite the past eminence of his family, "Nobody truly occupies a station in life any more. . . . There are displaced persons everywhere." As Henderson at fifty-five freely admits, he has always behaved "like a bum." His father, though, had been an impressive example of rectitude; he had known Henry Adams and Henry James; the family eminence goes back at least to Federal times. His father had followed the traditional life of public service. He had written books of social and literary criticism, defended persecuted Negroes, and in general regarded it as his inherited duty to help guide the national taste, opinion, and conduct in his day.

As for Henderson himself, he cheerfully admits that he is one of the "loony" members of the family—like the one that "got mixed up in the Boxer Rebellion, believing he was an Oriental" or the one that "was carried away in a balloon while publicizing the suffrage movement." Yet he still affirms—to the point of rainmaking for the parched inhabitants of Africa—the "service ideal" that "exists in our family." Like Wilhelm in *Seize the Day*, he has faced death, not in the war but while gazing at the soft white head of an octopus in an aquarium. "This is my last day," he thought on that occasion. "Death is giving me notice." But Henderson is strong, brutal, willful, with great stature and a big belly. Very much a creature of his time, he "seeks wisdom," believing that earlier generations have performed all the more practical tasks—"white Protestantism and the Constitution and the Civil War and capitalism and winning the West," all these things have been accomplished. But, he goes on, "that left the biggest problem of all, which was to encounter death. We've just got to do something about it . . . it's the destiny of my generation of Americans to go out into the world and try to find the wisdom of life." True, Henderson is often retrospective. He has moments of family nostalgia and piety, when he tries to get in touch with his dead father and mother. For this purpose he goes to the cellar and plays a violin (a genuine Guarnerius, of course) that had belonged to his father. He croons, "Ma, this is 'Humoresque' for you" and "Pa, listen—'Meditation from Thaïs.' " As we see, Henderson is not only musical but occult. He is "spell-prone . . . highly mediumistic and attuned."

But Henderson does not find fulfillment in such activities. He is bored and dissatisfied with his disorderly wife. Like most moderns he loves and pursues "reality" and yet he is just as strongly drawn to the mythic and the magical. He is alternately depressed and exalted by his inchoate notions, in describing which Bellow shows himself again to be an inspired interpreter of the eclectic, semi-literate mind of contemporary culture. Henderson needs new realms to discover, new opportunities of service and redemption. And so he is off to Africa, an Africa which is sometimes that of fantasy ("those were wild asses maybe, or zebras flying around in herds") and sometimes that of Sir James Frazer and Frobenius.

He finds in Africa that there is a curse upon the land. A terrible drought is killing the cattle of the first tribe he encounters, for although the cistern is full of water, the water is infested with frogs, which frighten the cattle away and which the natives have a taboo against killing. Henderson improvises a grenade to blow up the frogs, but blows up the whole cistern too. This is unfortunate because things had been going well for him. For example, Henderson had been absorbing animal magnetism from the natives, as when he ceremonially kisses the fat queen's belly: "I kissed, giving a shiver at the heat I encountered. The knot of the lion skin was pushed aside by my face, which sank inward. I was aware of the old lady's navel and her internal organs as they made sounds of submergence. I felt as though I were riding in a balloon above the Spice Islands, soaring in hot clouds while exotic odors rose from below."

But it is with the next tribe, the Wariri, that his most significant adventures occur. Here Henderson performs the ritual of moving the ponderous statue of the Rain Goddess, whereupon he is made Rain King, stripped naked, flayed, and thrown into the mud of the cattle pond, in the midst of the downpour he has summoned from heaven by his act. Humiliated, abject, yet gigantic, triumphant, visionary, an Ivy-League medicine man smeared with blood and dirt, Henderson dances on his bare feet through the cruel, hilarious scene. "Yes, here he is," cries our hero, "the mover of Mummah, the champion, the Sungo. Here comes Henderson of the U.S.A.—Captain Henderson, Purple Heart, veteran of North Africa, Sicily, Monte Cassino, etc., a giant shadow, a man of flesh and blood, a restless seeker, pitiful and rude, a stubborn old lush with broken bridge-work, threatening death and suicide. Oh, you rulers of heaven! Oh, you dooming powers! . . . And with all my heart I yelled, 'Mercy, have mercy!' And after that I yelled, 'No justice!' And after that I changed my mind and cried, 'No, no, truth, truth!' And then, 'Thy will be done! Not my will but Thy will!' This pitiful rude man, this poor stumbling bully, lifting up his call to heaven for truth. Do you hear that?"

There ensue several lengthy conversations on life and human destiny between Henderson and the philosophical King Dahfu—a somewhat pathetic monarch whom we often see surrounded by his demanding harem of naked women. He has read books like William James's *Principles of Psychology* and believes that when he dies his soul will be reborn in a lion, the totem animal of the tribe. Like the naturalistic novelists, Bellow is fond of characterizing people by analogies with animals. But Bellow, like Swift, follows the greater comic traditions of animal imagery. Tommy Wilhelm caricatures himself as a hippopotamus, yet the effect is to make him more human, more understandable, more complicated, rather than less so.

What might be called Bellow's totemistic style of comedy and character drawing gets a full workout in *Henderson*. A raiser of pigs and a self-proclaimed bum, Henderson has thought of himself as a pig. King Dahfu believes that what Henderson needs is rehabilitation in the image of the lion totem, and he therefore puts our hero through a course of what can only be described as lion-therapy, complete with psychiatric terms like "resistance" and "transference." This takes place in a cage under the palace, where the king keeps a magnificent lioness. The therapy consists in repeated exposure to the lioness, first getting Henderson to try to quell his fears of her and finally getting him to imitate the lioness, on his hands and knees, growling and roaring, so that by sympathetic magic he can absorb lion-like qualities. The scene in which he is finally able to roar satisfactorily, though still terrified, is a great comic moment. The king and the lioness watch Henderson "as though they were attending an opera performance." Henderson describes the roar he lets out as one which "summarized my entire course on this earth, from birth to Africa; and certain words crept into my roars, like 'God,' 'Help,' 'Lord have mercy,' only they came out 'Hoolp!' 'Moooorcy!' It's funny what words sprang forth. 'Au secours,' which was 'Secooooor' and also 'De profoooondis,' plus snatches from the 'Messiah' (He was despised and rejected, a man of sorrows, etcetera). Unbidden, French sometimes came back to me, the language in which I used to taunt my little friend François about his sister." In this abject, ridiculous, and yet eloquent roar we are impressed with the full pathos, the utter humiliation, and also the odd marginal grandeur of Henderson. After this he writes a letter to his wife directing her to apply for his admission to the Medical Center, signing the application "Leo E. Henderson" (although his name is Eugene). For now he is resolved to become the M.D. he has always dreamed of being since, as a boy, he had been inspired by the example of Sir Wilfred Grenfell. Of course the letter never arrives.

Henderson escapes from the Wariri after King Dahfu has been killed trying to capture the lion who is his father. One need hardly bother about the plot—the conniving witch doctor, the escape from prison, the hazardous flight of Henderson. It is all pleasant enough in the reading.

But the end is magnificent. Here we have Henderson walking around the blank, wintry airport in Newfoundland, where his plane has put down for refueling. He is paternally carrying in his arms an American child who speaks only Persian and is being sent alone to Nevada. He remembers how his own father had been angry at him once when he was a boy and how he had hitch-hiked to Canada, where he had got a job at a fair. His task was to accompany and care for an aged, toothless, and forlorn trained bear who was ending his days of performing by taking rides on a roller-coaster, though paralyzed by fear and vertigo and occasionally wetting himself, for the delectation of the crowds who watched from below. "We hugged each other, the bear and I, with something greater than terror and flew in those gilded cars. I shut my eyes in his wretched, time-abused fur. He held me in his arms and gave me comfort. And the great thing is that he didn't blame me. He had seen too much of life, and somewhere in his huge head he had worked it out that for creatures there is nothing that ever runs unmingled." Henderson the boy is long dead; Henderson the lion has disappeared, so has Henderson the pig. Henderson the bear remains, "long-suffering, age-worn, tragic, and discolored." Still a rather preposterous clown, he has nevertheless achieved a certain nobility by his way of "mingling" in the common fate of creatures. Will he remain Henderson the bear? Not if he can live up to the declarations of freedom and growth he made earlier in the book. "I am Man . . . and Man has many times tricked life when life thought it had him taped." And, though saddened, he had agreed with King Dahfu that "Nature is a deep imitator. And as man is the prince of organisms he is the master of adaptations. He is the artist of suggestions. He himself is his principal work of art, in the body, working in the flesh. What miracle! What triumph! Also, what disaster! What tears are to be shed!"

The king's words strike Bellow's "note." His main characters— Augie, Tommy Wilhelm, Henderson—are adept at imitation and at adapatation. They are different, to be sure. Augie remains young, strong, charming, yet emotionally soft. Wilhelm is wistful, unstable, romantic. Henderson is wild, brutal, a clown. But they are all malleable, emergent, pragmatic, and protean; they love freedom, development, pleasure, and change. They seek both natural and transcendent experiences that are expressive of their way of life.

What is so far chiefly missing in Bellow's writing is an account of what his heroes want to be free *from*. As Bellow is always showing, their very adaptibility lays them open to forms of tyranny—social convention, a job, a father, a lover, a wife, their children, everyone who may want to prey upon them. And all of these forms of tyranny, fraud, and emotional expropriation Bellow describes brilliantly. But only in *Seize the Day* is there a fully adequate, dramatically concentrated image of what the central figure is up against—the institutional, family, and personal fate that he must define himself by, as heroes in the greatest literature define themselves. *Augie March* is prodigiously circumstantial, but the circumstances are never marshaled into a controlling image, and Henderson is bundled off to Africa before we see enough of him in his native habitat to know fully, by understanding the circumstances of his life, what his character and his fate are. But who can complain when, once he is in Africa, we see him in episodes which make us think him the momentary equal, for tragi-comic madness, for divine insanity, of the greatest heroes of comic fiction?

DANIEL HUGHES

Reality and the Hero

Both Vladimir Nabokov's *Lolita* and
Saul Bellow's *Henderson the Rain King* are important novels, important in
theme and important in structure, important for what they reveal about
contemporary reality and for what they demonstrate about the novel itself
and its much-heralded crisis. Written by two of our finest novelists,
problematical, tragi-comic, appearing at crucial moments in the careers of
each writer, they put demands on our attention which we cannot ignore.
Yet despite the respectful press each has received, the numerous reviews,
and the best sellerdom of one of these novels, they remain baffling,
original, and sportive books, leaving each critic with his own theory, each
reader with his private experience. I would like to show how a reading of
these books in conjunction might throw light on what they are "really
about," and how, both as success and failure, each novel illuminates the
problems of the contemporary novelist.

I

The aesthetic bankruptcy of naturalism is a twice-told tale; even the kind
of realism we associate with the great nineteenth-century masterpieces of
the novel, Russian, French, and English, no longer seems viable as a
mode for our best novelists. After Joyce and Kafka, the novel, bitten by
poetry and teased into symbolism and allegory, has withdrawn from a
social milieu it can no longer describe or is no longer interested in. The

From *Saul Bellow and the Critics*, edited by Irving Malin. Copyright © 1967 by New
York University Press.

newest experimental writing moves in one of two directions, toward the pure evocation of objects in a hero-less world, as in Robbe-Grillet and Nathalie Sarraute, or toward a withdrawal from objects into an isolate self, a hero without a world, feeding on himself as in Samuel Beckett. Beckett's heroes, indeed, have even lost the ability to communicate the role of self, the hero of *The Unnamable* confessing that

> the fact would seem to be, if in my situation one may speak of facts, not only that I shall have to speak of things of which I cannot speak, but also which is even more interesting, but also that I, which is if possible even more interesting, that I shall have to, I forget, no matter. At the same time I am obliged to speak. I shall never be silent. Never.

The self collapses into incoherence here; the work of fiction exists only as a self-defeating triumph of method. But even when parody threatens to topple the whole enterprise, the formula of return to the world is suggested: "In the frenzy of utterance the concern with truth. Hence the interest of a possible deliverance by means of encounter. But not so fast. First dirty, then make clean." The encounter which the self desires here is the experience of something real, the real being defined as that which is not the self; the method suggested is the familiar purgative rite of withdrawal and return, the return giving us back a world which the novelist may still communicate and describe, although in Beckett this description does not exist.

Humbert Humbert and Henderson are not pushed so far out by their creators and they are brought back closer to the reality they seem to evade. Yet, as first-person narrators, as characters whose individual reality dominates the books in which they appear, they come closer to the solipsistic protagonists of Beckett than they do to the characterless consciousness of the hero in Nathalie Sarraute's *Portrait of a Man Unknown.* At the same time, they must be distinguished from the picaresque heroes of Kingsley Amis and John Wain whose existences serve largely the purpose of setting forth a sharply realized milieu which is under attack or criticism. Yet, even here, as Raymond Williams has pointed out concerning these "realistic" novels, "for all their genuine relevance and records of actual feelings, their final version of reality is parodic and farcical." *Lolita* and *Henderson the Rain King* begin with a version of reality that is parodic and farcical and end with a vision of parody overcome and farce turned to real anguish and real discovery. While we sense in Beckett's Malones and Molloys real anguish degenerating to unintentional farce and parody, in *Lolita* and *Henderson,* these traditional comic modes serve to exalt and define the potential reality the protagonist desires.

This, then, will be the grounds of our comparison: *Lolita* and *Henderson the Rain King* are novels about the quest for reality on the part of protagonists who completely fill the novels in which they appear but who are not satisfied with such a role. The nymphet Lolita stands in the same relation to Humbert Humbert that his symbolic African journey stands to Henderson; Africa and Lolita are realities which remain *outside* in the otherness which must be real because (1) the protagonist wants such reality, and (2) in the wanting, he discovers a world to live in. I would also suggest, without making it part of the subsequent analysis, that these novels are about the novelist himself wanting an actual world to describe.

Such an analysis as intended here must begin with the protagonists themselves, and, before we begin a reading of the content and structure of each book, it would do well to examine how Nabokov and Bellow set their protagonists in motion, and how their quests for reality, while comic in texture and incident, yet do not undergo satiric reduction.

Both Humbert Humbert and Henderson are characters *in extremis*, and both must face the charge of mental aberration; both admit this charge but in different ways. The great fun Nabokov has with psychoanalysis and psychiatry transcends mere personal pique: through this means Humbert resists the judgment of the fuddled normal. Who is there to judge him? Admitting that "I am writing under observation" and that "you have to be an artist or a madman" to perceive the reality of the nymphet, he presents himself with such complete knowledge of his condition that it is not possible for the reader to "interpret" his reality. This is emphasized in his re-enactment of the incident that presumably made him a pervert, the unconsummated seaside seduction of the earlier nymphet, Annabel, which he attempts to relive with Lolita, but, although he did look for a beach, he confesses "that even had we discovered a piece of sympathetic seaside somewhere, it would have come too late, since my real liberation had occurred much earlier." The beauties of Lolita herself had so transcended any psychological fixation that the original cause, a cause apparently demanded by the Freudian-mongering reader, is lost in the present experience. We can find no *reasons* with which to classify Humbert's behavior, however insane and aberrant it may seem both to him and to us. He simply is, and as Eros, as desire, we accept him for what he is, for the sake of the projected reality of Nabokov's comedy.

Henderson also poses the problem of insanity. Unlike Humbert Humbert, he does have a background and history which might account for his behavior, and he worries about this: "I, too, am considered crazy, and with good reason—moody, rough, tyrannical and probably mad." Henderson finds a familiar justification for his excesses: "Of course, in an age of madness, to be expected to be untouched by madness is a form of madness. But the pursuit of sanity can be a form of madness too." He can also plead hereditary excuses:

> Now, I come from a stock that has been damned and derided for more than a hundred years, and when I sat smashing bottles by the eternal sea it wasn't only my great ancestors, the ambassadors and statesmen, that people were recalling but the loony ones as well. One got himself mixed up in the Boxer Rebellion, believing he was an Oriental; one was taken for $300,000 by an Italian actress; one was carried away in a balloon while publicizing the suffrage movement. There have been plenty of impulsive or imbecile parties in our family.

Although Henderson characteristically worries about his mental condition more than does Humbert Humbert, and, although he spends most of the novel in a fever as much psychic as physical, no possibility for dismissing him arises from this situation; like Humbert Humbert he remains wholly defended through the expedient of admitting everything. No judgment can be made because there is no one to judge him, least of all, the hidden voice of the author.

Yet, we do have in these novels two protagonists who commit actions and express thoughts generally adjudged insane. How, then, do Bellow and Nabokov get us to accept the reality each desires? The reality of these novels, the social texture, the analogous "real" world each moves through does not exist, or, at least, does not come into being in the way this world normally comes to life in the novel. These novels are less about an actualized and possessed reality than they are about that area of experience between the potential and the actual, between dream and waking where all of us are partial madmen and comic Fausts. Between the potential and the actual falls the wish, and the most familiar form of the wish is the dream. Humbert Humbert and Eugene Henderson are scapegoats for everyman's grandiose desires and private itches; they live our dream, but they live this dream in a world they want and expect to be real, a theme which since Don Quixote, at least, has been more a subject for comedy than tragedy. As Erich Auerbach has pointed out in Mimesis, the reality of Cervantes' novel is not problematical: we know always where we are—the real is that which the Don has to make unreal; Cervantes never loses his ironic perspective. But, in the novels under discussion, the reality which may exist beyond the wish-engendered fantasies of Humbert and Henderson is not at all clear. Their presumed insanity or abnormality does not lead us to a countering rational world; like their heroes, we must discover a reality through their wishes, and we must participate in their serious dreams. Only the excessively confident reader could do otherwise, and these novels are not written for confident readers. As a result, below the comic surface of each book, a desperate tone emerges, and a serious purgation takes place. This process can best be described by a separate examination of the course of each book.

II

Lolita is certainly the more problematical of the two books. Among other things, it has been described as a satire on America, a parody of the romantic novel, a contribution to the *roman noir*, one of the last love stories, and by John Ray, Ph.D., as a "poignant personal study in which there lurks a general lesson." Mr. Lionel Trilling, in perhaps the best essay yet written on the book, does justice to its seriousness by reading it as a contribution to the tradition of passion-love seen through a comic and parodic perspective which does not reduce its actual intensity. But Mr. Trilling, like other critics and reviewers, expresses puzzlement and uneasiness over the shifts in tone which seem to occur in the novel, passages in which Nabokov seems to be either pulling the reader's leg or trying to exalt his novel into something it has not been, for example:

> I loved you. I was a pentapod monster, but I loved you. I was despicable and brutal and turpid, and everything, *mais je t'aimais, je t'aimais!* And there were times when I knew how you felt, and it was hell to know it, my little one. Lolita girl, brave Dolly Schiller.

Apparently, it is not easy to laugh at this passage, not because the basic incongruity is forgotten—middle-aged Humbert and the gum-chewing nymphet—but because this intensity, coupled with our knowledge that soon Humbert dies of a heart attack and Lolita fails to survive childbirth, leaves a comic response open to the charge of callousness. The intensity of the feeling here seems to overcome both comedy and satire reminding us of Keats's remark that "the excellence of every art is its intensity, capable of making all disagreeables evaporate from their being in close relationship with Beauty and Truth." That this witty, acerb, even slapdash and high-jinked book might have anything to do with Keatsian Beauty and Truth seems unlikely, yet the growing intensity of the novel is undeniable, and either we must regard this as misplaced or as part of an intention beyond the satiric and the funny. In a perceptive remark about the book, F. W. Dupee recognizes this duality: "*Lolita* is partly a masterpiece of grotesque comedy, partly an unsubdued wilderness where the wolf howls—a real wolf howling for a real Red Riding Hood."

The development of Humbert's sentimental education is a progress from fantasy to reality, in which the content of the wish remains the same, while the object of the wish slips away, leaving the desirer with the recognition of his self-induced folly. Whatever the content of his specific sexual perversion (and there is no psychological interest attached to it by Nabokov), Humbert's world, in which Lolita remains the sole content, arises *in spite of* tawdry surroundings and absurd misadventures, so much does the hero hunger to exist in a real world. Upon his arrival in Ramsdale, he learns that the house in which he was to stay has burned down, "possibly owing to the synchronous conflagration that had been raging all night in my veins." A joke, of course, but this internal conflagration is about to find its proper outlet. Humbert meets Lolita for the first time and experiences the epiphany which never leaves him.

Although, with the self-admitted naiveté of the pervert and like the tragi-comic hero of romance, Humbert is shocked to discover that his mistress is not chaste, the progress of Humbert's nympholepsy is self-induced, not self-deceived. The actual method by which Dolores Haze becomes Lolita is not a helpless reflex of perversion: "She was Lo, plain Lo, in the morning, standing four feet ten in one sock. She was Lola in slacks. She was Dolly at school. She was Dolores on the dotted line. But in my arms she was always Lolita." In Humbert's words, he *incarnates* her as all nympholepts apparently incarnate their nymphets. The process is part of a cunning epistemology: "It is a question of focal adjustment, of a certain distance that the inner eye thrills to surmount, and a certain contrast that the mind perceives with a gasp of perverse delight." Yet, paradoxically, Humbert would like to claim much for Lolita's external reality. Contrasting his memory of Annabel with the memory of Lolita, he writes:

> I see Annabel in such general terms as: "honey-colored skin," "thin arms," "brown bobbed hair," "long lashes," "big bright mouth"; and the other when you instantly evoke, with shut eyes, on the dark innerside of your eyelids, the objective, absolutely optical replica of a beloved face, a little ghost in natural colors (and this is how I see Lolita).

This adjustment is not perfect; and, in fact, the novel is the history of its increasing difficulty as Lolita ages into adolescence and Humbert's lust turns to love. The self-created vision nearly fails early in his quest when, seeing her at the summer camp where he has gone to pick her up after the death of her mother, he has to perform some mental and visual gymnastics to recover his vision. But the possibility of "a sound education and a healthy and happy girlhood" soon disappears. " 'In a wink,' as the Germans say, the angelic line of conduct was erased, and I overtook my prey (time moves ahead of our fancies!) and she was my Lolita again—in fact, more my Lolita than ever." That the real Lolita, or Lolita as someone else might conceive her, constantly threatens to break into Humbert's self-induced reality makes his journey an unhappy one, and I think it worth noting how little satisfaction Humbert gets from his delirious enchantment. He seems most triumphant after his initial sexual encounter with Lolita on the couch which, however perverse, has preserved her supposed purity.

The safety Humbert feels here is not mere safety from the police, but the safety one feels in preserving a wish intact; the experience has not diminished the wish because the *construction* remains standing: Lolita is still a controllable reality. Yet Humbert Humbert cannot remain in this blissful vestibule of being, for, though he claims shortly before he is seduced by Lolita in *The Enchanted Hunters* that "I had gradually eliminated all the superfluous blur, and by stacking level upon level of translucent vision, had evolved a final picture"—the comic anti-climax of his sexual plot introduces a new element into his carefully contrived world: the element of resistant chance, and as choice turns to chance, dream turns to nightmare.

At this point in the novel, the comedy of the basic situation darkens, although some of the funniest parts of the book still lie ahead: the parody of motels and highways, the monstrous Miss Pratt of the Beardsley School For Girls, and the climactic killing of Quilty. Humbert's increasingly agonized possession of Lolita begins to transcend its literary and parodic origins and becomes something more important. As usual, Humbert himself is fully aware of what is happening and gives us a later clue. When Lolita has left him, he finds that his perversion remains intact and that his greatest *pleasure* comes from unconsummated imaginings and visions, "the great rosegray never to be had," yet upon getting Lolita's letter asking for money, he doesn't hesitate to put away his dreams and set out again for the reality Lolita has become.

Two elements complicate the satiric and the comic perspective from which the book starts out, and both these elements are presented seriously by Nabokov because they belong to the underlying seriousness of the theme and not to the comic surface. One is the passage of time and the other is the related moral problem which surprisingly and superbly makes its appearance just when the joke *qua* joke threatens to become tiresome. Of course, Humbert, in his guise as perverted comic hero, is ready to meet the fact of Lolita's aging with his wildest and grandest flight.

But such bravado cannot sustain him. Like an Elizabethan sonne-
teer, he fears and fights against time's ravages of his ladylove: "I perceived
at once how much she had changed since I first met her two years ago."
And, as he enumerates how the approach of adolescence coarsens her and
sickens him, he still must recognize that "everything about her was of the
same impenetrable order." No matter how he has prepared himself for the
decline of his nymphet and her resulting abandonment, he continues to
love her even when "my alembics told me she should stop being a
nymphet."

The reader must now make a commitment to the characterization
of Lolita that he neither expected nor thought possible. Humbert Humbert's
concern and compassion undeniably involve the reader in a way he has
not been involved before. Although she is not a "real" character in the
usual novelistic sense, if we have been caught up in the cunning comic
rhythm of the whole, we cannot help lending our sympathy to the
unwinding of the plot. Until now, we have known two Lolitas 1) the
gumchewing, unindividualized comic caricature, and 2) the conscious
romantic distortion of her constructed by Humbert Humbert. Now we
meet a third Lolita, who is no more real than the first two, but in whom
we recognize the anguish of the narrator. Nabokov does not bring Lolita
to characterized "life"; rather, he brings his hero to a deep awareness of
her human situation. The comedy resulting from the incongruity of Lolita
One and Lolita Two gives way to the pathos of Lolita Three, without,
however, affecting the basic disparity of the first two. The important point
to recognize is that Humbert Humbert remains in control of the reality of
the novel; the reader still does not know any Lolita apart from him—he
does not know any Lolita at all; he responds wholly to the development in
the narrator, and this development, without destroying the comic surface,
suddenly presents us with the traditional moral problem of the novel: what
is the individual and social reality and how should we respond to it?
Nabokov has achieved a considerable feat here: the subsequent disquieting
passages referred to before now take their place in the whole—we have
been prepared for them, not only by the increasing intensity of the novel
but by the thinning out of the shocking joke which has borne us along
this far. Suddenly, the real wolf emerges and the real Red Riding Hood
demands our sympathy.

When I speak of "moral problems," I am not referring to the legal
aspects of Humbert's perversion, although there are numerous satiric passages dealing with the harmless pervert he thinks himself to be. The satire
is effective here, although Humbert is, as he says, writing under observation, and although the audience, as jury, is constantly present, the social

judgment does not much concern Humbert or his creator. In the key passage of the book, in which parody and satire come to suspension, Humbert commits himself to the reality and thus to the moral problem which Lolita has become for him, a reality not the product of his fantasy but of actual remembered experience.

Who wants to prove that life is a joke? Here Humbert's world is invulnerable to laughter. Lolita has becomes Dolores Haze, and whoever *she* is, she is not Humbert Humbert, and therefore has actually happened to him and is real. In the masterly scene in which Humbert Humbert visits the now married and pregnant Lolita all the devices are there: parody, wordplay, comic situation, and the marvelous excess characteristic of the whole, but the scene comes through with a new-found power; we attend to the scene with *both* comic detachment and the sympathy essential to pathos. And, because of our relation to the protagonist, our own sense of reality is called into question. What has been real in their relationship? As he later muses on their final meeting: "I was to her not a boy friend, not a glamour man, not a pal, not even a person at all, but just two eyes and a foot of engorged brawn." Lolita's reality is not in question here, but the reality of Humbert himself, and because of his complete control of the reality in the novel, *our* own sense of reality undergoes scrutiny and anxiety. For Lolita's reality has come into being through the perversion and fantasy of Humbert's genuine love. This progression is almost muffled by the verbal gymnastics and parodic situation of the whole, but the emergent theme cannot be ignored. It even makes an explicit appearance, though in typically disguised spoof. The play written by Humbert's rival, Clare Quilty, and in which Lolita makes her schoolgirl appearance, is described contemptuously by Humbert as a plot in which "barefooted Dolores was to lead check-trousered Mona to the paternal farm behind the Perilous Forest to prove to the braggard she was not a poet's fancy, but a rustic, down-to-brown-earth lass, and a last-minute kiss was to enforce the play's profound message, namely, that mirage and reality merge in love."

We are well aware that parody has its serious uses, that in satire from Petronius onward it can serve the severest purposes. But the relation of serious parody to comedy is more problematical. *Lolita* is a genuinely funny book at the same time that it is a serious comedy; part of its parody serves obvious enough satiric functions, whether Nabokov is lampooning psychoanalysis or American tourism, but its parody has an ultimately more important purpose because *Lolita*, paradoxically enough, is more serious in its comedy than in its satire. The satire is largely a matter of filling out the comic texture, while the basic parody of the love-novel relates to the serious comedy at the core of Nabokov's conception. As Northrop Frye points out, in the typical serious parody of apocalyptic symbolism, "the demonic erotic relation becomes a fierce destructive passion that works against loyalty and frustrates the one who possesses it." This is what happens in *Lolita*, but through a comic reversal, because we cannot at first take Lolita herself seriously as the harlot, witch, or siren of such forms. We have reached that decline in the form where the convention itself turns to irony. Yet, this very parody, through Humbert's developing relation to the reality of love, gives us back the value we thought we had lost. *Lolita* is a serious comedy because the value which the comedy threatened to reduce is maintained, is finally, and in spite of everything, upheld.

Mr. Trilling touches closely on the true theme of *Lolita* when he writes that the novel is not about sex at all, but about love. However, only the possibility of love is suggested, the beginning world of relation-ship. The novel is about the lover's quest for reality, a reality which he first creates out of himself, but which then is discovered to have an actual existence beyond him. We attend to this discovery because the form of the book is the form of discovery, and the reality, which appears in difficult splintered guises in modern fiction, here finds committed representation. The world of *Lolita*, then, is far more real than the Winchellian peepings of O'Hara or Cozzens; it is also more real, because more whole, than the highly intellectualized constructs of Robbe-Grillet and Sarraute. In this book, Beckett's underground man finds a possible way of relating to the world. That world itself does not emerge. We must look at another underground man of contemporary fiction to find a world that is closer to being born.

III

As *Lolita* uses the familiar progress of passion-love, seen through an unfamiliar parodic perspective, to discover a reality, so *Henderson the Rain King* uses the familiar rituals of quest and initiation, also from a comic perspective, to lay bare its reality. There is not the problem of mood in *Henderson* that there is in *Lolita*; for all the comedy and farce in the novel there is never any question that we must attend seriously to Henderson himself; we do not stand outside to judge him any more than we fail to give our confidence to Falstaff and other large comic heroes who fill the world in which they appear. Neither is the theme elusive in *Henderson*, although its ultimate working out requires an understanding of its struc-ture. Through Henderson's own, eventually repetitive, assertions, the theme comes clear: he is searching for a reality, a reality which, like Humbert's, can be shown conclusively to be something other than himself. Such a reality has nothing to do with adjustment or the small and orderly world in which mediocrity lives. Henderson makes huge claims on reality and reality answers him hugely back.

Henderson's relation to reality can be best approached through the argument which he has with his wife early in the book and which recurs to him throughout the novel. Having been told by her that she is glad that he seems more able to accept reality, he blusters back: "I know more about reality than you'll ever know. I am on damned good terms with reality, and don't you forget it." This boast sets up the familiar enactment of *hubris*, but Henderson is not easily cured. He does make large demands on the world, as the brilliant first fifty pages show, and his passionate sense of the real gives him the right to his boast. Later, when he is sitting with King Dahfu, he asserts that, while Lily neither likes nor loves reality,

Me, I love the old bitch just as she is and I like to think I am always prepared for even the very worst she has to show me. I am a true adorer of life, and if I can't reach as high as the face of it, I plant my kiss somewhere lower down.

Henderson as *alazon* goes through several phases, largely as a result of his relationship with the philosopher-king Dahfu. To his inborn and passionate sense of the real, Henderson adds spirit and imagination admitting that what we often call reality is nothing but pedantry and that he needn't have quarreled with his wife: "The world of facts is real all right, and not to be altered. The physical is all there, and it belongs to science. But then there is the noumenal department, and there we create and create and create."

The theme of a supra-reality finds its fullest expression in Dahfu's own paean to the imagination and how it becomes actualized in experience, one of Henderson's profoundest and most necessary lessons:

Birds flew, harpies flew, angels flew, Daedalus and son flew. And see here, it is no longer dreaming and story, for literally there is flying. You flew here, into Africa. All human accomplishment has this same origin, identically. Imagination is a force of nature. Is this not enough to make a person full of ecstasy? Imagination, imagination, imagination! It converts to actual. It sustains, it alters, it redeems!

Henderson's reality is complete when he encounters the lion Gmilo with Dahfu on the climactic lion-hunt. Even though Henderson has been trained by Dahfu to meet this contingency, even though he has assumed lionlike characteristics, it becomes apparent to him that, until now, he has not experienced true reality:

> The snarling of this animal was indeed the voice of death. And I thought how I had boasted to my dear Lily how I loved reality. . . . But oh, unreality, unreality, unreality! That has been my scheme for a troubled but eternal life. But now I was blasted away from this practice by the throat of the lion. His voice was like a blow at the back of my head.

The lion completes Henderson's quest; we understand that Henderson has come to know a truth because of the connection between suffering and knowledge insisted on throughout the novel. But what is this knowledge? What reality has Henderson discovered?

This discovery can only be described by an examination of the organization of the book itself. Paradoxically enough, though this is a novel about reality and the need for its rebirth, the world it presents is most akin to a dream. One almost expects Henderson to wake up at the end of the book and come down to breakfast with his wife and children. But it would be precisely this breakfast that would defeat the structure of the novel. We do not see Henderson "return"; the emphasis is on the content of the dream itself, not on the world which it abstracts, though Bellow tries to give the book the dimensions of a coherent world. As Henderson himself admits, "Still, an explanation is necessary, for living proof of something of the highest importance has been presented to me so I am obliged to communicate it. And not the least of the difficulties is that it happened as in a dream." A further complication to a realistic texture is the fact that Henderson's dream is both wish and prophecy. Bellow suggests the dual nature of his plot in the lightly-held identification of Henderson with Joseph. The wizened figure who leads Henderson and Romilayu into the trap set by the Wariri is identified with the figure who led Joseph into the trap set by his brothers. "Then the brothers saw Joseph and said, 'Behold the dreamer cometh.' Everybody should read the Bible."

Henderson's pursuit of reality arises from no scientific or philosophical impulse; as the development of the book shows, he is seeking the real because he is seeking salvation and he believes that the real will set him free. Through the ritual of initiation (and every incident in the book is either a prelude to initiation or the act itself) Henderson is successively reborn and brought closer to the truth. The quest is a successful one since he returns from his symbolic Africa in presumed possession of the selfhood he went to seek. But what success means here and how he has achieved it can be best understood by what his symbolic adventures and misadventures achieve. An actual process and method, akin to a religious experience, must be undergone.

In the beginning, a kind of stripping, a psychic and physical reduction, is necessary. Daniel's remark to Nebuchadnezzar, referred to throughout novel, gives us the clue: "They shall drive thee from among men, and thy dewelling shall be with beasts of the field." This reduction (or exaltation) to the animal defines Henderson's characteristic experience. He begins as a breeder of pigs and returns with a lion cub; in between he suffers degradation in faintly parodic imitation of Lear, who is also forced to the animal and undergoes an actual and symbolic stripping. Yet Henderson's degradation began long before his African adventure. When he was in the Army during the Second World War, he was stripped by Army medics because he caught the crabs and was left naked in the middle of a crossroads, swearing and roaring revenge. Again, after he has been made Rain-King, he is stripped by the village women and forced to accompany them on the Rain-King's rounds. " 'No, No!' I said, but by that time the underpants were already down around my knees. The worst had happened." In this state, poor bare forked Henderson is able to consummate the ritual that brings on the required rain. Again and again, Bellow calls attention to Henderson's tragi-comic seminudity. With dragging drawers and sweaty T-shirt, he goes about his salvation, even losing his bridgework, an occurrence which causes him more pain and agony than anything that happens to him. In the end, like Lear, he is reclothed. On his return from Africa he stops in Italy. "On Friday I got to Rome. I bought a corduroy outfit, burgundy colored, and an alpine hat with Bersagliere feathers, plus a shirt and underpants." The martial feathers provide an outward sign of Henderson's triumph, a hero's return. But first he had to become naked.

The stripping is the first step in the initiation, but the tests that follow actually do drive Henderson from men and force him to dwell with the beasts of the field. From bear to pig to cow to frog to lion, Henderson comes into successful or disastrous relationship with other forms of life. The tribe of his first encounter, the Arnewi, are a mild, pacific people who raise and worship cattle. Henderson, in his guise as a parody of Moses, attempts to rid the Arnewi of frogs who have infested their water-supply by blowing them from the water. But he suffers his first crushing defeat in Africa by blowing up the reservoir and losing what water the tribe already had. This is a directly personal failure: "That cistern of problem water with its algae and its frogs had entered me, occupying a square place in my interiors, and sloshing around as I moved."

Other tests on Henderson are met more successfully, tests which usually involve his impressive physical strength. He defeats Itelo, king of the Arnewi, in required wrestling; he carries away the body of the dead Rain-King of the vigorous Wariri; he lifts the stone idol Mummah, thereby becoming Rain-King himself. All these are of interest in examining the novel, but we only have room to discuss the key test: his relation to Dahfu's lion and to Dahfu himself, the king of the Wariri.

Dahfu, a problematic tutor in Henderson's fantasy, stands at Henderson's side, advising, cajoling, and warning him. This figure of the "prophet" is a familiar one in Bellow's novels, sometimes appearing as a threatening charlatan as well as a beneficent advisor to the hero; one thinks of Allbee and Shifcart in their relation to Leventhal in *The Victim*, of Tamkin in relation to Tommy Wilhelm in *Seize The Day*, of Einhorn and Mintouchian in relation to Augie March in his *Adventures*. Dahfu, as a climax to these symbolic prophets, shares their characteristics: he possesses their eccentric knowledge, he is partly comic, and he is excessive in thought and deed. Above all, like his forebears, there is an essential mystery about him. Dahfu is the most benign of these personages, and, in fact, undergoes a sacrificial death that Henderson may assume his characteristics. Indeed, the lion cub Henderson brings back with him from Africa is the symbolic representation of the dead king. But what does the king himself symbolize?

As with any resonant poetic symbol, no linear meaning can be attributed to the lion and lion-king of this novel. Indeed, this is a symbol wholly integrated with Henderson's quest, thus forming an interesting contrast with the eagle-ritual that Augie March undergoes in a partly real, partly symbolic Mexico. In the earlier novel, the symbol of the eagle, for all the brilliance of the writing, appears as a strange excrescence, but in Bellow's new book, the ordeal-by-lion does not put symbolic strain on a realistic content since the latter has only a tenuous existence in the novel anyway; moreover, the symbol gathers force and meaning throughout the whole novel. Henderson's relation to it begins in a characteristically daft comic manner when he tries to shoot the cat left by his disgruntled tenants; later, he sees Dahfu's insistence on his leonine education as a revenge plotted by the cat family. It soon becomes apparent that the lion kept under the throne by Dahfu is precisely what Henderson is not, something external, powerful, real. For all his boasting about reality, Henderson must undergo a savage encounter with something entirely foreign, and from this discover reality in himself. He asks, "How shall a man be broken for whom reality has no fixed dwelling?" By an encounter with the Other in the form of a lion.

The lion which Henderson encounters through Dahfu is actually a substitute for a second lion the king must capture in order to solidify his position, the uncaptured lion being the representative of Dahfu's father, the former king. His "practice runs" with the lion-surrogate annoy his councillors and, in fact, suggest that Dahfu himself, for all his magnificence, does not maintain a perfect relation to the real; indeed, Henderson must complete Dahfu's role after the latter's death. The lion will help him, as Dahfu explains:

> You ask, what can she do for you? Many things. First she is unavoidable. Test it, and you will find she is unavoidable. And this is what you need, as you are an avoider. Oh, you have accomplished momentous avoidances. But she will change that. She will make consciousness to shine. She will burnish you. She will force the present moment upon you. Second, lions are experiencers. But not in haste. They experience with deliberate luxury. The poet says, "The tigers of wrath are wiser than the horses of instruction." Let us embrace lions also in the same view.

This test proves the hardest for Henderson. On all fours in the posture of the comic and the beast, he fulfills the prophecy of Daniel, yet even this comes out in a comic guise. "Certain words crept into my roars, like 'God,' 'Help,' 'Lord have mercy,' only they came out 'Hoolp!' 'Mooorcy!' It's funny what words sprang forth. 'Au secours,' which was 'Secooooor' and also 'De profoooondis,' plus snatches from the 'Messiah.' " Yet Henderson preserves as much dignity as he can and comes upon his truth and his reality. In a letter to his wife just before he marches out with Dahfu to the climactic lion-hunt, he suggests one part of the answer: "I had a voice that said I want! *I* want? I? It should have told me *she* wants, *he* wants, *they* want. And moreover, it's love that makes reality reality. The opposite makes the opposite."

In his encounter with Gmilo, Dahfu's symbolic lion-father, Henderson meets his ultimate reality in the passage already cited. He moves from a life-long unreality to an immediate truth, for the lion symbolizes death. This confrontation, added to his insight into love quoted above (not unlike *Lolita's* buried theme of mirage and reality merging into love) completes his education. The rest of the novel—the escape from the mausoleum with the lion cub, the flight homeward with the American Persian waif Henderson picks up in a symbolic reversal of the earlier rejection of the Negro foundling brought home by his daughter Ricey, the joyous arrival in Newfoundland—all these complete Henderson's dreaming triumph, but add nothing essential to the theme or to the reality already discovered. However, we do not begrudge a Henderson triumphant; he has spent most of the novel in defeat.

I have used the word "symbol" frequently in discussing *Henderson* and there is no doubt that the novel cannot be understood without reference to the symbolic references and relationships established in the novel. Yet, the symbolism of *Henderson* is best described as light-hearted, though this characterization does not indicate a casual reading. Henderson himself calls up, either directly or in a parodic mode, Oedipus, Moses, Joseph, Jacob, Falstaff, Lear, etc., and his entire quest has a familiar mythic pattern. But the novel never sinks under its airy symbolic weight; as in *Lolita* the prevailing comic texture provides an atmosphere in which the serious symbol appears transparent, not as a revelation of inner meaning, but as a useful reference which, more often than not, increases the comedy.

Yet this comedy nowhere debases the symbol because Bellow's comedy is not ultimately critical of its protagonist. As in the presentation of Humbert Humbert, there is nothing in the novel with which Henderson is compared unfavorably. It is true that some of the comedy is less serious than the theme demands. Indeed, in its inheritance from *Gulliver's Travels* and *The Connecticut Yankee,* it sometimes sprawls into conventional aimlessness: a blustering American companioned by a wise but strangely articulate African, who, of course, knows more of the world than he does. But Henderson is a nobler comic hero than this. In the larger forms of comedy, as Northrop Frye says, "the comic hero will get his triumph whether what he has done is sensible or silly, honest or rascally." Henderson is doubly rewarded, both as a comic hero and as a hero putting his comedy behind him. He contains both *alazon* and *eiron* in himself; while he blusters, he suffers, and though he proves his own ironist, he never loses the huge sense of himself so necessary to his quest. When he discovers his reality, we attend seriously because we have the same doubleness in ourselves and rejoice to see it fulfill a pattern.

IV

I have argued that the two novels under discussion, using the devices of comedy, parody, and satire, still do not reduce their heroes to victims of emotionless observation; rather, we follow their return to reality with seriousness and sympathy. But how far this "return" takes us, how far a fused individual and social reality is restored to the novel form through these strategies remains to be seen. The complete circuit is not made for a variety of reasons. *Lolita* sometimes tends to fight off the serious bite reality has made in its parodic structure; the rather slick humor found in some of Nabokov's other stories and novels makes an appearance here in occasional aimless puns, undirected satire, and a certain thinness of event. At times the novelist seems weary of the whole idea, but with the abduction of Lolita the pace again quickens and the theme emerges strongly. Yet the reported death of Lolita in childbirth and Humbert's heart failure before trial seem expedients for closing out a troublesome situation. The artistic impulse has completed its cycle, but, as often in first-rate fiction, reverberations echo beyond the closed form. Of particular concern would be Humbert Humbert's subsequent mentality (we would not expect him to change his habits), the mind that wrote his manuscript, the impulse that made him an artist. Nabokov himself sees *Lolita* as rounding its effect: "For me a work of fiction exists only insofar as it affords me what I shall bluntly call aesthetic bliss, that is, a sense of being somehow, somewhere, connected with other states of being where art (curiosity, tenderness, kindness, ecstasy) is the norm." This attitude toward art can be related to Humbert's peroration: "I am thinking of aurochs and angels, the secret of durable pigments, prophetic sonnets, the refuge of art. And this is the only immortality you and I may share, my Lolita." Nevertheless, we are left in this novel with a compassionate murderer and pervert who has discovered the nature of reality. If we consider what the novel form still might be capable of, given such an astonishing possibility, the abrupt end must seem a disappointment. And if we accept Kenneth Burke's definition of form as the satisfaction of aroused desire, *Lolita* does not complete its structure. Like Humbert Humbert, we are left hungering for the reality he has finally begun to experience.

Henderson the Rain King appears similarly short-circuited. Bellow's unwillingness to show Henderson back in the society from which he fled makes his discovery and triumph less forceful. *Henderson* has the kind of comic structure which leads us to expect some kind of reintegration of the hero with his society. It is right that Huck Finn lights out for the territory, but it is not right that Henderson's drama, however brilliantly it may be rendered in terms of symbol and dream, remain wholly within the fantasy-world. The first four chapters of the novel are among the most striking in contemporary fiction for the manner in which the realistic life of a huge and suffering comic hero is presented. The flight to a symbolic Africa is inevitable, but so, according to the rhythmic expectation, is Henderson's return. Of course, the narrative problems of such a return are enormous, and I have no prescriptions to suggest. Neither am I suggesting that *Henderson* should complete the "moral closure" which Edwin Honig sees as characteristic of traditional allegory. Yet, Bellow is not writing satire, and a Gulliver-like withdrawal to the stables is not indicated, for Henderson seems about to begin where Gulliver leaves off. The ending in which Henderson runs around the grounded airplane in Newfoundland with his foundling by his side is unsatisfactory because the symbol consummates only Henderson's wish and not the reality he is about to re-enter: "I guess I felt it was my turn now to move, and so went running—leaping, leaping, pounding, and tingling over the pure white lining of the gray Arctic silence." Earlier in the novel, Henderson had experimented in living at home in an igloo and had dreamed of going to the Arctic like his boyhood hero Wilfred Grenfell. "But I don't think I would have found what I was looking for there. In that case, I would have overwhelmed the world from the North with my trampling." He is now ready for the Arctic silences, the same whiteness that disturbs Augie March at the end of his *Adventures* and which seems to represent pure potentiality in Bellow's world. But if Henderson is free to add his colors to the world we do not get a chance to see him do it.

A further problem in the representation of reality has to do with the texture of each novel. Elizabeth Hardwick has written of *Henderson*, "The scenery is too unreal for picaresque comedy; the events have too little resonance for symbolic fantasy." I think this criticism is too harsh because the area between picaresque comedy and symbolic fantasy is precisely the area Bellow is interested in depicting, and this is manifestly the area of the wish. But there is an undeniable thinness of texture in *Henderson* and in *Lolita* as well. This is surprising in view of the very rich texture we normally associate with these writers; indeed, Nabokov's short stories are often little more than exercises in texture, and *Augie March* is perhaps the richest of all American novels. There are exceptions, set pieces like the marvelous description of Lolita's tennis game or Henderson's experience with the sunlight on the wall of his hut before his battle with the frogs, but, for books so deeply concerned with reality, there is an insufficient concern with sensation in each novel: a world dense with sensory possibility and actuality is not built up as fully as the subject seems to demand. However, sensation as personal pain, shock, or withdrawal is constantly present in both books and that may be all that is needed.

When we turn back to the novels of Beckett, Sarraute, and other experimenters with the modern forms of the novel, we find parody, just as we do in Bellow and Nabokov. But parody in these writers is directed toward the destruction of the novel form as we understand it and involves a satirical and nihilistic view of reality. It is possible, as Erich Heller avers in discussing Mann's *Doctor Faustus*, that "the artist is condemned to the sphere of higher parody, the only thing that is still left when the 'real thing' has become impossible." But this "higher parody" need not take the nihilistic road of Beckett nor join in the desperate metaphysical jokes of Kafka. Mann's *Felix Krull* can be taken as a prototype of the kind of modern comic parody that is restorative as well as destructive, restorative of the form and the experience which the form encloses. *Lolita* and *Henderson the Rain King* are essentially serious parodies of comic parody itself because the initial value which the parody is meant to question is restored and with this restoration the unique reality of the experience sought reveals itself: we come into love in *Lolita* and into selfhood in *Henderson.* We are familiar with such a doubleness in an earlier writer like Stendhal: Fabrizio del Dongo, in particular, has this in common with Humbert Humbert and Henderson: the external reality in which he finds himself is less real than his sense of himself, is not large or various enough for his completest expression. As a result, many of his adventures and misadventures appear comic, but Fabrizio himself is always regarded with affection and sympathy: he discovers a world after all. Nabokov and Bellow do not possess, indeed, cannot afford, Stendhal's superb mixture of the tragic and the satirical, the comic and the pathetic. But the final effect of their novels is not unlike the mood of Stendhal's work, in which one not only comes into possession of the realist cake, but is also able to discover its inner romantic richness.

Of course, as I have said, neither of these novels comes back all the way into reality. Humbert Humbert and Lolita die conveniently and Henderson is left in his symbolic Newfoundland. These novels do not restore a full-bodied reality, but they encourage us to continue our search for one.

IRVING HOWE

Odysseus, Flat on His Back

Where shall a contemporary novel begin? Perhaps unavoidably: with the busted hero reeling from a messy divorce and moaning in a malodorous furnished room; picking at his psyche's wounds like a boy at knee scabs, rehearsing the mighty shambles of ambition ("how I rose from humble origins to complete disaster"); cursing the heart-and-ball breakers, both wives and volunteers, who have, he claims, laid him low; snarling contempt at his own self-pity with a Johnsonian epigram, "Grief, Sir, is a species of idleness"; and yet, amidst all this woe, bubbling with intellectual hope, as also with intellectual gas, and consoling himself with the truth that indeed "there were worse cripples around."

This is Moses Herzog, hero-patsy of Saul Bellow's extremely, if also unevenly, brilliant new novel. Herzog is a representative man of the sixties, eaten away by those "personal relations" which form the glory and the foolishness of a post-political intelligentsia. He is a good scholar, but cannot complete his books. He rips off imaginary letters to great men, finessing their wisdom and patronizing their mistakes. He is a lady-killer, "aging" at 47 and worried about his potency. He is a loving father twice-divorced, who each time has left behind him a child as token of good will. He is a true-blue Jewish groaner, and perversely, groans against fashionable despair. Inside or outside our skins, we all know Herzog: *Hypocrite lecteur—mon semblable—mein schlemiehl.* Hungering for a life of large significance, eager for "a politics in the Aristotelian sense," he nevertheless keeps melting into the mercies of women, each of whom, in sequence, really understands him.

From *The New Republic* (September 19, 1964). Copyright © 1964 by *The New Republic*.

Herzog is Bellow's sixth novel and in many ways the most remarkable. All of his books—whether melancholy realism, moral fable or picaresque fantasia—represent for him a new departure, a chosen risk in form and perception. Bellow has the most powerful mind among contemporary American novelists, or at least, he is the American novelist who best assimilates his intelligence to creative purpose. This might have been foreseen at the beginning of his career, for he has always been able to turn out a first-rate piece of discursive prose; what could not have been foreseen was that he would also become a virtuoso of fictional technique and language.

Behind Bellow's writing there is always a serious intention, but as he grows older he becomes increasingly devoted to the idea of the novel as sheer spectacle. His last few books comprise a hectic and at times ghastly bazaar of contemporary experience, they ring with the noise of struggle; characters dash in and out, glistening with bravura; adventures pile up merrily, as if the decline of the West had not been definitely proclaimed; the male characters plunge and rise, mad for transcendence; the women (a little tiresomely) are all very beautiful and mostly very damaging. And the language spins. . . .

Herzog himself is not, in the traditional sense, a novelistic character at all. He is observed neither from a cool distance nor through intimate psychological penetration. We experience him intensely, entering his very bones; yet, trapped as we are in his inner turmoil, we cannot be certain that finally we know him. For Bellow has not provided a critical check: there is no way of learning what any of the other characters, by way of Jamesian correction, might think or feel about Herzog. Bellow offers not a full-scale characterization but a full-length exposure of a state of being. We do not see Herzog acting in the world, we are made captive in the world of Herzog. The final picture is that of Herzog in cross-section, bleeding from the cut.

In one sense, then, there is a complete identification between Bellow and Herzog: the consciousness of the character forms the enclosing medium of the novel. But in a more important respect Bellow manages skillfully to avoid the kind of identification which might lead one to conclude that he "favors" his central character or fails to see through his weaknesses and falsities—a fault that could radically distort the line of vision by which everything is to be considered. That Herzog cannot accurately perceive the other figures in the novel and that we are closely confined to his sense of them, is true and in ways I shall later suggest, a limitation. But not a crippling limitation. For it soon becomes clear that, while totally committed to Herzog's experience, Bellow is not nearly so committed to his estimate of that experience.

For the most part, however, *Herzog* marks a notable advance in technique over Bellow's previous books. He has become a master of something that is rarely discussed in criticism because it is hard to do more than point toward it: the art of timing, which concerns the massing, centering and disposition of the characters and creates a sense of delight in the sheer motion of the narrative.

Bellow has also found a good solution to a technical problem which keeps arising in the contemporary novel. Most readers, I imagine, groan a little when they see a novelist wheeling into position one of those lengthy and leaden flashbacks in which, we know in advance, the trauma will be unveiled that is to explain the troubles of time-present. These flashbacks, by now one of the dreariest conventions of the novel, result in a lumpiness of narrative surface and blockage of narrative flow. But Bellow has managed to work out a form in which the illusion of simultaneity of time—a blend of past with the present-moving-into-future—is nicely maintained. Instead of the full-scale flashback, which often rests on the mistaken premise that a novelist needs to provide a psychiatric or sociological casebook on his characters, Bellow allows the consciousness of his narrator to flit about in time, restlessly, nervously, thereby capturing essential fragments of the past as they break into the awareness of the present. Through these interlockings of time—brief, dramatic and made to appear simultaneous—he creates the impression of a sustained rush of experience.

Bellow began his career as a novelist of somber intellectuality: his impressive early book *The Victim* asks almost to be read as a fable concerning the difficulties of attempting a secure moral judgment in our day. With *Augie March* he made a sharp turn, casting aside the urban contemplativeness and melancholy of his previous work, and deciding to regard American life as wonderfully "open," a great big shapeless orange bursting with the juices of vitality. Though in some ways his most virtuoso performance, *Augie March* suffers from a programmatic exuberance: it is fun to watch the turns and tricks the suddenly acrobatic Bellow can execute, yet hard to suppress a touch of anxiety concerning his heart-beat.

With *Augie March* Bellow also began to work out a new fictional style, for which there may be some predecessors—just possibly Daniel Fuchs and Nathanael West—but which in the main is an original achievement. By now it has come to be imitated by many American Jewish novelists as well as by a few gentiles trying wistfully to pass, but none of these manages it nearly so well as Bellow himself.

What Bellow did was to leave behind him the bleak neutrality of naturalistic prose and the quavering sensibility of the Jamesian novel: the first, he seemed to feel, was too lifeless and the second insufficiently masculine. Beginning with *Augie March*—but none of this applies to his masterful novella, *Seize the Day*—Bellow's prose becomes strongly anti-literary, a roughing up of diction and breaking down of syntax in order to avoid familiar patterns and expectations. The prose now consists of a rich, thick impasto of verbal color in which a splatter of sidewalk eloquence is mixed with erudite by-play. Together with this planned coarsening of texture, there is a great emphasis on speed, a violent wrenching and even forcing of images, all the consequence of his wish to break away from the stateliness of the literary sentence. Analytic refinement is sacrificed to sensuous vigor, careful psychological notation to the brawling of energy, syntactical qualification to kinesthetic thrust. (One is reminded a bit of action painting.) Psychology is out, absolutely out: for to psychologize means to reflect, to hesitate, to qualify, to modulate, to analyze. By contrast, the aim of Bellow's neo-baroque style is to communicate sensations of immediacy and intensity, even when dealing with abstract intellectual topics—to communicate, above all, the sense that men are still alive. Toward this end he is prepared to yield niceties of phrasing, surface finish, sometimes even coherence of structure.

It is a style admirably suited to the flaming set-piece, the rapid vignette, the picaresque excursion. But it is not so well suited to a sustained and complex action, or a lengthy flow of experience, or a tragic plot, or what George Moore, in discussing the nature of fiction, called the "rhythmic sequence of events." In *Augie March* there is a run of action but hardly a plot; in *Herzog* a superbly-realized situation but hardly a developing action; and in both of these novels, as well as in *Henderson*, not much of a "rhythmic sequence of events." That is why, I think, none of them has a fully satisfying denouement, an organic fulfillment of the action. In principle these books could continue forever, and that is one reason Bellow finds it hard to end them. He simply stops, much against one's will.

Finally, Bellow's style draws heavily from the Yiddish, not so much in borrowed diction as in underlying intonation and rhythm. Bellow's relation to Yiddish is much more easy and authoritative than that of most other American Jewish writers. The jabbing interplay of ironies, the intimate vulgarities, the strange blend of sentimental and sardonic which characterizes Yiddish speech are lassoed into Bellow's English: so that what we get is not a sick exploitation of folk memory but a vibrant linguistic and cultural transmutation. (Precisely at the moment when Yiddish is dying off as an independent language, it has experienced an astonishing, and not always happy, migration into American culture. In two or three decades students of American literature may have to study Yiddish for reasons no worse than those for which students of English literature study Anglo-Saxon.)

One of the most pleasing aspects of *Herzog* is that Bellow has brought together his two earlier manners: the melancholy and the bouncy, the "Russian" and the "American," *Seize the Day* and *Augie March*. *Herzog* is almost free of the gratuitous verbalism which marred *Augie March*, yet retains its vividness and richness of texture. The writing is now purer, chastened and a great deal more disciplined.

There is a similar marshalling of Bellow's earlier themes. For some years now he has been obsessed with that fatigue of spirit which hangs so dismally over contemporary life. *Seize the Day* shows a man utterly exhausted, unable so much as to feel his despair until the wrenching final page. *Augie March* shows a man composing a self out of a belief in life's possibilities. Of the two books *Seize the Day* seems to me the more convincing and authentic, perhaps because despair is easier to portray than joy, perhaps because the experience of our time, as well as its literature, predisposes us to associate truth with gloom. In any case, what seems notable about *Herzog* is that nothing is here blinked or evaded, rhetoric does not black out reality (Herzog declares himself "aging, vain, terribly narcissistic, suffering without proper dignity"); yet the will to struggle, the insistence upon human possibility, is maintained, and not as a mere flourish but as the award of agony. Herzog learns that

> . . . To look for fulfillment in another . . . was a feminine game. And the man who shops from woman to woman, though his heart aches with idealism, with the desire for pure love, has entered the female realm.

Not, perhaps, a very remarkable lesson, but worth learning when the cost comes high. More importantly, Herzog says about himself, wryly but truthfully, that he is a man who "thought and cared about belief." To think and care about belief: that is the first step toward salvation.

For all its vividness as performance, *Herzog* is a novel driven by an idea. It is a serious idea, though, in my judgment, neither worked out with sufficient care nor worked into the grain of the book with sufficient depth. Herzog, he tells us, means to write something that will deal "with a new angle on the modern condition, showing how life could be lived by renewing universal connections, overturning the last of the Romantic errors about the uniqueness of the Self, revising the old Western, Faustian ideology. . . ." This time clearly speaking for Bellow, Herzog declares himself opposed to

The canned sauerkraut of Spengler's "Prussian Socialism," the common-
places of the Wasteland outlook, the cheap mental stimulants of Alienation, the cant and rant of pipsqueaks about Inauthenticity and Forlornness.
I can't accept this foolish dreariness. We are talking about the whole life
of mankind. The subject is too great, too deep for such weakness,
cowardice. . . .

And in the magazine *Location* Bellow has recently written an attack on
"the 'doom of the West' [which] is the Established Church in modern
literature." It is a Church, he says, which asserts the individual to be
helpless among the impersonal mechanisms and sterilities of modern life;
it cultivates self-pity and surrender; and it is wrong.

Bellow has touched on something real. Talk about "the decline of
the West" can be elitist rubbish. The posture of alienation, like any other,
can collapse into social accommodation. Cries of despair can become mere
notes of fashion. Where the motif of alienation in the literature of
modernism during the late 19th and early 20th Centuries signified an act
of truth, courage and sometimes rebellion too, now it can easily become
the occasion for a mixture of private snobbism and public passivity. Yet
may not all ideas suffer this sort of outcome in a culture which seems
endlessly capable of assimilating and devitalizing everything? Suppose
Bellow's assault upon alienation becomes fashionable (it is not hard to
imagine the positive thinkers who will hasten to applaud): will it not then
suffer a public fate similar to that of the ideas he attacks?

Bellow is being just a little too cavalier in so readily disposing of a
central theme of modernist literature. Surely, as it was manifested in the
work of writers like Joyce, Flaubert, Eliot and Baudelaire, the sense of
alienation expressed a profound and even exhilarating response to the
reality of industrial society. (An imagining of despair can be as bracing as a
demand for joy can be ruthless.) And does not the sense of alienation, if
treated not as a mere literary convenience but as a galling social fact—
does this not continue to speak truthfully to significant conditions in our
life?

I raise these matters because Bellow, as a serious writer, must want
his readers to consider them not merely in but also beyond the setting of
his novel. When, however, one does consider them strictly in the context
of *Herzog*, certain critical issues present themselves. There is a discrepancy
between what the book actually is—brilliant but narrow in situation and
scope—and the sweeping intentions that lie behind it; or in other words,
between the dramatic texture and the thematic purpose. In the end one
feels that *Herzog* is too hermetic a work, the result of a technique which
encloses us rigidly in the troubles of a man during his phase of withdrawal

from the world. The material is absorbing in its own right; it is handled with great skill; but in relation to the intended theme, it all seems a little puny.

Bellow has conceived of the book as a stroke against the glorification of the sick self, but the novel we have—as picture, image, honest exposure—remains largely caught up with the thrashings of the sick self. One wants from Bellow a novel that will not be confined to a single besieged consciousness but instead will negotiate the kind of leap into the world which he proclaims, to savor the world's freshness and struggle against its recalcitrance, perhaps even to enter "politics in the Aristotelian sense."

Meanwhile, critics and readers, let us be grateful.

TONY TANNER

The Prisoner of Perception

His face was before him in the blotchy mirror. It was bearded with lather. He saw his perplexed, furious eyes and he gave an audible cry. *My God! Who is this creature? It considers itself human. But what is it? Not human of itself. But has the longing to be human.*

This is Moses E. Herzog, the central figure in Bellow's most recent novel, entitled *Herzog*. (His name almost certainly derives from Joyce's *Ulysses* where there is a minor character called Moses Herzog who is a put-upon Jewish merchant. It may also contain a distant reference to the famous and very brave mountaineer, Maurice Herzog.) This book—Bellow's most impressive to this date—seems to summarise and contain all the questions, the problems, the feelings, the plights, and the aspirations worked over in the previous novels, and it follows them out to their extremest reaches. It seems to be the result of a conclusive grappling with the gathering preoccupations of years. Herzog himself is clearly a descendant, if not a summation, of Bellow's other main characters—worried, harassed, brought down, messed up. His private life is at a point of chaos—for he is trying to recover from a disastrous second marriage which has just ended in divorce. He is condemned to perpetual compulsive introspection, the victim of memories which refuse to be shut out, racked by endless, nagging cerebration. He seems terribly isolated and cut-off, wandering the congested city streets, brooding apart in lonely rooms. The book contains few actual incidents in the present—an abortive trip to Vineyard Haven, a night with a girl friend, a visit to Chicago to see one of his children which ends with a car crash, the return to an old tumble-down house in the country which was where his second marriage reached its ultimate crisis. The significant action mainly takes part in his head. People and incidents teem through his memory, precipitating great bouts of agitated soul-searching and pounding speculation. More than that, his mind heaves under the weight and pressure, not only of his personal worries, but of the modern city, the innumerable problems of the modern age; ultimately it finds itself struggling with the deepest questions and mysteries of Man himself. His mind seems compelled to take on itself the burden of the whole world, the problem of mankind; yet as a physical being his relationships are fouled up, he is separated from his children, he is one of the struggling sweating mass—powerless, something of a failure, not a little lost. Yet his mind will not be stilled. There is irony as well as urgency in his predicament and Bellow excels himself in this book by presenting not only the importance, but also the curse and the comedy of intense consciousness. Herzog's is a representative modern mind, swamped with ideas, metaphysics and values, and surrounded by messy facts. It labours to cope with them all. The book enacts that labour.

At first sight, the meaning of the book might seem to be the sum of all the dozens of ideas that course through Herzog's mind. Yet a more careful view reveals a deeper, subtler intent. The book moves from a corrosive restlessness to a point of temporary rest, and the most important meaning is in that actual movement: the internal labour finally gives way to a glimpse of peace. A consideration of the form and technique of the book can help us to understand this better. A brief opening passage shows us a "tranquil" Herzog, alone in his old country house during the "peak of summer." Then it takes us back to the start of all his troubles. "Late in spring Herzog had been overcome by the need to explain, to have it out, to justify, to put in perspective, to clarify, to make amends." This compulsion to *understand*—typical of Bellow's protagonists—manifests itself in Herzog's habit of making endless notes and jottings, recording fragmentary thoughts, and observations. More than that he gets into the habit of writing letters—to friends, relations, dead ancestors, politicians, philosophers, finally even to God. Many of them are unfinished, none of them, as far as we know, is ever sent. Perhaps they are all imaginary, part of his internal continuum, sudden moments of excited hyper-consciousness when the mind engages in silent partnerless dialogues—"having it out," trying to clarify. Meanwhile Herzog is often sitting or lying down, "in the coop of his privacy." For the bulk of the book we are in that coop with him—going over things, witnesses of this endless, silent self-examination. It is not systematic: like his life it is mismanaged and patternless. He cannot organise the mixed swarm of facts, notions and ideas: "consciousness when it doesn't clearly understand what to live for, what to die for, can only abuse and ridicule itself." For much of the book Herzog suffers from "unemployed consciousness."

The book has to bring us not only the excitement of the ideas, but the strain, the futility, the near insanity which Herzog experiences. So the reminiscences and the thoughts and the letters flow, one into the other, like a troubled stream. There are sudden interruptions, extremely vivid, graphic evocations of New York or Chicago—unrelated, sudden heightenings of external pressure. The harsh noise and density of the city seem only to drive Herzog deeper into himself. He is never more lost in thought than on the subway. Significant human contact is minimal; even with Ramona, his current girl friend, he seems ultimately detached, only intermittently stimulated to a brief sexual activity accompanied by a little incipient emotion. He can recall many affairs; he loves his brothers and children; he has long talks with certain friends. But for the most part he seems quite incapable of any genuine relationships. His memory is densely populated—yet he moves like a solitary, sealed up in himself, ridden by a million thoughts. Writing letters to the void, while reality ebbs away from him.

But a counter-movement grows increasingly strong—a desire to re-engage simple reality, a yearning for a reprieve from this excess of solitary cerebration, a desire to pass beyond the impossible task of mental justification. His first instinct had been to explain. By the end he is meditating:

> A curious result of the increase of historical consciousness is that people think explanation is a necessity of survival. They have to explain their condition. And if the unexplained life is not worth living, the explained life is unbearable, too.

The book follows out his doomed attempts to explain and synthesise until we can feel with Herzog the need and the possibility for some new commencement and calm somewhere on the other side of "explanation." At the end Herzog is tranquil in his country house—as we glimpsed him at the start. Now we understand that tranquillity. But only because we have experienced to the full the turmoil which preceded it.

We shall have to look more closely at some of the ideas that Herzog wrestles with for they are crucial ideas in Bellow's work. But it must first be emphasised that Herzog is in no normal state: it is part of the meaning of the book that these ideas are being turned over by a mind in the throes of a riot of subjectivism. He is often in the state he finds himself enduring in Grand Central Station "both visionary and muddy . . . feverish, damaged, angry, quarrelsome, and shaky." On a train he will start various letters to people as various as Adlai Stevenson, Ramona, Nehru, Commissioner Wilson—and himself. His reaction at the time is typical:

> Quickly, quickly, more! . . . Herzog now barely looking through the tinted, immovable, sealed window felt his eager, flying spirit streaming out, speaking, piercing, making clear judgments, uttering final explanations, necessary words only. He was in a whirling ecstasy. He felt at the same time that his judgments exposed the boundless, baseless bossiness and wilfulness, the nagging embodied in his mental constitution.

The sealed window—the soaring mind: the certainty as to the importance of his thoughts—a suspicion that they result from a ridiculous tantrum. That is typical Herzog. He cannot select or filter his thoughts. "I am a prisoner of perception, a compulsory witness." This is a mind with no certainties, no calm programme, no sure focus. A mind in pain. "He wrote to Spinoza. *Thoughts not causally connected were said by you to cause pain. I find that is indeed the case. Random association, when the intellect is passive, is a form of bondage."*

Like many another alienated observer, he wonders if anguish and detachment are the necessary condition of his calling. "Moses had to see reality. Perhaps he was somewhat spared from it so that he might see it better, not fall asleep in its thick embrace. Awareness was his work; extended consciousness was his line, his business. Vigilance." Looking at his brother, a man immersed in business, Herzog contrasts himself—"a man like me has shown the arbitrary withdrawal of proud subjectivity from the collective and historical progress of mankind." But he says this in self-mockery, and by the end he drops the idea as a vain-glorious falsehood. Gradually, the prisoner starts to emerge. Here is a crucial moment after a heavy spell of speculation and vast generalisations:

> But then he realized that he did not need to perform elaborate abstract intellectual work—work he had always thrown himself into as if it were the struggle for survival. But not thinking is not necessarily fatal. Did I really believe that I would die when thinking stopped?

(Herzog alternates between addressing himself as "I" and "he," and even "you"; while not completely schizophrenic, it does suggest mental disturbance as well as comic detachment.) The habit of subjectivism, explanation, thought itself, becomes almost a plague, a genuine neurosis, of which he is at least partially cured by the end of the book as he moves towards reality's "thick embrace."

But his self-communings and memories compromise the bulk of the book. True, the city-scapes are incomparably vivid, detailed, and pungent; essentially *there* so we can really feel the background against which the modern mind works, and has to work. Herzog feels part of the New York mess, and indeed there seems to be at times an intimate connexion between the city and his thoughts. Perhaps the teeming confusion of its chaos agitates his mind into a state of over-excited emulation—the city triggering off the spasms of unrelated thoughts, just as the thoughts sometimes grind to an inconclusive halt in the congestion of the city streets. Thus in Chicago: "He was perhaps as midwestern and unfocused as these same streets. Not so much determinism, he thought, as lack of determining elements—the absence of a formative power." For all that, the most important reality in the book is inside Herzog's head, in the ramifications of his ungovernable memory and the fretful reachings of his mind. It is there that we meet most of the characters in his life, and relive some of his most intense experiences. It is there that Herzog establishes contact with his ancestors and re-enacts his "ancient times." As though he is trying to form some sort of community in his head to compensate for the absence of it in society at large. It is part of his effort to "make steady progress from disorder to harmony," to capture a sense of lineage out of the welter of the past—the past of Moses Herzog, of his family, his race, his culture, Man himself. Many of his letters are to the dead. "But then why shouldn't he write the dead? He lived with them as much as with the living—perhaps more." He knows what an "insidious blight" nostalgia is, but his prolonged excursions into the past are only partially self-indulgence and escapism. For it is in his memory that Herzog is seeking some lost reality, some necessary key which will help him to align himself with the norms from which he has wandered and blundered into his personal chaos and separation. He must expose himself to everything, excluding nothing (not even the traumatic sexual assault he suffered as a child) before he can learn true acceptance and a new orientation. Mental regurgitation is part of his therapy: the way back to a point at which life can be resumed lies through memory. "Engrossed, unmoving in his chair, Herzog listened to the dead at their dead quarrels." Some of the most powerful and moving scenes are of his family, his youth, the sufferings of his "late unlucky father": scenes and characters are re-created with an astonishing and compelling wealth of circumstantial detail, while Herzog seems to go into a sort of catatonic trance, engulfed by the past.

Note that Bellow is not concerned to give a straight-forward, chronological biography of Herzog. He is concerned to show a middle-aged confused man beset by teeming fragments of the past, trying to relate them, seeking coherence, trying to disentangle from them all some sense

of necessary ancestry, and stabilising orientation. Similarly with the characters and events of Herzog's own adult life—they are recalled, summoned
up in love or anger, or allowed to drift in and out of the periphery of his
mind. There are well over a score of characters, who loom into focus with
extreme individual vividness—his wives, his women, psychiatrists, lawyers, fellow academics, brothers, writers, childhood friends, as well as his
parents and older relations. Inevitably many of the incidents he recalls
with these people are essentially conversations, discussions, disagreements,
rows. Apart from sex, and some travel, most of Herzog's more recent
experience has been mainly verbal. This indeed, is perhaps part of the
disease—his own, his age's. "People legislate continually by means of
talk." Like Augie, Herzog is surrounded by people who want to give him
advice, manipulate him, impose their view of things, their realities, on
his. Some of them—his second wife, her lover, her lawyer—actually plot
against him for his money, and his children, but most of the pressures are
verbal. Augie found himself surrounded by Machiavellians: Herzog is set
down among "Reality-Instructors"—people who positively enjoy thrusting
forward the low view of truth, cruel in their relish of the nastiness of life.
And even Moses himself recognises that he, too, wants to teach his ideas.
"A very special sort of lunatic expects to inculcate his principles. Sandor
Himmelstein, Valentine Gersbach, Madeleine P. Herzog, Moses himself.
Reality Instructors. They want to teach you—to punish you with—the lessons of
the Real." But one question abides with Herzog which he silently puts to
the world of Reality-Instructors. "What makes you think realism must be
brutal?" Part of his quest is for a higher view which nevertheless does not
blink the brutality which is undoubtedly there.

Herzog recalls people and incidents as often as not because he
wishes to take issue with their views, or consider the implications of their
acts. We get very little external reality straight—indeed it is possible that
the whole book is a reminiscence. (There is a slight, perhaps deliberate
ambiguity, about the time lapse between the start and the end. One is not
sure whether something is actually taking place or being remembered.
Indeed, it is possible that Herzog is remembering previous memories. The
book ends where it began.) Situations, characters, and events for the most
part come to us coloured by his memory, penetrated by his questioning:
often broken up or interrupted by a burst of letter writing. Herzog calls his
letter-writing and scribbling of odd notes "ridiculous," but he falls into it
continually. Some of the letters are comic, some angry, some desperate,
some urgent, many of them theoretical and pedagogic. They are a way of
relieving the accumulating pressures on his mind; also they are part of his
vast attempt to take stock, understand, and clarify. Into them he puts his

needs, his resentments, his quarrels with the creeds of his age; through them he expresses his inchoate beliefs and tentative faith. Perhaps also they not only help him to come to terms with the dizzying clutter of his life and times, but also serve as a means whereby he can disburden himself of that clutter. But as a phenomenon, irrespective of what Herzog writes in them, these letters and notes are symptoms of a plight and desire which are basic in Bellow's work. Herzog says to himself, in words which remind us of so many other Bellow protagonists: "I seem to have been stirred fiercely by a desire to communicate, or by the curious project of attempted communication." All those prolific letters simply serve to emphasise Herzog's silence, his basic isolation and apartness and indrawnness. He carries the world in his head. But the desire to communicate is real and points the way to a possible redemption from a habit of introspection which could lead to solipsism.

Herzog's thoughts and concerns are too various to summarise; indeed their profuse, unrelated multiplicity is an essential part of the meaning of the book. But a few concerns which have always seriously engaged Bellow recur, and Herzog wrestles with problems and ideas that other characters in Bellow's work have also attacked and pondered, and that Bellow himself has discussed in many articles. Some of these should be mentioned. For instance Herzog returns continually to the question of the value and importance of the individual self. The great work he was meditating before he started to go to pieces was going to show "how life could be lived by renewing universal connections; overturning the last of the Romantic errors about the uniqueness of the Self," and he thinks back with some irony to the time when as a student he gave an Emersonian address maintaining "The Main enterprise of the world . . . is the up-building of a man. The private life of one man shall be a more illustrious monarchy . . . than any kingdom in history." On the other hand he is disgusted by the slick contemporary pessimists who maintain that you must "sacrifice your poor, squawking, niggardly individuality which may be nothing anyway (from an analytic viewpoint) but a persistent infantile megalomania, or (from a Marxian point of view) a stinking little bourgeois property—to historical necessity." Against low sneering realists, Herzog prefers Romanticism. But on the other hand the objections to the cult of selfhood remain. Herzog oscillates continually and decides "perhaps a moratorium on definitions of human nature is now best." But secretly he really resists taking the view which degrades human worth, even though he knows what it is to long to escape from the burden of individuality. Secondly, the problem of freedom worries him: "people can be free now but the freedom doesn't have any content. It's like a howling emptiness."

Technology has "created private life but gave nothing to fill it with."
What does personal freedom mean; how much are we historically determined? Herzog thinks of Tolstoy's concept of freedom, and would seem to
sympathise with it. "*That man is free whose condition is simple, truthful—
real. To be free is to be released from historical limitation.*" A dignified
ideal—yet to step out into the street is to be buffeted by evidence of
limitations.

   Thirdly, Herzog refuses to believe the modern age is worse than
any other and will not endorse pessimism. Spengler's notion of the decline
of the West with its implication that the great age for Jews is gone forever,
made him sick with rage as a youth: and when he reads that Heidegger
talks about "the fall into the quotidian," he writes a letter to him asking
"*When did this fall occur? Where were we standing when it happened?*" The
potentialities of human life must be perennial. Though there is evil in the
world he refuses to concentrate on it as the sole reality. He hears the most
appalling evidence of sheer evil in the court room. The description of how
a woman, without any tears or remorse, killed her child while her lover
lay on the bed, watching and smoking, makes him feel violently sick. It is
inexplicable, irremediable evil. "He opened his mouth to relieve the
pressure he felt. He was wrung, and wrung again, and wrung again,
again." It is this incident which makes him go to Chicago, intending to kill
Madeleine and her lover because he has a notion they are mistreating his
child. Of course, he has no murder in his heart and transcends his
moment of aggressive impulse. His attitude to life is essentially creative
not destructive. There is evil but he feels we must look away from it,
beyond it. He feels that our age is too fond of regarding itself as monstrous, that an insidious prestige is now attached to "the negative."
Vengefully, we deny all possibility of transcendence. The human imagination has been deflected and feeds on murder and death: "*Safe, comfortable
people playing at crisis, alienation, apocalypse and desperation, make me sick,*"
writes Herzog to a fellow professor. All this is the wrong path for civilisation.
"*We love apocalypses too much, and crisis ethics, and florid extremism with its
thrilling language. Excuse me, no. I've had all the monstrosity I want.*" To
another he writes:

> Has the filthy moment come when moral feeling dies, conscience disintegrates,
> and respect for liberty, law, public decency, all the rest collapse in cowardice,
> decadence, blood? . . . I can't accept this foolish dreariness. We are talking
> about the whole of mankind.

He thinks that "*mankind is making it—making it in glory though deafened by
the explosions of blood.*" This is not callousness in Herzog; rather it is an

insistence not only on the futility but on the dangers of dwelling on evil and death, nourishing the imagination on suffering and despair. Herzog wants to get away from the insidious attractions of nihilism. He is working for a change of heart.

These, then, are some of the ideas that possess Herzog. He is convinced of their importance; he wants to change the world. And Bellow is careful to show that there is some comic presumption in all this along with a fair amount of egotism. Not for nothing is Herzog often caught looking at his own reflexion—he is unusually self-absorbed and self-important. Balance is restored by continual reminders of Herzog as a struggling physical creature; and he himself is continually mocking himself, undercutting his high mental intentions. We catch him at a transition point, waking to the ludicrous side of his conviction that "the progress of civilization—indeed, the survival of civilization—depended on the successes of Moses E. Herzog." He has it in him to want to be a new law-giver to mankind (as his name suggests) but his mind has reached a dangerous point when it can think "If I am right, the problem of the world's coherence, and all responsibility for it, becomes mine." Herzog himself comes to smile at himself, mentally legislating for the whole world while crammed into a subway car. After all, his own life is a "catalogue of errors"; he has been self-righteous, conceited in his suffering, monstrously egotistical, mediocre and merely "flirting a little with the transcendent." These are rigorous self criticisms; more usually it is the comic futility of his thinking that strikes him. At the same time his notions are precious and not invalidated. But for all his absurdity he is Herzog for good or bad. "I am Herzog. I have to be that man. There is no one else to do it. After smiling, he must return to his own Self and see the thing through." And properly to be that self he has to move beyond ideas, temporarily at least, and re-establish contact with ordinary reality.

This provides the ending of the book. Taking his daughter out, he has a car crash. He has some exhausting, troublesome hours with the police because of the revolver found on him. And this is where he really starts to relax, to descend "from his strange, spiraling flight of the last few days." He asks himself:

> Is this, by chance, the reality you have been looking for, Herzog, in your earnest Herzog way? Down in the ranks with other people—ordinary life?
> By yourself you can't determine which reality is real?

Bailed out by his brother he returns to his old country house. Taking an inventory of its great disorder and mess, he seems at the same time to be taking stock of the mess of his own life. He feels a strange joy, relaxed and liberated. Liberated, not only from Madeleine, but from excessive exhausting egotism, the curse of unending thought, the compulsive desire to explain everything and legislate mentally for the whole world. Madeleine said he was "sick with abstractions," and another woman tells him his "ideas get in the way." He feels there is some truth in this. He realises that perhaps he has been making an error in "going after reality with language."

A new calm starts to grow in him because he gradually ceases to strive for comprehension. "Go through what is comprehensible and you conclude that only the incomprehensible gives any light." He is sure that life is more than "mere facticity." Faith grows in him, as he starts to move beyond his verbalising, intellectualising, self-preoccupation and self-importance. Quoting approvingly the Whitman line—"Escaped from the life that exhibits itself"—he comes to a realisation of the dangers of that narcissism which makes an individual set himself up as a witness, an exemplar. He is learning a new humility, reacquainting himself with the ordinary with deep gladness. The curse is lifting and he is on the verge of a new health, stirred by "indefinite music within." Instead of worrying at the world with his theories he relaxes, "feeling that he was easily contained by everything about him." To calm his imagination, excited by a new happiness, he paints a piano for his daughter. At the same time "To God he jotted several lines":

> How my mind has struggled to make coherent sense. I have not been too good at it. But have desired to do your unknowable will, taking it and you, without symbols. Everything of intensest significance. Especially if divested of me.

He decides to "lay off certain persistent torments. To surrender the hyperactivity of this hyperactive face. But just to put it out instead to the radiance of the sun." He starts thinking about a more ordinary, sane future; instead of perverse self-communing—"work. Real, relevant work." "I mean to share with other human beings as far as possible and not destroy my remaining years in the same way. Herzog felt a deep, dizzy eagerness to begin." The prose of this last chapter is extremely specific and at the same time brimming with lyricism. It communicates Herzog's new delight in the simple objects in his house, and the loveliness of the summer garden; his dawning reverence for the concrete, the rich plentitude of the seen world. At the same time it catches his inner, trembling fervour as he moves beyond thought to a mood which is almost mystical. He is surcharged with a strange joy—mortal, but with transcendent intimations.

"This strange organization, I know it will die. And inside—something, some-thing, happiness. . . ."

The "spell" of the last few months is passing. "Perhaps he'd stop writing letters. Yes, that was what was coming, in fact. The knowledge that he was done with those letters." The last scene of the book leaves Herzog, stretched out on a couch, for the first time experiencing a true pervading quiet after the remorseless inner clamouring which has racked him throughout the book. "At this time he had no messages for anyone. Nothing. Not a single word." So the book ends. The resolution is completely internal. Externally there is still mess extending in all direc-tions, but he has won through to a new attitude to it and seems at least able to re-enter it in a more tranquil spirit. His new good intentions are not shown in action; we do not see the common life he intends to lead nor do we see him sharing his life with other human beings. The book takes Herzog to the end of his sickness and the promise of cure. The inward work has been done. He has endured thought and memory to the point of madness and breakdown: now he is passing beyond them into a mood of calm quiescent readiness. More genuinely than in any previous book by Bellow, we feel a novel, joyous sanity growing out of the neurotic exhaus-tion. No new meanings, no solutions: rather a change of heart, a turning to the sun. Not resignation but a profound "let be," accompanied by peace and a prayer of praise such as can only be uttered the other side of suffering.

JOHN JACOB CLAYTON

Alienation and Masochism

Bellow affirms. But if Bellow affirms so *hard*, it is because he has to compensate for so much that he sees in the culture. But let me go further: it is not only what Bellow *sees* in the culture but what he *brings* to the culture. He has within him the seeds of the despair which he attacks. He is reviling that side of himself which concurs with the prophets of doom and hucksters of the void.

Partly this despair derives from a frustrated idealism. Bellow is like the humanist he criticizes in the *Times Literary Supplement* for judging by a system of ideals deriving from eighteenth century humanism (and nineteenth century romanticism) and therefore seeing the life around him as bitterly disappointing, as absurd. Believing in nobility, Bellow looks around him—and within him—and fears it isn't there.

Of course, Bellow is aware of the fallacy of setting impossible standards—for example, as in his "Sermon of Doctor Pep" or the satire on idealism in *Augie March* and *Henderson the Rain King*. But beneath the satire he is like Augie: "You want there should be Man with a capital M, with great stature." He lyricizes over Father Herzog: "His *I* had such dignity." He sorrows over a world from which nobility and greatness and dignity seem to be missing. The complement of such idealism and love of greatness is an anguish at what society and the individual really are.

Perhaps this anguish is particularly Jewish. The other side of Jewish hope for the individual and faith in the common life is Jewish despair, Jewish guilt and self-hatred, Jewish masochism. As Maurice Samuels has written of the Jewish people with their lofty idealism: "It was because they had undertaken to be so much better that they felt themselves to be so

From *Saul Bellow: In Defense of Man.* Copyright ©1968 by Indiana University Press.

much worse." Here again, in Rosenberg's phrase, is the "Jewish vertigo" —but this time with its tragic side: the Jew's "refusal to accept from life less than the full satisfaction in the face of all obstacles,"—a refusal leading to despair.

Bellow's despair is typically Jewish. For while it is true that the Jew has transformed suffering by means of irony and a celebration of endurance, it is also true that Jews are expert sufferers. Howe says, "The virtue of powerlessness, the power of helplessness, the company of the dispossessed, the sanctity of the insulted and injured—these, finally, are the great themes of Yiddish literature." In each phrase of this statement we see the underside of *bitochon* (faith in life): helplessness, alienation, injury. We think of the tradition of suffering on the Yiddish stage, of stories of helplessness such as Schneour's "Revenge"—the "revenge" for the murder of a young man's family in a pogrom being only the killing of a gentile's dog—followed by anxiety: "the gentile must have overheard!" We think of the stories of sorrow like that of "Munie the Bird Dealer": openly cuckolded by his wife, "Munie sat down with his hands on the floor, and remained there, motionless, not like a human being, but like a piece of broken gray stone." We think of Kafka's projections of guilt and masochism, of Henry Roth's *Call It Sleep*, a novel of guilt, of a child's punishment and misery, of a victory achieved at the cost of a retreat into the self. Indeed, when critics say that the Jewish writer now speaks for all men and that this is the root of his current popularity, they refer primarily to the "voices of powerlessness speaking in situations of humiliation, nakedness, and weakness. . . ." This is the Jewish voice "that speaks most directly about the nature of present experience." Fiedler agrees: "It is the Jew who has been best able to recast this old American wisdom (that home is exile, that it is the nature of man to feel himself everywhere alienated) in terms valid for twentieth century Americans, which is to say, for dwellers in cities." Similarly Isaac Rosenfeld sees the Jew as the perfect "insider" in a complex age precisely because he is so much an "outsider."

Hence, in attacking the tradition of alienation and despair in modern literature, Bellow is attacking also a Jewish tradition very much his own. The *diaspora*—the scattering of the Jews into exile—is threefold: from the promised land to the shtetl, from the shtetl to the Jewish slum (Napoleon Street in *Herzog*), from the ghetto to the modern world (Chicago in *Herzog*). (We remember the hero of Philip Roth's "Eli the Fanatic" discovering his alienation in the midst of the suburbs by being forced to recognize his identification with the refugee in the black suit and hat.) Swados, like Bellow in asking writers to rejoin the human race, attacks the Jewish writer's "tradition of alienation" and argues, "The

reader who does not approach these Jewish writers with romantic preconceptions finds himself continuously stumbling on their ill-concealed self-
hatred, despair, and masochism." This is reminiscent of Wallace Markfield's
To an Early Grave, which, while it treats with gentle irony the suffering of
the sensitive, ego-ridden, world-beaten hero, also celebrates that suffering. In a beautiful prayer to the dead "Leslie" (a character modelled after
Isaac Rosenfeld), Morroe thinks:

> Leslie . . . intercede for me.
> I am no big intellect. I am no bargain. I watch too much
> television. I read, but I do not retain. I am not lost, exactly, but still I
> am nowhere. I am the servant of no great end. I follow the recommenda-
> tions of the *Consumer's Research Bulletin*.
> But do me this favor, anyway. Keep them off. For they hem me
> in from all sides now. They wait deep in the dark. They put in my
> mouth the taste of darkness. They set grief and despair upon me like
> savage dogs. They give me queer feelings, they get me all balled up.
> When I turn my head or open an eye they will rip me with tooth and
> claw. They will throw me from awful heights. They will drown me in
> a drop of water. They will put me in a grave.

The following line—"And then he got a whiff of far-off ocean"—is a
portent of hope, showing that Markfield is not wallowing in despair. But
the novel is in the tradition that Swados attacks. So too is Friedman's
Stern about a man "whose Jewishness," as Fiedler says, "survives only as a
psychological disease. . . ." Weighted down with guilt for paying too little
for his house, for not fighting his anti-Semitic neighbor, for being a Jew,
he may buy his son a trampoline to watch him rise free into the sky, he
may cultivate sophisticated Negro friends, he may join the Air Force—but
he is *nach-shlepper, a shlemiel*, guilty still. And still alienated, he gets sick
aboard a general's B-17: "Cowardly Jewish vomit staining a golden air-
craft." For Malamud in *The Assistant*, to be a Jew means to accept
suffering. Frank Alpine, converting to Judaism at the end, must undergo
circumcision, the pain of which foreshadows his life as a Jew (which is to
say, for Malamud, as a *man*: the Jew is simply the prototypal human
being).

Noting the positive and negative sides of the Jewish tradition,
Maxwell Geismar feels that "Judaism in Bellow's work is a source . . . of
guilt and anxiety rather than of pride and pleasure." He feels that Bellow
is *oppressed* by his moral tradition of Judaism. Indeed, he says (mistakenly)
of *The Victim* that

> the whole 'Jewish' concept in this hero (and in the author?) is so close to
> paranoia and madness, so fraught with guilt, anxiety, and fear and so

lacking in warmth, humor and joy, that it is no longer in the historic sense, Jewish. There is all the Jewish guilt without the Jewish pride, there is all the agony of life but no enjoyment, there is the heavy vestigial morality with none of the deep or wild human impulses which necessitated this morality.

This attack is unfair (what of Schlossberg? what of the humanizing, the learning to love, that Asa goes through?), and so one-sided that the criticism seems personally motivated and looks forward to Geismar's vicious personal attack on Bellow in *Ramparts*. But Geismar is not totally wrong; the guilt and the agony are strong in Bellow's fiction. Indeed, Norman Podhoretz calls the tone of *The Victim* "oppressively pessimistic." "I call it oppressive," Podhoretz goes on, "because it is a pessimism over the human condition even darker than Freud's in *Civilization and Its Discontents*. In *The Victim*, the making of a settlement (that is, the stifling of the instincts) is seen as bringing no positive rewards or compensations of any significance—no increase of energy through sublimation, no powerful Faustian drive; it merely has the negative virtue of preventing the outbreak of 'cannibalism.' " Certainly Bellow's view of the world includes what he calls "the darkness"—the presence in nature and in the human heart of that which has no concern for man; the presence of death under the "social sugars"; the presence of cannibalism under the breaded chickenburger; the chaos under the civilized ego. And so, he isn't speaking out of facile optimism when he asks: "After absurdity, what? After nakedness, what?"

Bellow himself has said, "Well, I am a melancholic—a depressive temperament. But I long ago stopped enjoying melancholy—I got heartily sick of my own character about fifteen years ago. Sometimes I think these comic outbursts [in *Augie March*] are directed against my own depressive tendencies." I would argue that his affirmation of man is also directed against his own bitter nature.

II

In spite of his desire to be affirmative, Bellow's depressive tendencies are seen in nearly all his fiction. One would expect in a writer who wishes to affirm human life and to defend the individual to find characters with strength, grace, even nobility. But Bellow's characters are lonely, despairing, cut off not only from society but from friends and wives. Moreover, they are pathological social masochists, filled with guilt and self-hatred, needing to suffer and to fail.

"A Father-to-Be" is a good example. Filled with despair and masochism relieved only by the humanity of the sufferer and the humor of his imagination, it contains in short form many of the essential elements of Bellow's characters.

The sufferer, Rogin, is like Tommy Wilhelm in his awkward bulk and like Herzog in his masochistic submission to a "bitch." In Joan, indeed, we have the first glimpse of Herzog's Madeleine—beautiful, with a Roman nose, sociable, aristocratic, money-devouring, man-devouring. Just as she now locks up her dog in the bedroom "where he jumped persistently against the door with a rhythmic sound of claws on the wood," so she will, when they marry, lock up Rogin.

The story tells of Rogin's subway ride to his fiancee's—what he sees and thinks. Rogin feels annoyed by the bills Joan is already piling up before marriage. Paying for her psychiatrist (a whim), her gifts to her rich roommate, her food, he feels weighed down, "under pressure." He generalizes, "Who is free? No one is free. Who has no burdens? Everyone under pressure. The very rocks, the waters of the earth, beasts, men, children—everyone has some weight to carry." Similarly, he sees two tall men, "shapeless in their winter clothes, as if their coats concealed suits of chain mail."

As in *Seize the Day*, the world is a loveless one. Rogin, a person with a warm heart, sees one man indifferent to his friend's confession of heavy drinking, sees a father fussing with his daughter "as if he were trying to change her into something else." Another child comes in with the same muff. The parents are annoyed; and "it seemed to Rogin that each child was in love with its own muff and didn't even see the other." His own mother, who had always spoiled him, was becoming difficult. "She had sat at the table motionless, with her long-suffering face, severe, and she let him cut his own meat, a thing she almost never did."

Indeed, Rogin is not sure, as he recalls his dream of carrying a woman on his head, whether the woman was fiancee or mother. He feels that they both are extracting their price—"Oh Lord, how he had to pay, and it had never even occurred to him formerly that these things might have a price"—leaving it uncertain as to what the price is or why he must pay it.

His most awful vision is of a fellow-passenger, handsome but empty looking, well-dressed—a dandy of respectability—cold: "he seemed to draw about himself a circle of privilege, notifying all others to mind their own business and let him read his paper." As Rogin, who is an inventor and possessor of strange notions, watches, he imagines that this respectable fellow-passenger might be his own son by Joan, a son in whom his own traits are recessive. He feels not like an individual but like an instrument working toward ends "we thought were our own. But no! The whole thing was so unjust. To suffer, to labor, to toil and force your way through the spikes of life . . . only to become the father of a fourth-rate man of the world like this. . . ." It is a vision of his own extinction—and not only his, but of the human future, in which his kind of man would be gone. We are reminded of Rogin's other dream—of refusing to allow an undertaker to cut his hair—that is, of refusing to die. Now this subway vision of his own death makes him irate; the reader wonders, will he be able to throw off his burdens or will he submit to "death"?

As the tragicomic fantasy continues, Rogin grumbles at Joan's door: " 'I won't be used. . . . I have my own right to exist.' " But quickly we know that he *will* be used. She plies him with baby talk—" 'Oh my baby. You're covered with snow. Why didn't you wear your hat? It's all over its little head'—her favorite third-person endearment." And although he thinks of telling her, " 'Do you think . . . that I alone was made to carry the burden of the whole world on me? Do you think I was born just to be taken advantage of and sacrificed?' " he says nothing.

And so, he defends his individuality, his dignity, his manhood— but only in his thoughts. When Joan comes back, he bows his head and lets her shampoo his hair; his "secret loving spirit" overflows into the sink, and he forgets the words he had rehearsed.

Certainly the "water-filled hollow of the sink" is meant to be a symbol of the womb and his "pink" scalp a symbol of infancy. This is Rogin's birth, but an ironic birth: he, not the man in the subway, is his son, Joan's son, in whom his own traits will be recessive and hers dominant. In effect this "spoiled child" is changing his mother. His uncertainty over which woman shall be "on his head" is over; it will be Joan, who is shampooing him. However, in a more important sense, Rogin is here acceding to death. In his dream he had refused to let the undertaker cut his hair; now he accepts Joan's shampoo.

Thus Rogin will never drop his burdens. He has submitted to a masochistic relationship, submitted to being "bled" like Tommy Wilhelm and Moses Herzog. Unlike *Seize the Day* and *Herzog,* this short story does not delve into the origins of Rogin's masochism. What is clear quite simply is the masochism; and it is clear too that the story, despairing of saving Rogin from his burdens, illustrates Bellow's own depressive temperament. Further, in his defeat as an individual, Rogin is symptomatic of a larger defeat of humanity. "Would this [cold, indifferent dandy] perhaps be general forty years from now?" Bellow, then, finds himself unable to defend the ordinary individual whom he so desires to vindicate. The masochism of Rogin makes it impossible for him to affirm the potentialities of his humanity, as it makes it impossible for Bellow to defend the human being.

It would be helpful now to consider these attitudes in three of the novels: *Dangling Man, Augie March,* and *Seize the Day.*

Isolates and depressives appear in all Bellow's novels and often his heroes are cut off from those who love them. There is, for instance, Joseph in *Dangling Man,* who can talk only to himself, and that fact accounts for the form of the novel as a journal, the proper form for an isolate. Bellow says of Gide in a review article, "he is an autobiographer, in fact, who hopes to be transformed into an historian, an excellent monologist who wants to advance to dialogue. . . . Sadly enough, the number of intelligent people whose most vital conversation is with themselves is growing." This criticism of Gide applies to the Dangling Man (and to most of Bellow's characters): Joseph is an intelligent monologist. He is living with Iva, his wife, but she might as well be visiting her mother, as does Asa's wife in *The Victim:* there is only one conversation between them and that is an argument. He is as alone as Asa, as Tommy Wilhelm, as Herzog. He has to invent a Spirit of Alternatives to talk to so that his ideas can have a sounding board—his friends, he affronts; his family, he rejects. There is no organized plot, no dramatic interaction among characters working toward a resolution: the problems and their resolution remain internal. The journal entries are flat, unemotional, yet quietly ironic; for example the January 16 entry: "Fairly quiet day." In the midst of so many fairly quiet days, this entry is self-lacerating. As Hassan says, the book leaves the impression "of a man who screams out in laughter to see his guts dangling from his belly." In quiet laughter: the screaming is internal.

It seems especially strange that Bellow, a defender of Man against writers of alienation and the void, should create in *Dangling Man* a novel so close in form and spirit to that classic novel of alienation and the absurdity of existence, Sartre's *Nausea.* There are so many similarities that it seems certain Bellow in 1944 was consciously drawing on Sartre's 1938 novel. Both novels are in the form of journals. Roquentin and Joseph start their journals for the same reason: an important change has come over them. "Something has happened to me," both heroes say in effect; they are trying to understand what it is. Both men are isolates: Roquentin has occasional sexual intercourse with Françoise the café owner, Joseph is married to Iva, but we hear little of these relationships; the emotional lives of the two men are equally barren. Each one is "pushed upon [himself] entirely," and for both this puts "the very facts of simple existence in doubt." Both feel boredom and weariness, a disgust for life.

Both are amateur writers studying eighteenth century figures. Both are unable to continue their writing, feeling, in Joseph's case (besides paralysis) that the ideas of the eighteenth century cannot answer his questions, and in Roquentin's case that his M. Rollebon had been only false security—a way for Roquentin to avoid feeling his own existence, a "Purpose" in life. Neither acts purposefully while he writes his journal; Joseph reads the newspapers, goes for walks, Roquentin walks, eats, thinks. Around them they see a fragmented and trivial environment: Roquentin sees disjointed hands, cards, teeth, hears pieces of fatuous conversation; and Joseph:

> Since eleven I have been growing restless, imagining that I am hungry again. Into the silence of the house there fall accentuating sounds, the closing of a door in another room, the ticking of drops from a faucet, the rustling of the steam in the radiator, the thrum of a sewing machine upstairs. The unmade bed, the walls are brightly striped. The maid knocks and pushes open the door. She has a cigarette in her mouth.

Joseph, like Roquentin, wonders who he is. Roquentin feels he is "No one. Antoine Roquentin exists for no one. That amuses me. And just what is Antoine Roquentin? An abstraction. A pale reflection of myself wavers in my consciousness. Antoine Roquentin . . . and suddenly the 'I' pales, pales and fades out." Is there a self? The more Roquentin writes about Rollebon, the more he finds that it is he himself who creates this character. Rollebon seems to have no fixed ego. Reports of his conduct do not seem to be about the same person. Joseph "suffers from a feeling of strangeness, of not quite belonging to the world, of lying under a cloud and looking up at it." No longer "the sort of person I had been," Joseph looks at himself, stands back and examines himself through the occasional use of third person description: "Joseph, aged twenty-seven, an employee of the Inter-American Travel Bureau, a tall, already slightly flabby but, nevertheless handsome young man, a graduate of the University of Wisconsin. . . ." What is this strange object "Joseph"? "Only for legal purposes," he says, is he his old self. This is not the same, certainly, as to deny the existence of a self; but it is to question with Sartre its consistency and unity. How strange for a writer committed to the defense of the individual!

Joseph and Roquentin are separated from the world, and so too is Tommy Wilhelm in *Seize the Day*. Tommy is legally separated from his wife; his father has rejected him as a slob; he has no friends, and (with reason) he doesn't trust his one acquaintance, Tamkin; he feels that his children's affections have been poisoned against him; he believes that his wife wishes him dead. He is bitter, weighed down by grief, living on self-pity and pills; alienated from himself, accepting the world's values and rejecting himself, he sees himself as a swine, an elephant, a hippopotamus. Like Herzog, like Joseph, like Asa, he sees a cold, alien world which reflects his own isolation; what he sees, he is.

> And was everybody crazy here? What sort of people did you see? Every other man spoke a language entirely his own, which he had figured out by private thinking; he had his own ideas and peculiar ways. If you wanted to talk about a glass of water, you had to start back with God creating the heavens and earth; the apple; Abraham; Moses and Jesus; Rome; the Middle Ages; gunpowder; the Revolution; back to Newton; up to Einstein; then war and Lenin and Hitler. After reviewing this and getting it all straight again you could proceed to talk about a glass of water. "I'm fainting, please get me a little water." You were lucky even then to make yourself understood. And this happened over and over and over with everyone you met. You had to translate and translate, explain and explain, back and forth, and it was the punishment of hell itself not to understand or be understood, not to know the crazy from the sane, the wise from the fools, the young from the old or the sick from the well. The fathers were no fathers and the sons no sons. You had to talk with yourself in the daytime and reason with yourself at night. Who else was there to talk to in a city like New York?

Of course Tommy, like all of Bellow's heroes, does not want to cut himself off from other men. Just as Joseph longs for a "colony of the spirit" and believes that "Goodness is achieved not in a vacuum, but in the company of other men, attended by love," so Tommy longs for merger into community, and, as we shall see, knows moments of loving communality. But in general his attachments have been to the cold nipple of the coke bottle and to the fantasy father who, even more terrible than the real father, persecutes him.

Happy-go-lucky Augie March may seem an exception, but he, too, is an alienatee. He has, it is true, many friends, many loves. Bellow turned to the affirmative *Augie March* after discarding a novel in progress, "The Crab and the Butterfly," of which one section, "The Trip to Galena," was published in *Partisan Review* in 1950. The hero is an alienatee like Joseph, only more aggressive and verbal, who rejects the practical advice of his sister, angry that she accepted a mediocre marriage. At the house of his future in-laws, he becomes sick, embarrasses everybody, and leaves early. Much more naturalistic then *Augie March*, the published excerpt offers few hints of the later novel's affirmations. The hero hates "romantic Hamlet melancholy," but unlike Augie, he exemplifies it. As Bellow said later, "It was a grim book, in the spirit of the first two, when I suddenly decided, 'No.' Actually my feeling wasn't as mild as I'm describing it. I felt a great revulsion." The result of this revulsion was the affirmative *Augie March*. But while Bellow seemingly discarded completely "The Crab and the Butterfly," we can see, comparing the published excerpt with *Augie March*, that the earlier novel is hidden away in the shell of the later one. In both there is a young man who had dealt with the black market in Europe, who had run with a rough crowd. In both, the hero's disreputable appearance and behavior bring shame to a sibling (brother in *Augie*, sister in *Crab*) who has accepted middle class life, which the hero rejects. In both, this sibling and spouse claim a kind of greatness, of nobility. In both, this sibling and also an old woman (an aunt in *Crab*, Grandma Lausch in *Augie*) want to plan the hero's life; the hero rejects these plans and strikes out on his own, criticizing the sibling for accepting too little, "While I, you see, was still campaigning." We remember Kayo Obermark's question to Augie: "How is your campaign for a worthwhile fate . . .?" But, far more important, in both the hero is, finally, a lonely outsider. As Tony Tanner says of Augie, "Underneath his exhilarating rhetoric one sometimes hears a faint echo of that saddest of lines from that loneliest of characters, Melville's Bartleby, who could only say, 'I would prefer not to.' "

Augie cannot commit himself to anyone. After Thea leaves, Augie groans, "Me, love's servant? I wasn't at all!" Even at the end he is by himself, his wife in Paris, and driving alone he is a stranger in exile.

III

Bellow's heroes are not only alienated; they alienate *themselves*. Filled with guilt, they loathe themselves and, in most of the novels, need to heap suffering and indignity on their own heads. Joseph, Asa, Tommy, Henderson, Herzog—all are moral (social) masochists. Their literary ancestors are in the fiction of the underground, especially in Dostoyevsky. Bellow borrowed, for instance, the entire plot of *Eternal Husband* for *The Victim*, and in all his novels he uses Dostoyevskian imagery, imagery of almost psychotic strain—vivid, seemingly irrelevant impressions that touch at the antennae of the unconscious.

Dangling Man has even closer affinities of spirit to Dostoyevsky's fiction than to Sartre's. By pointing out these affinities, I will show that Bellow is close to the underground tradition he attacks. Like the Underground Man, Joseph is a self-alienated moral masochist:

> But what can a decent man speak of with most pleasure?
> Answer: of himself.
> Well, so I will talk about myself.

So the Underground Man talks about himself, as does the Dangling Man. He does so from a wretched room—he seems pleased with its wretchedness and pleased with his own—at least he recites in detail all his disgusting traits, all his frustrations. He revels in his alienation, in his loathsomeness, in his spite. "People do pride themselves on their diseases." Joseph is like that too. As acidly self-analytic as Dostoyevsky's hero, he writes down every detail of his paralysis, of his disgust and boredom, of the frustrations that he faces. Like the Underground Man he is filled with self-hatred which reveals itself in his imagining or enlarging offenses against him. Both are "as suspicious and prone to take offence as a hunchback or a dwarf." Joseph is certain the maid disregards him; he is sure Iva is disgusted with him and wants him to earn his keep. The Almstadts treat him like a loafer and affront him by leaving a chicken feather in his orange juice. If Joseph reveals self-hatred by these projections, he demonstrates it also by explosive scenes very much like those the Underground Man indulges in with his friends from school. And as the Underground Man broods for years over the officer who, ignoring him, pushes past, so Joseph has to repay Burns, the Communist who ignores him presumably because Joseph is now a "renegade." Embarrassing the friend he is with, Joseph shouts that Burns is an "addict" and an "idiot"; then, going up to him, he makes Burns admit he knows him. Joseph, like the Underground Man, has a "great deal of *amour proper.*" He does not *openly* delight, as the Underground Man does, in "the enjoyment of despair," but like him Joseph has "a mad fear of being slighted or scorned, an exacerbated 'honor,' " a sign not of self-love but self-hatred.

Their self-hatred is the other side of their gigantic idealism. Both, trying to be more than human, are less. The Underground Man wants nothing more than to be good. He has the noblest, loftiest sentiments; he is full of loving-kindness, and, although he is the first to recognize his baseness, he feels superior to those who ridicule him. Joseph, too, is a moral idealist: he sees himself as the thoughtful, good man. He asks, "How should a good man live?" In spite of his recognition that he has changed, that he is not so mild as he once was, he is terribly self-righteous. He thinks of his friends as having failed him because of their weaknesses; he feels morally superior to his successful brother, rejecting his friendship and help. He believes he has not understood the "likelihood of baseness in other people," and although recognizing that "the treasons I saw at the Servatius party were partly mine," he generally keeps the stance of the moral man in an immoral world. It is largely because they cannot sustain their ideals that the Underground Man and Dangling Man hate themselves so much and act as badly as they do.

Their guilt and self-hatred are especially responsible for their desire to suffer. Joseph's suffering really has two effects: it expiates guilt and it forms a stance of moral superiority. If it is true, as I have said, that Joseph does not *openly* delight in suffering as the Underground Man does (who goes into a tavern hoping to be thrown through the window), nevertheless Joseph secretly seeks to suffer, just as do Tommy Wilhelm, Henderson, and Herzog.

First, simply to write the journal is in itself to choose to lacerate oneself—though at the same time to give oneself comfort by admiring the size of the wound. On the first page Joseph rejects the Hemingway code of "hard-boiled-dom" current in America. He is not going to be afraid of expressing weakness: he is going to moan, he is going to open himself up. Actually he is bitterly terse, but his anguish is clear.

He comes to the world with a desire to *not achieve*. He prefers a menial job at a travel agency to a good position with his brother. He prefers poverty to luxury. He would rather die in war than benefit from it, would rather be "a victim than a beneficiary." He does not want to raise himself by war, nor by anything else. Partly Joseph's sufferings are meant to assuage his guilt: it is significant that after his blood test—after blood has been taken from him—he is able for the first time to read all day. Partly, too, his suffering is a sign of his higher nature—he raises himself up by keeping himself down. He writes of Myron, whom he has just embarrassed in the scene with the Communist—"But then I may be expecting too much from Myron. He has the pride of what he has become: a successful young man, comfortable, respected, safe for the present from those craters of the spirit which I have lately looked into." Thus, although he has just embarrassed Myron, he is superior because of what he has gone through.

We find, then, that the defender of the dignity and freedom of the individual, he who affirms humanity, is none other than an alienatee and a masochist similar in a number of ways to Dostoyevsky's anti-hero, the Underground Man. One scene in *Dangling Man* reveals with particular clarity a Dostoyevskian psychology from which emerge behavior patterns associated with figures like Raskolnikov and Velchaninov. This scene also shows the conflict between Joseph the spokesman and Joseph the dramatic character. Keith Opdahl has spoken of the difficulty of creating ironic distance in the journal form. He points to various kinds of incongruities as enabling Bellow to separate author from character. Bellow is, in general, successful in making this separation; but in doing so, he makes it difficult for us to see Joseph as the reasonable defender of Western values.

Joseph takes Iva to his brother Amos' house for Christmas. Amos is disappointed in Joseph's choice of career—his choice of failure. After a quarrel at the dinner table during which Joseph refuses to consider becoming an officer, believing that to succeed would be to climb "upon the backs of the dead," he rejects both Amos' present of a hundred dollars and Amos' way of life; then, climbing to the music room, he listens again and again to a Haydn divertimento for cello—a record he had given the family the year before. Interrupted by his teen-aged niece Eta, who wants to play a Cugat record, he becomes angry. "Beggars can't be choosers," she tells him, and, furious, he spanks her. When the family rushes upstairs to stop him, he is irate that they think him a rapist and thief (he had taken a pin from his sister-in-law's drawer and Eta had seen and reported him). After they go home, Iva weeps on the bed. " 'Dearest!' I shouted. "It's so nice to know that you at least have faith in me.' "

Somehow through all of this he feels essentially pure. He had gone upstairs to return the hundred dollar bill, had stayed to gain the knowledge of life that Haydn could give him, treated Eta like the spoiled brat she was, and left because his own family implied that he was a thief and a pervert.

But the reader isn't convinced. First, the humble voluntary poverty and refusal to advance himself over the backs of the dead are ways of gaining secret superiority over his brother and society at large: he will be—it is his comparison—like Socrates, a common soldier. This superiority is revealed by his quoting Isaiah with regard to his sister-in-law Dolly, and Eta: "Because the daughters of Zion are haughty, and walk with stretched forth necks and wanton eyes, walking and mincing as they go, and making a tinkling with their feet: therefore the Lord will smite with a scab the crown of the head of the daughters of Zion, and the Lord will discover their secret parts." It is revealed too by his "missionary eagerness" to save Eta from her family when she was twelve.

As Joseph introduces the scene he remembers the last time Amos offered him money. When he refused, Amos said, "I'd take it, by golly. I wouldn't be so proud and stiff-necked." A few lines further on Joseph quotes from Isaiah about "stretched-forth necks." Thus he is projecting his secret pride onto "the daughters of Zion," Eta and Dolly. On the following page Joseph reflects that Eta resembles him physically and later wonders about (though he rejects) affinities of another kind. Thus his judgment of Eta's pride is a displaced judgment of his own, and a displaced anxiety that he will be smitten for pride.

At the end of the scene Joseph's anger at his family's unspoken accusations is again projection. No one says or even hints that he was handling the girl for perverted sexual satisfaction; no one says—Dolly in fact denies—that he is a thief. Yet in some sense he must feel guilty of both crimes. Joseph mentions the passage from Isaiah in connection with the graceful necks of Dolly and Eta. He is astonished that Isaiah, like himself, associates the graceful delicate neck of a woman with her "secret parts" her "ancient machinery of procreation." Thus he does see both Dolly and Eta as sexual objects. Upstairs, angry at Eta, he calls her an animal, and pulls her over his knees, "trapping both her legs in mine." As she struggles, it is her neck he remembers pressing down—and then he describes "her long hair reaching nearly to the floor and her round, nubile thighs bare" in his lap. Of course not all his description of the girl is sexual, but there is enough to make us feel that the hint of sexual offense is his own projection. The situation is not so clear concerning the charge of "thief." But in a general way, Joseph's attitude toward life is that of a guilty thief. As a moral masochist, anything Joseph takes feels like theft to him, just as in *The Victim*, Asa Leventhal feels that he has stolen his moderately good place in life.

Joseph's own place in life, he feels, is to suffer.

> I have never found another street that resembled St. Dominique. It was in a slum between a market and a hospital. I was generally intensely preoccupied with what went on in it and watched from the stairs and the windows. Little since then has worked upon me with such force as, say, the sight of a driver trying to raise his fallen horse, of a funeral passing through the snow, or of a cripple who taunted his brother. And the pungency and staleness of its stores and cellars, the dogs, the boys, the French and immigrant women, the beggars with sores and deformities whose like I was not to meet again until I was old enough to read of Villon's Paris, the very breezes in the narrow course of that street, have remained so clear to me that I sometimes think it is the only place where I was ever allowed to encounter reality.

We are reminded strongly of Herzog, who recalls

> Napoleon Street, rotten, toylike, crazy and filthy, riddled, flogged with harsh weather—the bootlegger's boys reciting ancient prayers. To this Moses' heart was attached with great power. Here was a wider range of human feelings than he had ever again been able to find. . . . What was wrong with Napoleon Street? thought Herzog. All he ever wanted was there.

For both heroes reality is the world of their childhood, and this reality is one of suffering. Late in the book Joseph receives a letter from John Pearl, nostalgic for Chicago. Joseph interprets Pearl's feelings: "He thinks he would be safer in Chicago, where he grew up. Sentimentality! He doesn't mean Chicago. It's no less inhuman. He means his father's house and the few blocks adjacent." It is the security of his own father's house that Joseph, like Herzog, longs for: two Jews yearning for the time their personal temples stood and the diaspora had not yet begun. Joseph remembers cleaning shoes at home as a child: the feeling of the room "closed off from the wet and fog of the street." He says, "nothing could have tempted me out of the house." It is this shutaway, secure world he is trying to recapture in his isolation and suffering. It is only a partial truth, but a truth nonetheless, that isolation and suffering are Joseph's ticket home.

This truth sheds light on the passage in which Joseph listens to Haydn in the music room.

> It was the first movement, the adagio, that I cared most about. Its sober opening notes, preliminary to a thoughtful confession, showed me that I was still an apprentice in suffering and humiliation. I had not even begun. I had, furthermore, no right to expect to avoid them. So much was immediately clear. Surely no one could plead for exception; that was not a human privilege. What I should do with them, how to meet them, was answered in the second declaration: with grace, without meanness. And though I could not as yet apply that answer to myself, I recognized its rightness and was vehemently moved by it. Not until I was a whole man could it be my answer, too.

It is a beautiful passage, affirming the possibility of communication and of human nobility in the face of suffering. To say that Joseph finds what he needs in the music is certainly not to negate the truth of what he finds, any more than the wisdom of Dostoyevsky's Underground Man is negated by *his* masochism. But let us see Joseph as he is: isolated from others, gaining by his suffering self-justification, moral mastery, the reflection of childhood security, the reduction of guilt. If goodness is achieved not "in a vacuum but in the company of other men attended by love," Joseph is not achieving it; he removes himself from the others, isolates himself with *dead* company—Haydn—leaving Iva alone with Amos, Dolly, and Eta. He speaks of grace and the lack of meanness as the way to meet suffering and humiliation, yet ten minutes before, he met the "humiliation" of being handed money by attacking his brother, and five minutes later he will throw a tantrum and attack a teenaged girl for the humiliation he receives at her hands. True, he admits that he has not yet become capable of applying Haydn's answer to his own life; but that is just the point: there is a schism between Joseph the spokesman and Joseph the character; the defense is qualified by the defender.

The defender is much like the Underground Man, who also yearns to love and to have faith in men (as is evident in the long, only partially ironic sermon to the prostitute), but whose pride leads him to scorn men and hate himself. Of course Dostoyevsky does not negate man. His characters are, like Joseph, alienatees, but also like Joseph, alienatees with souls. Bellow, like Dostoyevsky, does not want to plunge us into the void but to guide us away from it. But both authors have ambivalent attitudes toward life; much of Bellow's sympathy lies with Joseph the masochistic sufferer, despairer, alienatee, just as Dostoyevsky's sympathy is partly with Raskolnikov and Ivan. But when we say this, we must remember that Raskolnikov and Ivan, and Joseph, too, are themselves divided characters. Joseph, therefore, represents a good example of Bellow's desperate affirmation—his longing to affirm, but his inability to do so fully.

Seize the Day is still more obviously about a moral masochist, Tommy Wilhelm. Tommy is his own most difficult obstacle, his own worst enemy. What he believes to be his troubles are not his real troubles. He allows Margaret to place burden upon burden on him, when he knows that "no court would have awarded her the amounts he paid." He chooses to live with a cold, carping father in a hotel for retired people. He chooses, out of pride, to leave the company where he had been employed, and does not look for other work.

Nor is it only present troubles that are self-imposed. Throughout his life Tommy has made bad decisions he knew in advance to be bad. "He had decided that it would be a bad mistake to go to Hollywood and then he went." He did not accidentally give Tamkin his last $700. "From the moment when he tasted the peculiar flavor of fatality in Dr. Tamkin, he could no longer keep back the money."

He constantly provokes his father into punishing him. Knowing his father's attitude toward his drug-taking, Tommy nevertheless (or rather, therefore) waits until they are together to swallow a phenaphen. He indulges in sloppy habits which disgust the old man. When he makes a scene in the restaurant, choking himself in demonstration of what Margaret does to him, he certainly knows that his father will snap, "Stop that—stop it!" He begs for pity, "almost bringing his hands together in a clasp," although he knows he can expect no pity. "Look out, Wilky, you're tiring my patience very much," his father says before he finally explodes. Tommy knows he is tiring his father's patience, and he wants to do so.

Yet Tommy only dimly suspects his self-destructive impulses. He, like Asa, sees himself as a victim: "It isn't my fault"—fate, the world, the hotel clerk are against him. He has bad luck at cards, takes a licking on the stock market. As Napoleon once told a young officer, *"Bonheur est aussi une qualité."* Tommy, however, believes that he is simply unfortunate. He is being murdered: "You must realize, you're killing me," he tells his wife. "Thou shalt not kill! Don't you remember that?" When his father gives him advice, he reflects on how much the old man is *not* giving him. When his father says, "Well, Wilky, here we are under the same roof again, after all these years," Tommy is suspicious: "Wasn't his father saying, 'Why are you here in a hotel with me and not at home in Brooklyn with your wife and two boys?' " The city itself is against him, slapping parking tickets on his car or frightening him with handbills that look like tickets.

But Tommy sees in the city what he is himself. Is the city grasping, money sucking, self-centered? So too is Tommy, who tries to drink or eat his way back to childhood security, who begs for love and pity. Tommy hates the city as he hates his own "pretender" soul.

Yet he has chosen the city. He remembers idyllically the suburbs around Boston. But no, "to be here in New York with his old father was more genuinely like his life." Indeed, he believes that to suffer is his fate, therefore his true occupation:

> He received a suggestion from some remote element in his thoughts that the business of life—the real business—to carry his peculiar burden, to feel shame and impotence, to taste these quelled tears—the only important business, the highest business was being done. Maybe the making of mistakes expressed the very purpose of his life and the essence of his being here.

What better summation could there be of the life of a moral masochist—or, in Reik's terminology, of a social masochist?

Still, it is important to note that Tommy's masochism does not warp *Seize the Day*, and that this is not a novel expressing the author's masochism but a novel about a masochist. There is, to be sure, a persecuted little man here, but as in *Dangling Man* and *The Victim*, it is a *self*-persecuted individual, created with the full awareness of the author. In other words, this is a far different thing from the authorial self-pity and masochism which Harvey Swados feels and attacks in Jewish writers.

Tommy needs to destroy himself and wants to see himself as a victim. There is social masochism, too, in the origin of his behavior and in its reinforcement.

According to Bernard Berliner, masochism does not result from the individual directing early sadism against the ego, but rather begins with another person and is from inception a pattern, literal or symbolic, directed toward a figure of both love and authority, a strong superego figure, generally a father. The masochist, acting out his childhood relationship, fulfills the expectations of the father. As Weiss says, "Wilhelm has the masochistic necessity to fail, to be destroyed at the hands of the punishing father, in order, under the terms of the moral masochistic commitment, to retain his love, and, in less obvious ways, to memorialize certain events in the past." It is for these motives that Tommy lives in New York, resides in his father's hotel, dresses and acts sloppily, behaves with cringing self-pity. I am reminded of Reik's discussion of the "provocative factor" found in both sexual and social (moral) masochism. Tommy acts the little boy; he provokes by childish behavior the punishment he needs to reproduce his childhood relationship with his father. Tommy uses Tamkin as a substitute father (*Tamkin* Tom-kin). Both are doctors, both give advice, and Tommy sees himself riding on the backs of both; thus to lose under the influence of Tamkin—to "take a licking" on the market—is to take a symbolic licking from his own father, a punishment which is a form of love. As Wilhelm Reich puts it, the masochist makes "demands for love in the form of provocation and spite."

This explanation does not cancel Freud's idea that masochistic behavior is self-punishment to remove guilt, generally oedipal. "You have lots of guilt in you," Tamkin tells Tommy. He judges himself by his father's criteria, from his father's perspective. "When he was drunk he reproached himself horribly as Wilky," his father's nickname for him: " 'You fool, you clunk, you Wilky!' " And although in Hollywood he tried to break away from his father's judgment by changing his name (Wilhelm Adler to Tommy Wilhelm), he was unable to do so: "Wilky was his inescapable self." He "knows" his father is right, "knows" he should not have trusted Tamkin, or gone to Hollywood, or married Margaret, or left Margaret, or resigned from his job.

But as Reik and Berliner both show, the masochist gets positive rewards as well as guilt-reduction. Berliner says, "suffering has come to mean being worthy of love." "When I suffer—you aren't even sorry. That's because you have no affection for me, and you don't want any part of me." This is the baldest statement of Tommy's secret goal. And although Dr. Adler does not provide pity, or phenaphen, he does provide a duplication of the more or less secure father-child relationship. Tommy's worthiness of pity is in itself rewarding—whether or not he is actually pitied. It makes him feel, like Joseph, morally superior to his cold father. Thus, again like Joseph, Tommy refuses to dodge the draft during the war, becoming an ordinary GI rather than an officer. And, like Joseph and

Augie, he feels superior to his father and Mr. Perls "because they adored money." But Tommy's suffering must seem to come from outside sources, and therefore he must keep "his troubles before him." If he did not, "he risked losing them altogether, and he knew by experience that this was worse." Worse not only because specific fear is milder than vague anxiety but also because his self-justifying construction might break down and, in confusion, his real motives would threaten to emerge.

Tommy luxuriates in his suffering. He sees himself as a sacrificial victim, remembers poem fragments like "Come then sorrow/Sweetest Sorrow! Like an own babe I nurse thee on my breast!" He does not know why he remembers these lines, but it is clear to the reader: his vision of himself as dead, his invitation of sorrow, his identification of sorrow with the state of infancy. Both doctors, his own father and Tamkin, tell him: "You make too much of your problems. . . . They ought not to be turned into a career" (his father); "Don't marry suffering. Some people do" (Tamkin).

Tommy has married suffering. Even more than Joseph, he moves toward death. He is in a hotel with old people waiting to die. He constantly feels pains in the chest, or choked, or suffocated, as he shows his father by strangling himself and telling him, "Dad, I just can't breathe. My chest is all up—I feel choked." He is being bled to death: "When I had it, I flowed money. They bled it away from me. I hemorrhaged money." Margaret is "trying to put an end to me." Tommy feels like the Brahma bull eaten by the piranha. "When I have the money they eat me alive, like those piranha fish. . . . when they ate up the Brahma bull in the river."

The bull in the river—Tommy also refers to himself as "wallowing hippopotamus"—connects the images of death by being devoured and death by water. Drowning is the most common image of death in *Seize the Day*. Tommy remembers from a college literature course the line, "Sunk though he be beneath the wat'ry floor" from *Lycidas*, about the drowning of Edward King. His father suggests a water cure, and in telling him to forget his troubles, says, "Concentrate on real troubles—fatal sickness, accidents," a statement which seems an accidental invitation to die. Later, Tommy is afraid, "the waters of the earth are going to roll over me." When he discovered the loss of his investment, "his washed tears rose and rose and he looked like a man about to drown." It is as if he were going to drown in his own tears—a very precise symbolic statement. Choked, he visits his father by the pool in the steam room, and there he is, in a sense, told to die: "I'll see you dead Wilky . . ."; and at the stranger's funeral he symbolically does die by drowning: his eyes are blind and wet, there is heavy sealike music which pours into him, he sinks "towards the consummation of his heart's ultimate need." Weiss exaggerates in believing that this scene represents Tommy's acceptance of the role of victim; but it is true that Tommy's self-pity and his drive toward self-destruction and even death are brought to climax here.

Augie March is not a novel about a social or moral masochist. As was pointed out earlier, Bellow developed in this book a conscious opposition to his own bitter nature. Yet in the conflict which Robert Alter considers between *Augie March* as a picaresque novel and *Augie March* as a *Bildungsroman,* there are still hints of Bellow's depressive, masochistic characters.

The conflict of interests is present from the beginning: we are concerned both with the characters Augie meets, and with the adventures, as well as with his process of education. For much of the novel this education is secondary: Augie's "larkiness" carries him—and us—through. But from the beginning of the Mexican adventure with Thea, Augie grows more and more self-critical, less buoyant, less able to sustain himself by larkiness.

Bellow has admitted that he cannot plan a whole book, that he gets "a book two-thirds done and I don't know how it is going to turn out." Increasingly Bellow shows his dissatisfaction with Augie by his hero's self-criticism, criticisms by others, ironic contradictions, and apparent self-indulgence. *Self-criticism:* "I actually did intend to be as good as possible. That's how much I myself knew. But Jesus, Lord! Dissembling! Why, the master dissemblers there are around!" *Criticism of others:* Thea tells him, "By a little flattery anyone can get what he wants from you, Augie. . . . I can't out-flatter everyone in the world." *Ironic contradictions:* although Augie criticizes the ideal constructors with their monomanias, he says, "Clem had urged me to be engaged for six months. . . . but this advice was good for people who were merely shopping, not for someone who had lived all his life with one great object"; and although laughing at Utopians, he wants to form a community of orphans with his retarded brother as shoemaking instructor and charming, social Stella as housemother. *Self-indulgence:* when Thea leaves him, Augie carries on like an infant, ready to kill when he finds out that Thea has gone off with Talavera; and to a Russian who dares doubt that he, Augie, has suffered more than anyone, Augie says, "What do you mean, you runt! You cheesecloth cossack you! After I've told you how I feel—" *I.* Augie has to recognize, "Why, he too had a life."

Thus the quality of Augie's speech questions the image of adventuring picaro and at the same time questions the affirmation, as more and more strongly come refrains of the Darkness facing the individual. Late in the novel Augie looks over Chicago from the roof of a hospital:

> Around was Chicago. In its repetition it exhausted your imagination of details and units, more units than the cells of the brain and bricks of Babel. The Ezekiel cauldron of wrath, stoked with bones. In time the cauldron too would melt. A mysterious tremor, dust, vapor, emanation of stupendous effort traveled with the air, over me on top of the great establishment, so full as it was, and over the clinics, clinks, factories, flophouses, morgue, skid row. As before the work of Egypt and Assyria, as before a sea, you're nothing here. Nothing.

Here Augie, as much as any of the prophets of doom Bellow scourges, prophesies the end of the city, and *in* the city the negation of the individual. In contradiction to Bellow's style and in contradiction to his willed affirmation, the novel has sinister undercurrents.

In more subtle ways, as well, Augie is similar to Bellow's typical heroes. For instance, like Joseph and Asa, he cannot accept success. Augie may be like Huck, "lightin' out for the Territory" when Mrs. Renling or brother Simon want to tame him, but he is also suspiciously like Joseph, rejecting high position, insisting on a loser's role. And just as Tommy leaves Margaret, and Joseph is unable to accept the love of Iva *or* Kitty; just as Asa shuns Mary, and Henderson flees Lily, and Herzog runs from angelic Sono and domestic Daisy or sensual Ramona—so, too, Augie is unable to accept the love of Thea or to stay with Sophie. I am reminded of Herzog running frm the Sisslers, "not able to stand kindness at this time." Even at the end, Augie driving through Europe on business has dropped a few hints that Stella, like Thea, is being unfaithful to him; Augie, like Herzog, sets himself up for being cuckolded.

Thus there is more similarity than appears between Bellow's overtly masochistic heroes and Augie. Augie is not a typical Bellow hero; Bellow produces enough noise and gaiety with the role of the picaro to mask alienation, self-hatred, and masochism. But in spite of him, hints of them appear.

What is true of Augie seems equally true of Bellow. Bellow, like his hero, is life-affirming, love-affirming, individual-affirming. But underneath the "yea" is a deep, persuasive "nay"—underneath belief in the individual and in the possibility of community is alienation, masochism, despair.

JOHN BAYLEY

By Way of Mr. Sammler

M r. Sammler and, still more, his
cousin, Elya Gruner, are honest men in the fine old bourgeois meaning of
the word: they are deliberately created to be such; not heroes of our time,
but heroes reconstituted to see if they can acclimatise to our time, take
root in the mulch of its fiction, and inhabit the consciousness of that
fiction without drawing too much attention to themselves. For such an
experiment the American-Jewish novel offers the best available—indeed
the only possible—conditions for success. It has the obvious but enormous
advantage of continuity not only with the almost pre-fictional traditon of
the *honnête homme*, but with the great humanistic liberal and Victorian
novel world of Dickens, Thackeray and George Eliot, carried from the
Anglo-Saxon heartland to every European country, naturalised especially
in Russia, and grafted—though not altogether securely—to the developing
American culture. A certain kind of Jewish image in fiction today is the
product not of the Torah and the Hasidim but of *Little Dorrit* and John
Stuart Mill.

What keeps this inheritance alive and vigorous is that it is not only
an intellectual affair, a tradition of culture handed on to the most intelligent and receptive heirs available: it also appeals to a tribal and communal
life-style. It is just conceivable that some pillar of the country-club could
be celebrated by the spokesman of a wasp novelist as Bellow through Mr.
Sammler celebrates Elya Gruner.

Sammler in a mental whisper said, "Well, Elya. Well, well, Elya". And
then in the same way he said, "Remember, God, the soul of Elya

From *Salmagundi* 30 (Summer 1975). Copyright © 1975 by *Salmagundi*.

Gruner, who, as willingly as possible and as well as he was able, and even to an intolerable point, and even in suffocation and as death was coming was eager, even childishly perhaps (may I be forgiven for this), even with a certain servility, to do what was required of him. At his best this man was much kinder than at my very best I have ever been or could ever be. He was aware that he must meet, and he did meet—through all the confusion and the degraded clowning of this life through which we are speeding—he did meet the terms of his contract. The terms which, in his inmost heart, each man knows. As I know mine. As all know. For that is the truth of it—that we all know, God, that we know, that we know, we know, we know".

He might do, but what should we have to think if he did? Our alert fragmented sensibilities, all programmed to "the modern", would have to look in every direction except that in which the words pointed. If intelligence were there irony would also have to be present, the ritual a parody of some well-meaning, but also well-heeled, Episcopalian parson; but that, and every other obvious lead would merely bring us back to the really terrible irony of contemporary form: there would be no way in which the words could not be referred to some intention or aspect of technique brooded in the book's—that is the writer's—consciousness. The unspeakable thing about the modern consciousness in fiction is the fact that it cannot refer to anything outside itself. Like Lawrence's "him with his tail in his mouth," it lets us into its continuum of every kind of possibility, every talking point for the seminar, except the presumption of a firm contract elsewhere.

Indeed it is obvious that the modern consciousness is not capable of taking the last paragraph of Mr. Sammler's Planet seriously. How could it? Why should it? Founded on what Lionel Trilling has defined as the concept of "authenticity", it cannot afford to look outside its own instincts without becoming inauthentic: it can only be instructed and diverted by new somersaults of stance, new departures in form. These can be presented in terms of a critical vocabulary of exchangable counters, the counters of pseudo-order and pseudo-morality—the discerning, the passionate, the compassionate, the committed, the horrifyingly funny, the deeply concerned. Those are some of the squarer ones. But since the authentic is by definition incapable of insincerity, and since these terms all carry some semantic assumptions about the sincere, they cannot be taken very seriously. Authenticity should be purely egocentric, its logical emotional expression sadism and masochism of various kinds, the destruction or mutilation of the self, or of others as a respite from the self. An element of indulgence has always secretly accompanied the composition of fiction, but it has now become the principle of the form: for the novelist a duty and an imperative. His indulgence authenticates the reader's.

The born writer of today—a Mailer or Burroughs, Hubert Selby, or Joyce Carol Oates—methodically explores this indulgence. It is also logical that his expression of the authentic consciousness should resemble—coincide rather—as far as possible with itself. If bored, it should be boring: language must mirror its obsessions, its paranoia: the opposite process from say, Jane Austen, where boredom and constriction are converted by an equally conscientious principle of art into entertainment and liberation. The coincidence was observed by Simone Weil, who remarked that the modern consciousness naturally took the form of fiction, and *vice-versa*. The world which consciousness turns into itself naturally has no idea of an absolute contract external to that world. Elya Gruner on his death-bed is not merely not a character seen in fiction (Tolstoy's Ivan Ilyich is also not such a one) but he is a character who does not—cannot—see his own consciousness in fictional terms.

Why not? The short answer is to be found in the ancestry of this novel. The progenitors of Bellow-Sammler did not have to answer the question why Little Dorrit is so staunch in looking after her father, or why the selfishness of young Pendennis is a disagreeable quality. They knew it "as all know"—even the reader. Bellow parodies this knowledge in the remarkable scene in which the huge negro pickpocket silently exhibits his penis to Mr. Sammler in the hall of the latter's apartment. "We hold some things to be self-evident, man". This is a scene straight out of the consciousness, the fictional consciousness, in which Lionel Feffer—existing as he does on another planet than Mr. Sammler's—lives and has his being. He is, of course, fascinated by the scene as fiction, and wants Mr. Sammler to tell him all about it. "How marvellous! what a . . . a sudden glory. It could be straight out of *Finnegan's Wake*. 'Everyone must bare his crotch' ". Feffer's reaction is exactly typical of the consciousness as fiction, or the fiction as consciousness. The scene he reacts to is self-evidently authentic, and it also neatly illustrates the difference between the authentic as fiction and the thing we are all supposed to "know", the thing that fiction once could only dramatise and repeat to us because it assumed we did know.

Mr. Sammler is himself aware of the validity, as fiction, of his experience with the big negro. "Objectively I have little use for such experiences, but there is such an absurd craving for actions that connect with other actions, for coherency, for form, for mysteries or fables . . . And I don't like it. I don't like any of it". How right he is. The experience in modern fiction always connects, not so much in accord with the famous precept of E. M. Forster as because it cannot help it. The critic today can always see unity in any novel he thinks good: he is not defining its quality but identifying its nature. This is particularly true of the American novel, which has always been dominated, even in the rambling composite world of Moby Dick, by the solitary Hegelian *geist*, whether that spirit manifests itself like Melville's in metaphysical terms, or—as in the case of Hemingway—through the absolute fiat of a new style. To occlude the spirit would also be to disperse its identifying unity, and in terms of the American tradition this is an exceedingly difficult thing to do. The admirable thing about Mr. *Sammler* is its successful evasion of this spiritual unity, which it parodies and makes use of for fictional purposes, its own point being way outside the united states of fiction.

Bellow courts with equanimity the fate of ostracisation as a modern novelist; and my own experience is that intellectuals whose inclination or duty compel them to welcome novelty in any form are indeed apt to look sideways at Mr. Sammler. So at least it is in England, and there is plenty of indication that this is also the standard reaction in America. I have already referred to Lionel Trilling's study in the ideology of the self, *Sincerity and Authenticity*, which makes brief mention of Bellow in dubious not to say doleful terms. There is not just the implication that Bellow has given up the struggle, turned his head aside from modernity, but that in attempting to reconstitute in fiction the idea of the good and sincere man—instead of exploring the possibilities of his modern authentic counterpart—Bellow is perpetrating something aesthetically ludicrous, vulgarly inapposite. So brilliant and persuasive is Trilling's general argument, and so unanswerable is his quiet rejection of any attempts to be "humane" or "compassionate" within the framework of the modern sensibility, that it is difficult not to agree. But the point does remain: Bellow's heroes are not competing in the same league with anything going on today: Sammler's disenchantment with the modern fictional image (confirmed by the brutal fiasco of his academic lecture) is as total as Elya Gruner's ignorance of it. The great thing about Bellow and his heroes is that they do not try to have it both ways, to be with it and "humane" at the same time.

It is of course true that Bellow has been a modern novelist, and that aspects of Mr. *Sammler*—his liking for Orwell and English mustard, his love of Bloomsbury and H. G. Wells—are excellent ways of shrugging off the burden of a "message" by making it appear more than a trifle absurd, even if endearingly so. They are perennial ways. Old-fashioned morality in Mr. *Sammler* is concealed behind the slightly prissy meticulous quality sometimes associated with it. Bellow's beautifully fastidious and discriminatory use of language is rightly abandoned in the emotion felt by Mr. Sammler in the last paragraph of his book, which I quoted. The contract cannot be made more acceptable by style. But in general Bellow's style is nowhere more emphatic than in this book, sardonically underlining the complex working out of moral intelligence required to nourish a society in which "all know". Delicacy and discrimination are not the same thing as knowing how to meet the terms of one's contract, but they have a sort of Jamesian association with it, which it pleases Bellow to define. He shows that style and language can exhibit all the stigmata of tradition and at the same time appear both tough and timeless; it is the language which really endorses and gives weight to the meaning, shows that the apparently reactionary is still very much alive.

Trilling's argument, based as it is on the survival or non-survival of *ideas,* overrides this obvious point: of course it is no good sounding humane and compassionate oneself—that is indeed to get left behind in a world that no longer exists—but while language can be reciprocally used and appreciated as it is in *Mr. Sammler* it makes no sense to talk of our cultural state as one in which only the authentic consciousness can prevail. George Steiner and others, more despairing than Trilling even, have foretold that the consciousness of today will dissolve and corrupt even the arts and discriminations of the written word. It may happen, but it is also the case that the patient is alive and well and probably living in New York.

Angus Wilson's recent novel, *As if by Magic,* seems apposite here. It is, as one might expect, a work of great brilliance, and the stratum of meaning that underlies it abuts also on Sammler territory. Both novels are aware that the modern consciousness is and requires to be its own state of fiction: both record the fact with a degree of sarcasm and satire: Bellow through his radical discrimination of different worlds and life-styles, Wilson—more obviously and more dangerously—by equating the idea of magic with the fictional "solution": his young persons think that seminars on Lawrence and George Eliot will teach them magically how to live; his middle-aged agronomist hopes that his new strain of "magic" rice will cure the world of poverty. Bellow's young man extolling the bizarre threats of pickpockets as "a sudden glory" or Wilson's young woman bedding down in the parental couch with two male fellow-students—both regard themselves as liberated and egged on by the images of consciousness that fiction brings; in the latter case, indeed, the girl sees herself as completing on her own initiative and in the conceit of her own apotheosised *savoir-vivre,* a model of living and loving not fully in the tableau of *Women in Love.*

The drawback to Wilson's method, however, is the absence of any detachment or radical distinction within the world of the novel itself. Whether by intention or by instinct its style and manner collude too deeply with the kinds of magic that its sights are supposedly set on; for it is written badly, as if the author were aware (which he no doubt is) that in a TV world words don't get paid much individual attention to—the programme merely rushes on, getting in as much frenetic entertainment and viewing time as possible. Wilson's object is compromised by his desire to produce a wholly contemporary work that is also there to take off the contemporary. He is clearly in mortal fear of being left out, of not being where the action is; and thus the texture of the work becomes as slovenly as everything in it. The irony is that he can make the kind of conscious use of Victorian fiction—its spaciousness, organisation and breadth of attack—that appears much more obliquely and interestingly in Bellow's Jewish background of serious culture and the moral contract: but his horror of seeming in any sense to recreate or make use of the Victorian fictional tradition leaves him in the end out on a limb. Clarity and focus disappear from the method, even as the message attempts in its own peculiar way to endorse them.

The interest of this is that it shows to what extent Wilson, like almost every other modern novelist, takes for granted the idea of unity, the "organic wholeness" of a work of art, a novel in particular. The oneness of his style with his characters' attitudes and responses is depressing, indeed claustrophobic, as it is in most other modern fiction. Bellow, by contrast, succeeds in Mr. Sammler in producing a masterpiece in which none of the pieces especially fit together, or have any need to do so. Dr. Lal and his moon theories, which appeal to Sammler's old fondness for H. G. Wells (himself of course an almost grotesque example of an impure and "non-unified" approach to fiction) are simply around in the slightly mad way in which so much else is today. Bellow would no doubt go along with the Hegelian view of modern art as presenting a bunch of alternatives and possible diversions too variegated to allow the use of any yardstick of quality and kind; significant, though, that Wells is not "placed" as a writer, but left hovering as an aspect of the culture that set out to make sense of things.

Since discrimination holds its pieces together like embroidery, it becomes almost willy-nilly a parody of works to which the symbolism of "wholeness" is avowedly essential. Difficult not to believe that Bellow, who in his time has tried out almost every style of fictional approach, did not here intend the signs and symbols of fictional earnestness to act as self-born mockers of fiction's enterprise. I have never "taught" Mr. Sammler, but I can imagine with what routine alertness the seminar would move off on the scent, turning from the moon symbolism with raised eyebrows to Angela and Shula (they would be prepared to accept that for Sammler himself the moon is not a sex symbol) and then in full cry after Eisen, the powerful mechanical young Israeli, with his ruined marriage and his horrible baize bag full of metal objects. The climax of meaning here would come when Feffer is struggling in the grip of the great negro, the exiled African prince, whom he has snapped with a minox camera in the act of pickpocketing. The fictional consciousness doing its thing on life. Up steps Eisen, and at a word misunderstood from his father-in-law Sammler, slams the negro's head with his bag of modern bronzes, modishly rough pseudo-art replicas of tanks and other artifacts of progress. Young crude Israeli smashes out at older but more dignified kinds of malignancy, whose normal thing is to be left to their bad selves. Meanwhile Wallace, turning father Gruner's place upside-down in his search for stashed Mafia currency, accidently severs a watermain. Gruner himself, in hospital, dies when the screw on his carotid artery fails to stop an aneurism flooding his brain with blood.

Already in such a paraphrase fiction has arrived: and with it all the usual kinds of falsity. But by letting such matters protrude, Bellow had disarmed them of any occult fictional power. If I am right that *Mr. Sammler* offers us a specific rejection of the modern fictional image, it certainly does not reject the devices of art, and particularly of the arts of formalism. Bellow makes symbolism work for him even as he depreciates it: its effect is to remind us that life is not like the images of it such devices draw: instead of involving us in a novel they coolly remind us it is not one. The simplicity and the candour of the book, and especially of its ending, do not depend alone on the ease with which Bellow and his cast skip into the Victorian moral framework but also on the skill with which the techniques of the novel form are used against it.

This skill is as old as *Tristram Shandy* or *Evgeny Onegin*, both of which share with *Mr. Sammler* the disconcerting gift of imparting a very plain sense of life—its "contract" in fact—through a highly sophisticated and amused art contrivance. Not for nothing is this admonition—not stated openly, as Bellow in his last paragraph nerves himself to do— conveyed through an epigraph in Pushkin's verse novel: "Il n'y de bonheur que dans les voies communes". Nabokov's error, an astounding one, which only so solipsistically brilliant a leprechaun could be stupid enough to make, is not to see that such a plain revelation is the only point of formalism, that without that bread and butter to fall back on everything else at the tea-party turns sickly and boring.

It seems to me a fact of great importance that no single conscious-ness broods over *Mr. Sammler* and is co-extensive with the book. The distinction here would be between the novel in which everything—and not merely Madame Bovary herself—is *moi*; and the novel in which the author has as it were made the acquaintance of, and got on terms with, a person whom he can use as a narrator and explorer. Sammler is in no sense Bellow's *alter ego*, but a formal projection of aspects of Bellow's awareness of things, which enable him—and this is the secret of success probably—to diminish and refine judgment. Judgment is all the clearer because the judge is cranky, odd, distinctly out of things. Herzog and Bellow's other previous *consciences*, back to the Dangling Man, encroached too much upon author and novel alike—they became the fictional con-sciousness. Mr. Sammler does not do that; he is too evidently *a côte*, as, for example, Fanny Price is in *Mansfield Park*. Jane Austen does not so much say things through Fanny Price as see what the world looks like through her eyes. She is a more helpless as well as a more partial viewer than the author, and the world she sees is all the more clearly focused for that reason—judged too, with a judgment that does not pretend to be anything than partial and non-unified, appealing as it does to sources outside the novel's world.

Mr. *Sammler* succeeds by being partial and incomplete, by rejecting the modern novel's paradigm of totality in the act of consciousness. But it is not a symposium or *Bildungsroman*, full of wise saws and modern instances. They are there, each with an appropriate mouthpiece, but the novel's exquisite sense of place and person, its shapely but unemphatic perspective, provides without any need for an aggressive display of whole-ness the magic circle within which, as James laid down, all relations happily appear to stop. Bellow also rejects the meaningful, putting as little weight behind his imputations as behind his symbols. Every implication is of course tendentious. As a Jewish partisan in the misery of wartime Poland Mr. Sammler was entitled, we gather, to the relief and rapture of violence which modern man claims as a right in itself, one neither earned by persecutions nor justified by contemporary conditions. These past/present contrasts do possess an external authenticity however: they do not depend on being part of a novel. Compare again with *As if By Magic*. Having trounced modern magic, in its various forms, Wilson ends by giving his heroine an enormous legacy, and this liberates her as no attempts at hippy culture or communal love-making had done. Money is the only true magic; but this banal conclusion, which cannot be avoided by the novel, cannot be openly endorsed by it either; it remains in the limbo between the novel's autonomous consciousness and the assertions that might be said to float free of it.

This is the dilemma of the unified novel consciousness. Hard and clear pieces of separable intelligence and insight get lost in it. But Bellow does not lose them. They remain detached from the narrative, constellated only with the twin planets of civilisation and style. This, admittedly, is only a fancy way of saying that one likes Bellow's personality, which is that of a man, not of a novel, and makes his work well suited to the *ad hominem* approach. And indeed, where the novel is concerned, is there— should there be—any other? What sort of a man is the novelist? Is he really worth getting to know?—it is these queries that get overlaid by our acceptance of the consciousness as fiction, as by any of the ensuing preoccupations of formalism.

In the words of Wallace (everyone in Mr. Sammler is rightly given a crisp, discriminatory turn of phrase; is endowed by the author not with dominant consciousness but with his separable skills) our recollecting and discussing with Mr. Sammler "helps to keep the wolf of insignificance from the door". There seems to me the possibility that it is by meeting his people in appraisal and speculation, outside fictional metaphysic, that we can apprehend their virtues; with certainty, and yet without their author seeming to be under strain to produce "a good man". The "goodness" of characters in art depend more than is usually recognised on our ability to converse with them. We talk with Pierce, Prince Andrew, Levin, Dostoevsky's Alyosha: his Myshkin, on the other hand, like his Svidrigailov and Stavrogin, we merely contemplate with fascination as we would an actor, in Mr. Sammler's words "a man with a bit to play, like so many modern individuals". Mr. Sammler is firmly in agreement with Simone Weil that the modern consciousness takes to the form of a fiction, doing its thing, "Acting Human", laughing and crying and getting others to laugh and cry.

"But supposing that one dislikes all this theatre of the soul?" Mr. Sammler's query is pertinent, for it might be thought: how in that case write novels, absorb us, and move us? Again the sap in the tradition behind Sammler and his author provide the answer. In steely fashion he seals off the modern, magic persons, those who are fuzzy with "Acting Human"—Shula, Angela, Wallace—from those who, like Margotte and Elya Gruner, know the human contract by not playing Human. Sammler knows the world, not by doing his thing in it but by being—as most by tradition are and must be—its victim: his war-time experiences are not only traditional and local—like the irruption of the Slav Question at the end of *Anna Karenina*—but endless and timeless. Bellow has succeeded in creating a hero who in terms of feeling, emotion and experience represents—if one may be forgiven the phrase—the silent majority, even while his capacity to reflect on and give words to these things is that of an intellectual. Sorel's famous dictum does not have the last word here: Mr. Sammler is a clerk, but a clerk who commits no treasons.

JOHN HOLLANDER

"To Jerusalem and Back"

"Of all possible subjects, travel is
the most difficult for an artist, as it is easiest for the journalist," remarked
W. H. Auden of Henry James's itinerary of his return to the United States in
1906, *The American Scene.* "For the latter, the interesting event is the
new, the extraordinary, the comic, the shocking, and all that the peripa-
tetic journalist requires is a flair for being on the spot where and when
such events happen. . . . The artist, on the other hand, is deprived of his
most treasured liberty, the freedom to invent." In 1967 Saul Bellow went
to Israel to cover the Six-Day War as a journalist; it was a moment of
triumph, and the Holocaust seemed to have been sealed in the past. In
1975, he returned to Jerusalem as an artist, after eight years during which
America, Israel, and their relations to each other and to the rest of the
world had saddened. His account of the journey is by turns comic, bitter,
nostalgic, meditative, earnest, flighty, and tragic, but perhaps its central
strand involves Bellow's lack of any need for "the freedom to invent."
Three moments in the histories of Israel—the quarter-century-old modern
state, and the several-thousand-year-old people—and the advent of the
chronicler himself seem to have coincided with imaginative consequences:
Bellow's journey there and then could take him to a world many of whose
scenes, characters, and significances are like those of his fictions.

This fine book (it appeared in slightly different form in *The New
Yorker*) starts out in London on the way to Jerusalem, and at the end
returns briefly to London again and then home to Bellow's Chicago. But
the trip is a journey inward and backward as well; the author is an
important novelist, a Chicagoan, a literary intellectual, a Jew, a lover of

---

From *Harper's* 20 (Spring 1976). Copyright © 1976 by John Hollander.

Russian literature, and it is these regions of identity through which he voyages. The "To . . . and Back" of the title signifies not the search of a reporter for a story, but the ironic questing of a firmly-rooted artist of the Jewish diaspora in his travel abroad to a lately marked-out center, and safely home to a periphery of exile again. The title comprises as well an additional series of narrative and speculative oscillations between Israel and America, emotions and ideologies, things and texts, private lives and public roles, which give the book its energy and its structure, and which fill it with rewarding asides, at first glance seeming almost irrelevant, on literature, politics, and the life of the mind.

Every artist's "personal account" is personal in its own way. The opening pages of Bellow's book may mislead us a bit into thinking that its mode of ironic perception, half-affirming, half-disclaiming the author's identification with his subject, will be maintained throughout. On boarding the plane in London with his gentile wife, Bellow is seated next to one of a group of ultra-orthodox Hasidim, living and working in America but unable to speak English or to see the need for it. The author engages this young man in Yiddish, and, not to offend so fiercely innocent an orthodoxy, endeavors to order a kosher meal for himself, fails because the supply has been exhausted, and finds the combination of his fluent Yiddish and ignored dietary laws evoking a baroque conversation with his neighbor. As the plane lands, the state of Israel absorbs them both. The acutely assimilated American writer with a zest for the heroic, and the even more acutely intransigent sectarian (whose customary dress preserves nothing more Judaistic than the middle-class clothing of nineteenth-century Poland): together they stand for the diaspora itself, disembarking on the ancient soil of an inconveniently belated nation-state. For the unworldly one, the secular republic primarily extends an ease of access to sacred ground, shadowed perhaps by its use of the holy language for mundane purposes, possibly not excluding the abominable. For the chronicler sitting beside him, committed neither to mending walls nor smashing them, but rather to meditating the ways in which walls make sense of the unbounded, the fact of the nation state as a democratic republic is itself a sacred point. "Where there is no paradox, there is no life," says one of his Israeli acquaintances some pages later. A lesser writer might have allowed this to sum up the range of his experience. But Bellow does not, and the structure of his account leads him as much into personal affirmation as ironic withdrawal, into moments of joy and stretches of skepticism, and even into one glimpse, proper to sacred ground, of a transcendence of time and place.

His book is no travel diary, although its episodes are shaped by walks, visits, encounters, excursions, consultations, and formal inter-views. The book is full of talk: Bellow records the differing views of his informants on the book's central question—the survival of Israel—often commenting himself, but always leaving the reader at once uncertain of the correctness of the reading of events, and yet convinced of a kind of humane authoritativeness in most of the speakers, if only perhaps because they are all dwelling on the shores of a nightmare of annihilation. These speakers are full of theories about Israel and the Arab nations, the U.S., the U.S.S.R., the Palestinians, Israel itself. An almost Dostoevskian excitement—kindled by the relations of character to ideology—frequently occurs. But the scenes and anecdotes can lead, often wittily, into personal association: autographed pictures of Hubert Humphrey presented to the barber at Bellow's hotel prompt Bellow to remember, with nostalgia and chagrin, how at a White House banquet he was not recognized by Hum-phrey. In another instance, he is led into a meditation on Jean-Paul Sartre and contemporary French culture.

Throughout all this is a sense of the grotesque awkwardness of Jewish survival having to be intimately associated with Middle Eastern politics since World War I. "Wouldn't it be the most horrible of ironies if the Jews had collected themselves conveniently in one country for a second Holocaust," observes an American academic, and Bellow's recur-rent theme frequently causes the reader to wonder if the Holocaust is not perhaps merely suspended in a forty-year lull. But the book is held together by a vision of something more universal as well: "I sometimes think there are two Israels," says Bellow at a late point in the account. "The real one is territorially insignificant. The other, the mental Israel, is immense, a country inestimably important, playing a major role in the world, as broad as all history—and perhaps as deep as sleep."

The "sleep" is all the more meaningful here, since Bellow has characterized as a kind of undogmatic slumber the attitudes of many Jews toward Israel and, more generally, of Westerners toward their own as yet unpoliced states. Sartre, particularly, exemplifies for him the state in which "a great deal of intelligence can be invested in ignorance when the need for illusion is deep." Henry Kissinger is another of the book's trimmers; and Joseph Alsop and the late Arabist Marshall Hodgson display a *sarcta simplicitas* in these pages. There are palpable heroic types from Saul Bellow novels as well. Teddy Kollek, the energetic mayor of Jerusa-lem, gets an almost Emersonian characterization: "A force of nature, without coaxing he makes his feelings clear." Meyer Weisgall, founder of the Weizmann Institute of Scientific Research, is for him another entrepreneurial adventurer; and a ship's engineer and Kibbutz-dweller exemplifies a type of endurance beyond achievement.

Life and literature, past and present, are confronted also in the shadow of Russia, which falls across so many of these pages; it surrounds Bellow's own world as Islam does Israel, a complex presence. The spiritual home of Dostoevsky, Solzhenitzin, Sinyavsky (who appear as ironic points of light), it is also the center in this book of a totalitarian darkness, of an ideological cloud which can almost take amusement from the temporary status of a bit of territory through which a remnant of rootless cosmopolitans have drilled to reconnect their roots, thereby incidentally infecting the Middle East with a touch of serious but eradicable bourgeois democracy.

Bellow's interlocutors are doves and hawks, optimists and prophets of some kind of destruction; he takes no position himself on the Arab world, but only hums a kind of refrain throughout this book: the problematic existence of Israel as a nation "means only that the Jews, because they are Jews, have never been able to take the right to live as a natural right." Bellow's deep involvement with Jewish survival is somehow connected in these reflections with a fierce loyalty to American democratic pluralism (notwithstanding the destructive necessity of Israel's political dependence on the U.S.). He finds them both threatened from within and without, and reacts with continuous distaste to what he interprets as overripe innocence, and the weariness and satiation of the West with its own noblest traditions.

What gives *To Jerusalem and Back* a unifying tone is in some measure the presence of the author's personality as a referee, a supplier of historical facts and provider of a ruminative literary sensibility. There is no trace of the bitterness toward women we see in his later novels. And there seems to be no need, in this particular mode of personal reportage, for rhetorical devices of distancing and framing the narrator—one thinks of Norman Mailer's "he," which is sometimes engaging, sometimes presumptuous like a historical *passé defini* in French. Bellow's own dialectic of identities is itself emblematic of the whole milieu of his journey, and the many speakers seem at the end to have been internalized as a chorus of hopes, fears, and pledges. The controlling ironies are ultimately those of history rather than those of personality.

FRANK McCONNELL

Saul Bellow and the
Terms of Our Contract

If the postwar American novel really
exists as a body of fiction with specific aims, common problems, and
distinctive ways of confronting those problems, then the work of Saul
Bellow should occupy a special eminence therein. He received his B.S.
from Northwestern University in 1938, beginning his adult career on the
eve of the war which was to cast such long and dark shadows over the
century's life. He has continued to produce fiction and cultural criticism
of major importance—and undiminished energy—from the midst of that
war into the seventies.

In the context of American writing, the sheer longevity of Bellow's
talent is a remarkable thing. For some years now, it has been a cliché of
criticism—and a popular mythology—that American novelists tend in an
extraordinary degree to be one-book geniuses. There appears to be something in our cultural climate which encourages or even necessitates the
fate of writers who, after initial and brilliant success, either spend the
remainder of their lives trying vainly to repeat and recapture their first
glory, or simply find it impossible to write any more at all. Fitzgerald and
Hemingway, before their canonization by the academy, were continually
faulted—both by the critics and, it seems, by their own private demons—
for not living up to the achievement of *The Great Gatsby* and *The Sun
Also Rises*. Norman Mailer's violent love-hate affair with the novel seems
to have been generated in large part by his inability, throughout the

From *Four Postwar American Novelists*. Copyright © 1977 by The University of Chicago
Press.

fifties, fully to satisfy the expectations aroused by *The Naked and the Dead.* And the forties saw at least three brilliant writers—Ross Lockridge of *Raintree County,* Thomas Heggen of *Mr. Roberts,* and Paul Bowles of *The Sheltering Sky*—who fell prey, in varying modalities of violence, to this complex fatality. Even Faulkner, whose gift survived past all expectation, can be seen not so much as a denier of that nemesis, but more as a clever manipulator of it. Faulkner's strategy is to make his work a single "first novel," spinning out the immense tale of Yoknapatawpha County in a series of books which are less individual novels than chapters of one encyclopedia and sustained vision.

It would be overreaching to suggest that Bellow has singlehandedly defeated the "one-book fate" for a whole generation of American novelists; but it is nevertheless true that his books, from *Dangling Man* (1944) to *Humboldt's Gift* (1975), form a consistent, carefully nurtured *oeuvre* not often encountered in the work of American writers. And it is equally true that the productions of John Barth, Thomas Pynchon, and—frenetically—Norman Mailer all display the same sort of continuity, the same sense of cultivated and constructed fictive argument, as do Bellow's books. There is something European about Saul Bellow's series of novels, in the fiction's openness to the widest range of philosophical, historical, and political debate and in the openness of each single fiction to further development and debate in subsequent tales. And we can argue that one of the great achievements of American fiction generally in the postwar period has been its acquisition of just such a feeling of expanse. Whether Bellow influences such a subtle development is, naturally, beyond proof and pointless to discuss. What cannot be denied is that he is the first American novelist of his generation to raise both the special problems and the special possibilities of postwar fiction, even though he may be the first of a generation which has often found cause to disown and repudiate his primacy.

The case of Saul Bellow is an interesting incident of that nebulous thing, the history of taste. His first two novels, *Dangling Man* and *The Victim* (1947), were successful if not earthshaking books, earning high critical praise even in a decade which seems to have produced more than its share of original young writers. But *The Adventures of Augie March,* which won the National Book Award in fiction for 1953, established its author beyond all question as the important writer of his time: comparisons of *Augie March* to the best of Twain and Melville were commonplace by the middle of the fifties. *Seize the Day* (1956) and *Henderson the Rain King* (1959) consolidated Bellow's hegemony over American prose. It is a safe bet that if an English teacher or graduate student of the fifties was asked, "Who is the greatest living American writer?" the answer would be, "Saul Bellow." If the answer was "Norman Mailer," it was to be assumed that the respondent was being coy; if it was "William Gaddis," "William Burroughs," or "John Barth," he was being perverse.

But 1959, the year of *Henderson*, was a fateful year: the last of the Eisenhower decade, and the earliest of America's full-scale involvement in the politics of North and South Vietnam. And the last, in many ways, of Bellow's undisputed preeminence in his country's letters. Five years were to intervene between *Henderson* and the publication of his next novel. And they were five years which saw, not only the internal and external erosion of the nation's public self-confidence, but the reemergence of Norman Mailer, the maturation of John Barth, and the appearance of Thomas Pynchon. By the time *Herzog* appeared in 1964, the contours of American fiction had changed since Eugene Henderson took his fantastic voyage to darkest Africa. Bellow came to appear, to some, less and less at home in the new climate; to others, more and more curmudgeonly. Celebrants of the absurdist fiction of "black humor" could contrast the riotous comedy of *An American Dream* or *The Sot-Weed Factor* to the solemnities and *longueurs* of *The Victim* or *Seize the Day*—quite forgetting, in the contrast, the rich and often outrageous sense of comedy in *Augie March* and *Henderson*. Bellow's fiction, regnant throughout the Eisenhower era, could be unfairly invoked as a literary symbol of those years, a symbol of the political mediocrity and moral timidity which spawned Richard Nixon, Ed Sullivan, and *Confidential* magazine. And Bellow himself, in some ways, appeared to concur in the eclipse of his influence. After the comic fantasy of *Henderson*, *Herzog* could be regarded as a retrenchment in the direction of realism and high seriousness. *Herzog* is, at least, the first novel in which Bellow's main character is an academic intellectual rather than a free-ranging, canny and unattached jack-of-all-trades. And though *Herzog*, like *Augie March*, won the National Book Award for its year, the award this time could be thought of as the cautious honoring of an emeritus rather than the joyful recognition of a vital and originating talent. *Mr. Sammler's Planet* (1970) is Bellow's own recognition of and ironic statement upon this emeritus status. Artur Sammler, his septuagenarian, European hero living through the manic sixties in the heart of New York City, is unmistakably a vision of his own fictive career, ignored or (worse) pensioned off by the very writing it has generated: "What was it to be entrapped by a psychiatric standard (Sammler blamed the Germans and their psychoanalysis for this)! Who had raised the diaper flag? Who had made shit a sacrament? What literary and psychological movement was that? Mr. Sammler, with bitter angry mind, held the top rail of his jammed bus, riding downtown, a short journey."

In the question "Who had made shit a sacrament?" we can hear Bellow's own cultured, traditionary revulsion against the scatological metaphysics of Mailer's *An American Dream*, Barth's *Giles Goat-Boy*, and Pynchon's *V*. But if we also choose to see in the novels of Mailer, Barth, and Pynchon an earnest concern with the resurrection of the art of fiction as a living enterprise, an attempt—however varied—to turn fiction to use in living with the everyday and the everyday to use in the construction of saving fictions, then the answer to Sammler's question is a curious one. For it is Bellow himself, as much as any contemporary American writer, who has helped make "shit"—the omnipresent, tawdry materiality of middle-class life—into a sacrament, or into the matter of serious myth. And Bellow's own resistance, then, to the development of fiction becomes itself an important feature of the fruitful but dangerous territory his work has mapped out.

There are at least two ways of looking at Bellow's position in American fiction, each of which contradicts the other and both of which, at times, are true. The development of the novel form represented by Barth, Pynchon, and the later Mailer is characterized by a riotous sense of fantasy and a deliberate flaunting of the conventions of naturalistic narrative. We may say, then, either that Bellow's novels avoid, out of timidity or pomposity, the allurements of this fantasy-vision of the world; or that such fantasy, while present in his best work, is nevertheless triumphantly contained therein—a suburb of nightmare in which other writers may be forced to dwell, but which Bellow visits only occasionally and when it suits his larger purpose. If the word can still be used in any but a derogatory sense, Bellow is a realist: his characters all have names, families, dull (usually nonacademic) jobs, and live in recognizable locales. One could learn a good deal about Chicago from reading *Humboldt's Gift* and about Manhattan from *Mr. Sammler's Planet*—a claim that cannot be made for the Maryland of *The Floating Opera* or the New York of *V*. But at the same time—and this, not the geography, is the permanent interest of his characters—they lead intense, gloomy mental lives which continually threaten to break the comfortable reality of their surroundings, casting them adrift in a sea of hallucination, romance, and guilt. Nowhere is this delicate balance of tendencies better caught than in *The Victim*, as the hero, Asa Leventhal, crosses the ferry to Staten Island to visit his sister-in-law and her sick child:

> The towers on the shore rose up in huge blocks, scorched, smoky, gray, and bare white where the sun was direct upon them. The notion brushed

Leventhal's mind that the light over them and over the water was akin to the yellow revealed in the slit of the eye of a wild animal, say a lion, something inhuman that didn't care about anything human and yet was implanted in every human being too, one speck of it, and formed a part of him that responded to the heat and the glare, exhausting as these were, or even to freezing, salty things, harsh things, all things difficult to stand.

The inhuman glare of the lion's eye, the color of the beast, is the ultimate fate and the ultimate test which awaits not only Leventhal, but all of Bellow's heroes. Two of them, in fact, will actually meet an emblematic beast who either consumes or purifies their pretensions to civilized humanity: Augie March encounters the bald eagle Caligula, and Henderson is forced to stroke the lioness Atti. But the beast need not be literally, physically there. At any moment, as one walks down a city street, talks to a lover or a friend, has a bland breakfast with one's aging father, the abyss may open, the world turn ugly and murderous, and the carnivorous ape within each of us reassert his primacy over all we have invented of civilization and decency. Moses Herzog, that agonized and self-betrayed scholar, is trying to write an intellectual history of the modern world "investigating the social meaning of Nothingness." But Herzog's book can, finally, achieve no more than Leventhal's Staten Island epiphany: the shuddering recognition of how little distant we actually are from the savagery of our origins, how fragile a thing is the civilization which makes, we continue to tell ourselves, our life worth living.

But this denuding confrontation with the inhuman is, in one form or another, the common denominator and common originator of most contemporary fictions; and what distinguishes Bellow is not only his firm and unusually "realistic" articulation of this theme, but the distinctively traditional moral context in which he articulates it. His training as an anthropologist equips him—as it does another former anthropology student, William Burroughs—to understand the arbitrary, eternally endangered quality of civilized society. But unlike Burroughs, Bellow insists in book after book that that delicate, arbitrary thing, civilization, is still possible, still capable of being asserted, even in the face of the beasts our own civilization has loosed against itself in the forms of dehumanized labor, political and economic terrorism, and imaginative stultification. The passage I cited from The Victim is, in this respect, characteristic of Bellow's style. For while the color of the beast is there, in all its implied threat to the certainties of Leventhal's existence, it is there only as metaphor, or better, as an image at second remove: the towers on the shore have, at sunset, a curious color, like the color one can see in the eyes of lions, the color of the inhuman. As serious as the threat is, it is nevertheless contained within and disciplined by the very prose which articulates it. In an age of excess and apocalypse, an age which has in many ways turned the end of the world into its most important product, Bellow remains a resolutely antiapocalyptic novelist, defending the value of the human middle ground when most of us, much of the time, seem to have forgotten that territory's very existence. But the efficiency of his defense of normality is a function, absolutely, of his powerful sense of the impingements of the abnormal, of his ability to imagine, as chillingly as any novelist writing today, the manic horrors of solipsism and nightmare which lurk around every corner, down every street, of our artificially daylit cities.

The Victim, again, contains an extraordinary and perhaps intentionally prophetic allegory of Bellow's own position vis à vis the novelists who have succeeded him. Leventhal is taking his young, neglected nephew Philip out for a day in Manhattan, attempting to cheer the boy with sunshine and snacks. But when Leventhal suggests walking from Pennsylvania Station to Times Square, Philip wants to ride the subway. The boy is fascinated by the technical details which honeycomb the city's underground—"water pipes and sewage, gas mains, the electrical system for the subway, telephone and telegraph wires, and the cable for the Broadway trolley"—details whose allure Leventhal cannot understand. And when they finally debark at Forty-second Street, Leventhal reluctantly agrees to take Philip to a movie—whereupon the boy immediately chooses his uncle's least favorite genre, a Boris Karloff horror film.

When we remember the fascination of writers like Mailer and Pynchon with the dark underground of urban life—both literal and figurative—and the powerful fascination of so many contemporary novelists with the metaphor of modern existence as an immense horror film (Mailer's *The Naked and the Dead,* Burroughs's *Nova Express,* Donald Barthelme's *City Life,* Brock Brower's *The Late Great Creature,* Pynchon's *Gravity's Rainbow*), it is difficult not to see in this episode Bellow's own accurate forecast of where American fiction is headed and of his position in that movement. Both the boy and the man are concerned with survival of the most elemental sort, with finding, at the center of the urban desert, an image of the truth and a reason to go on. But while the younger survivor seeks out, embraces, the dangerous complexities of the underground and the too real fantasies of the horror film, the older man participates in both with a cool distaste, a humanist's wry reluctance.

This is to say that to read Bellow intelligently we must call into serious question our time-honored prejudices about the nature of "realism" and "fantasy" as varieties of narrative. Like all good novelists, Bellow not only educates us about the parameters of our own lives, he also educates us in the craft of reading novels. The fantastic and the realistic modes are carefully and continually intermingled in his tales. And, far from being a relic of the Eisenhower decade, Bellow appears more and more to be an artist who had to wait for the absurdist explosion of sixties fiction for his novels to be put in a true perspective. Rereading, from the vantage point of *The Sot-Weed Factor* or *Gravity's Rainbow*, even the comparatively tame narrative of *The Victim* or *Seize the Day*, we can see that those fifties-style celebrations of Bellow's "accurate eye" or "sense of life" were only part of the story. For, at his best and most characteristic, he is a true and brilliant fabulator of the American postwar variety—and one whose distinctive and firm commitment to literary tradition renders his fabulations all the more powerful and valuable.

There is, indeed, one specific tradition of this sort, a mingling of fantasy and realism, to which Bellow is more properly the heir than are many other writers. That is the tradition of the Jewish tale, found in the legends of the Hasidic rabbis, the marvelously pure folk stories of Sholem Aleichem, and the more sophisticated, bitter parables of Isaac Bashevis Singer. In these stories, the interpenetration of the everyday, creatural life of the *shtetl* and the high magic of man's reconciliation with Yahweh is at the very center of the narrative's power. Bellow's talent for the realistic-fantastic mode undoubtedly owes something to this highly developed, urban folk art, though not as much as do the fictions of a Jewish writer like Bernard Malamud in *The Natural* or *The Assistant*.

That Bellow's work can be characterized by "Jewishness" is another of those truisms which, while they contain a good deal of significance, may be ultimately misleading. The fifties saw an extraordinary efflorescence of what was heralded at the time as the "American Jewish novel," much as the sixties were celebrated as the era of the underground, absurdist black humorists. While it is true that Philip Roth (*Letting Go*), Edward Wallant (*The Pawnbroker*), Bruce Jay Friedman (*Stern*), Malamud, and Bellow all used the figure of the American Jew as a central symbolic feature in their explorations of the national soul (or lack of same), it is impossible to assign to that figure any meaning consistent from one writer to another. American fiction has always been obsessed with the idea of the outsider, the man who, for one reason or another, can never quite assimilate himself to the unself-conscious optimism of the classic American dream and who therefore becomes a living test of that dream's pretensions to a truly universal liberty and peace. (This obsession in the

American novel was, of course, most brilliantly traced in the work of another great Jewish writer of the decade, Leslie Fiedler in *Love and Death in the American Novel.*) From the Indians of James Fenimore Cooper through the vatic adolescents of Mark Twain to the blacks of Leroi Jones and Ishmael Reed, the outsider figure has always been among the most familiar in our literature. But the Jew, in his special complexity, was an unusually powerful, suggestive version of the outsider for the emerging sensibility—or better, emerging panic—of the fifties.

The American Jew, in many ways, was the red Indian of Levittown. The period after World War II was not, of course, the first great era of urban expansion in America, but it was the first era in which urban expansion came to be a central, disturbing facet of the American imagination. Sociologists, economists, politicians, and novelists began to realize, during the forties and fifties, that the growth of the city had become the most important fact for the future of democratic man. The city was no longer the center for weekday trade and weekend carousing it had largely represented to the nineteenth-century mind, nor was it the morally arid wasteland of the post-World War I imagination. It had become, quite simply, the essential context in which life, for better and worse, was henceforth to be lived out in America. The decade of Bellow's first triumphant novels was also the decade which saw the belated discovery of urban existence as a special kind of life, as well as the emergence of that peculiar amalgam of technologist and visionary, the "city planner." If Bellow's fiction is an instance, that is, of the Europeanization of the American novel, one reason for this is that his period is the period of the Europeanization (or urbanization) of American culture.

In the new city of postwar America, the new society taking account of its own immense technological sophistication, what better outsider-figure could be invented than the Jew? Unlike the Indian, his "outsideness" is not a function of his physical separation from the center of culture. The Jew, traditionally, lives within and is brilliant within the very heart of urban life. Unlike the black, his response to the culture which subtly excludes him is not anger or revolution (one thinks of Bigger Thomas in Richard Wright's *Native Son*), but rather acceptance coupled with silent disaffiliation and a wry irony which—at least imaginatively— can be more devastating than a Molotov cocktail. The Jew, in European as well as American tradition, is the man in whom history has become incarnate: the man whose very existence calls the infinitely progressive future into question by his reminiscence of an infinitely disappointing past, of diaspora, pogrom, the idea of *Rassenschade*. He is the ideal red Indian of an urban culture since, like Chingachgook and Uncas in Cooper's novels, he knows the topography of his own peculiar jungle better than the pioneers, cowboys, explorers, and goyim who condescendingly enlist his loyalty.

It is no surprise, then, that the "Jewish novel" enjoyed the splendid realizations it did in the fifties. Throughout the decade, in fact, the only outsider-myth which offered any alternative to it was that of the total dropout, the beatnik: the often less than noble savage whose disaffiliation was so programmatic and so idealized that he could brook no mode of separation but a return to the absolute nonparticipation of the fictional Indian himself. It is not without significance, indeed, that the two most permanently valuable members of the Beat Generation, Allen Ginsburg and Norman Mailer, are both outsiders of one kind—Jews—whose rage for separation leads them finally to disown that variety of outsidership for something at once purer, more deliberately chosen, and thence perhaps more self-defeating.

But unlike Mailer, his only serious rival in the fiction of the fifties, Bellow is content with Jewishness. And yet his use of that heritage and that myth sets him apart from any putative "Jewish" school of writing, just as it sets him apart from the more banal complacencies of so much other fiction of the age. Bellow's Jew is an urban outsider, an alien at the heart of, and living almost unnoticed within, the urban meltingpot; but as a Jew he is also the heir and avatar of a moral and ethical heritage which is at the very origin of the civilization that rejects him. And he is therefore the heir and avatar of diseases of the soul—and their potential cures—which have less to do with Jewishness than they do with the larger business of living at all in this age of the world. Bellow is a "Jewish" novelist, that is, in just the degree to which a writer like Graham Greene is a "Catholic" one. The aura of historical tradition and moral rigor is, for both men, an inescapable condition of their storytelling—and yet only as a model, a testcase, for the chances of any tradition's, any morality's survival in contemporary reality. Neither writer, one would think, can have made many converts to his particular religion. For the very great force of both writers is precisely in their sense of the difficulty and ambiguity of the theological norms—precisely, in a theological sense, in their gift for heresy.

The archetypal situation of a Bellow novel, then, may be paraphrased in this way: a man, always an American and usually a Jew, often an intellectual and never less than highly intelligent, discovers chaos. The chaos he discovers, moreover, is not the romantic, Nietzschean abyss nor the existential gulf of the absurd, but a homegrown variety of those monstrosities, implicated in the very texture of his personal relationships, his everyday hopes and acitivities, his job. The plot of the characteristic Bellow fiction, then, is the story of the hero's attempt to live with, survive within, the void that has opened at his feet. That is to say, Bellow's heroes, like the novelist himself, are concerned with finding a way to revivify the sanctions and values of Western culture in the context of the terrible complexity of the new megalopolis and the "lonely crowd." They are not—like some of the characters of Mailer and Pynchon, among others—mythmakers, questing for a new order and a new morality adequate to the crisis of contemporary history. They are mythpreservers, whose greatest efforts are bent toward reestablishing the originating values of civilization even against the nightmare civilization threatens to become.

Bellow is an ideological novelist. For all his vaunted "realism," for all the authenticity of his locales and the convincing ring of his characters' urban speech, he is a writer for whom thought, ideas, the concepts we hold of what goes on around us, are ultimately more important than "what goes on" itself. If inauthenticity is the besetting disease of mid-twentieth-century man, Bellow articulates the violent crisis of that disease in what must be its most classical form. It is the fever that comes more severely to intellectuals than to others, the horrifying discovery that, for all your thought, all your balanced and well-learned sense of the terms of life, nothing—nothing—really avails when you have to face the wreckage of a love affair, the onslaught of age, the unreasoning hatred of the man staring you in the face. That is the color of the beast, the senseless, brute throbbing of reality which waits within the insulated city. And that is the color which Bellow's narrative dialogues seek, if not to obliterate, at least to make tolerable, tamed once again to the systems of thought which have been evolved over the millennia for the very purpose of taming it.

The dialogue form, indeed, is the most perennial and perennially creative form of Bellow's narrative. Not a great natural storyteller—not a great delineator of raw action, movement, physical violence—he is a consummate inventor of conversation, either between two people or, more often, between the quarreling halves of a single personality. Like the Talmud, his books are full of passionate talk, the debates of earnest and ironic teachers over the myriad possible interpretations of the lesson of the text—only, in Bellow, the "text" is not the divine text of Torah, but the quotidian text of a single mind in its warfare with the material world. His fiction, that is, while it deals realistically with real characters, is also continually capable of making ideas themselves the most active and most interesting "characters" of the action.

This tendency of Bellow's work achieves, in his most recent books, a level of originality, complexity, and strangeness which is one of the most remarkable events of recent American writing. But it is a tendency which has been present in his work from the beginning, and which, from the vantage of the present, accounts for the sometimes clumsy quality of his earlier books. *Dangling Man* and *The Victim* set out the perimeters of his moral concerns with graphic, occasionally inelegant precision. And in both novels the presence of dialogue as an austere collision of viewpoints and philosophies plays a central and organizing role. . . .

. . . The self-image most frequently in Henderson's mind is that of King Nebuchadnezzar in the Book of Daniel, the king who was punished for his presumption against God with the fulfillment of the prophecy "They shall drive thee from among men, and thy dwelling shall be with the beasts of the field."

It is, in fact, among the beasts—not of the field, but of the jungle—that Henderson makes his final attempt at confrontation and self-vindication. The myth of Nebuchadnezzar is never far from the surface of his story. Previous Bellow characters had shudderingly recognized the presence of the beast, the heraldic monstrosity of whatever does not tolerate man, in the curious color of a sunset over Staten Island or, like Augie, actually met an avatar of the beast in the ferocious-looking but cowardly eagle Caligula. But Henderson actually seeks out such a confrontation and in so doing becomes Bellow's closest approximation of what we shall see to be the permanent ethic, existentially foolhardy, of Norman Mailer. And if Henderson falters and moans when the confrontation finally comes, with the lioness Atti, he nevertheless persists in that confrontation to a point which is equally heroic and buffoonish.

It was Thomas Hobbes—and after him, virtually the entire eighteenth century of political theorists—who argued that man in the state of nature, denuded of the reassurances of the social contract, is little better than a ravenous animal. The romantic revolution itself arises out of eighteenth-century reasonings and is brooded over by Rousseau's celebration of the nobility of "savage" man before his corruption and betrayal by social artificiality. But romanticism never really makes peace with the Enlightenment idea of "natural" civilization as the brutally uncivilized war of all against all. The noble savage of Rousseau, Chateaubriand, and to some extent Shelley is not so much a positive myth of pure anarchism (as it became in such later versions as Edgar Rice Burroughs's Tarzan) but is, rather, a negative, pastoral judgment on the present unreformed state of society. The high romantic contemplates the vision of Edenic, natural man the more efficiently to plan a reorganization of present man which can approximate, on the willed, artificial level of culture, the intuited freedom and dignity of that mythic, metahistorical nature.

This is an aspect of so-called romantic primitivism which is often misunderstood. But Eugene Henderson, though he manages only fumblingly and with comic distortion to articulate his insights, lives out a precise and brilliantly planned drama of the romantic political dialectic. At one point, after wandering through Africa with only his guide for company, he comes upon the outskirts of a native village, where a young girl, upon seeing him, bursts into uncontrollable weeping. His disconcerted reaction, in all its engaging clumsiness, is a parable of romantic man's anguished introspection before the sheer, overwhelming fact of politics, the fact of other people:

> Society is what beats me. Alone I can be pretty good, but let me go among people and there's the devil to pay. Confronted with this weeping girl I was by this time ready to start bawling myself, thinking of Lily and the children and my father and the violin and the foundling and all the sorrows of my life. I felt that my nose was swelling, becoming very red.

His trip to Africa itself is impelled, if not ultimately caused, by a particularly shocking version of that opening of the insane at the heart of the everyday which is, by now, a familiar aspect of Bellow's work. One day on his farm Henderson is in the midst of a violent quarrel with Lily, his second wife. He shouts, pounds the table—and kills a woman in his wrath:

> Miss Lenox was the old woman who lived across the road and came in to fix our breakfast. . . . I went into the kitchen and saw this old creature lying dead on the floor. During my rage, her heart had stopped.

Society, indeed, is what beats Henderson—beats him so severely that he must regard his egoistic anguish as a murderous force. There is even something brilliantly Hobbesian (or Lockean, or Humean) in the very articulation of Miss Lenox's demise. He does not say, "Because of my rage, her heart had stopped," but rather, "During my rage." But, causal or not, this awful coincidence is enough to send him on his manic quest. At the beginning of the next chapter, he begins the narrative of his sojourn in Africa.

Like many other questers in contemporary American fiction, Henderson does not even have a clear idea of the object of his quest. But, taking the story in the double context of the myth of Nebuchadnezzar and the heritage of eighteenth-century liberal thought, we can say that his search is actually for a principle of rationality—for an order which will enable him to believe in himself and in the dignity of his immense passions and yearnings, and, at the same time, to collaborate in the realization of the dignity and independence of other people in a cohesive, charitable society. If Augie March is a "saint of charity" striving to realize his own separate existence, Henderson is the reverse: a saint (or monster) of egoism trying to realize the claims of other people.

One can say, in fact, that Henderson goes to Africa to learn the wisdom of Tarzan and, instead, discovers the mirror of Hobbes—discovers, that is, his own ineluctable moral involvement with others, even at the heart of supposedly the most "savage" country in the world. The rationality he discovers, then, is a rationality which condemns his own egoism, even though it is his very egoism, his heroic insistence on seeing things through, which leads him to the discovery of that rationality. This is the romantic revolutionary paradox and the shape of Henderson's experience.

Bellow, here as elsewhere, remains a faithful enough student of anthropology to ridicule our comfortable Western belief in the exclusiveness of our claims to rational civilization. The two tribes Henderson encounters exhibit not only the richness and complexity of so-called primitive societies as they actually exist, but also the possibility of producing sensitive human beings fully as compelling as the self-confident and self-accusing Henderson. More important, though, the two tribes offer a schematic diagram of Henderson's own, quintessentially Western and "enlightened" idea of Natural Man. Eugene Henderson's first name means "well-born": as the heir of the romantic ideal of universal aristocracy, this civilized nobleman in doubt of his own nobility seeks, in Africa, a natural, primal kingship which will substantiate the lessons he has learned (and unlearned) about his own separate destiny. We remember the con-man version of that promise in Seize the Day, Tamkin's assurance that "Thou art King. Thou art at thy best." Henderson's journey may be thought of, then, as an attempt to rediscover and re-prove the heroic tradition so cheapened in Tamkin's poem. Hence the ironic title of the book, for Henderson does, indeed, become a "Rain King," a ritual monarch of the warlike tribe of the Wariri, but finds that kingship fully as artificial, fully as fraught with the complex, agonizing dubiety of social existence as was the life of New England he had thought to transcend.

The first tribe Henderson visits, the peace-loving, bovine Arnewi, are a parody of the Rousseauist and Chateaubriandesque idea of the "savage": affectionate, sensual in a prepubescent way, the perfect subjects, in their Edenic innocence, for Henderson's Faustian desire to lead. But this very desire thwarts itself and in so doing incidentally destroys the Eden of the Arnewi. Trying to rid their water supply of the ritually untouchable frogs which infest it, Henderson blows up the reservoir. Self-exiled from the now doubly melancholy Arnewi, he enters the coun-

try of the more dangerous Wariri, where he meets his double, the splen-
didly ego-consolidated King Dahfu, master and lover of the lioness Atti,
who needs to prove his kingship by capturing the male lion believed to
reincarnate the spirit of his father. Dahfu, however, comically disappoints
Henderson's quest for a truly natural, pastoral state of human nobility. For
Dahfu, as Henderson learns, has given up a promising career as a doctor to
return to the kingship of his people and is much given to reading the
European psychologists and physiognomists of the nineteenth century,
with a view to elaborating his own theory of spiritual and physical
correspondences. He is, in other words, a very Cartesian savage indeed,
and as he traps Henderson into assuming the role of "Rain King" or
water-giver of the tribe, we realize that he is—cleverly and perhaps
educatively—using the leverage of Henderson's own naive ideas of the
"primitive" against him.

Dahfu is killed in the climactic, liturgical lion hunt which would
have solidified his kingship. He is, in fact, the victim of a palace conspiracy no less complicated or sinister than those which have beset Versailles
and St. Petersburg. And here again the parody of the novel is unmistak-
able. An earlier voyager and explorer of the possibilities of civilization,
Swift's Gulliver, found himself a cumbersome, self-destructively immense
giant among the Lilliputians and a minuscule, eternally victimized atom of
personality among the Brobdignagians. Bellow's later but equally gullible
mental traveler finds himself, first, a carrier of that very impulse to power
which he seeks to escape among the Arnewi, and then an innocent victim
of the *Realpolitik* he refuses to recognize—till it is too late—underneath
the exotic trappings of Wariri culture. More than any other Bellow hero,
Henderson tries to escape the killing dichotomy of romantic individualism
and politics by escaping politics altogether—and finds politics (almost in
the Platonic sense of our spiritual responsibility for others) everywhere.
The last, wonderfully inconclusive scene of the novel gives us Henderson,
temporarily grounded en route back to America, leaping exultantly around
an icy airfield in Newfoundland (what more ironically named place for
this book of frustrated discovery to end?), clutching in his arms a lonely
Persian orphan boy, also voyaging to the New World. It is a moment
which may be either a breakthrough into an elemental charity or the
despairing expression of an impossible ideal of love. But, as either or both,
it is one of the most powerful and enigmatically metaphysical scenes in
Bellow's fiction.

EARL ROVIT

Saul Bellow and the Concept of the Survivor

In one of his pontifical remarks on Art, Life, and Other Higher Matters, Ernest Hemingway offered his blueprint for the making of A Great Writer, reserving as his capstone requirement that "above all he (the artist) must survive." Hemingway, of course, was suggesting that the bourgeois artist in a modern affluent society had special problems in this respect. In large part he was invoking the romantic notion that the writer works best when he is hungry, running scared, and allowed to do his work free from the blandishments of publicity, Hollywood offers, cafe-society, and the insidious corruption of his own self-esteem. In the scope of his own work Hemingway was enormously successful at projecting an heroic figure, staunch in individuality, embattled against the world, intent on carving out a tiny sphere of autonomy that might hold eternal resonance even as it was physically swept aside by the forces it fronted. In this context I am reminded of the argument that Terrence Des Pres, author of The Survivor, carries on with Bruno Bettleheim on the behavior of concentration camp victims. Bettleheim has recorded the story of a woman ordered to dance in front of the gas chamber who, complying with the order, managed to seize a gun and shoot a guard. She was, of course, immediately killed. Bettleheim cites this action as a luminous model of heroic behavior—which it certainly is. Des Pres points out, however, that under such circumstances it was the only alternative to passive obedience; nonetheless, for all of its courage and moral beauty, it was still suicide. And he suggests further that Bettleheim's very traditional notion of heroism "dovetails with the view of man as victim." "In fact," he continues, "the celebration of man's 'indominable spirit' and our acceptance of victimhood are rooted in the single belief, as old as Western culture, that human bondage can be transcended only in death. Death is at once the entrance to a world of fulfilment unobtainable on earth and the proof of a spirit unvanquished by fear or compromise." In Des Pres' study of survivor-behavior, he argues that there may be an alternative to heroic or cowardly victimization. That in situations of utter extremity, man is stripped to a state of "radical nakedness" where everything means precisely and only what it is. And one may entertain the possibility that on this level there may be a biological "talent for life" that cuts below moral and intellectual questions of accommodation or rebellion. In other words, there may be a mode of behavior appropriate to the survivor other than that of victim or rebel.

I introduce these references with deliberate cunning. Not only is Hemingway the immediate Chicago predecessor of Saul Bellow, but in his life and work he offers a curiously illuminating contrast—a kind of negative fatherhood—to Bellow's achievement. Hemingway, who eventually took his own life for reasons that may have appeared heroic to him at least, always had a soft spot in his heart for victims who fought back—and it is fair to suggest that this is one legitimate way to define the Hemingway hero: a victim who rebels; a loser whose integrity is validated by his defeat. That such a moral principle is tantamount to an approval of suicide on a sheerly physical level is mitigated by the fact that the terms of the game, in Hemingway's case, are safely symbolic—nor do I say this with any desire to degrade Hemingway's stunning achievement. Born in an upper-middleclass suburb of Chicago, nurtured on the just expectations that socio-economically he was and always would be a "have" rather than a "have-not" and that his risktaking would be a matter of voluntary choice, Hemingway viewed the world in a way that coincided perfectly with that of his generation and class. And thus when Hemingway talks of the writer's need to survive and the hero who dies "well," he is clearly thinking in terms of a transcendence and a performance of conquest that stir rich resonances in the Western tradition. In Hemingway's dramas, the hero can draw sustenance from both sides of the archetypal dialectic— from the Christian sacrifice and the Faustian defiance; and, most important, the artist himself can luxuriate in the honorific identities of his own heroic creations.

Saul Bellow, resembling in curious ways the older Chicago novelist, Theodore Dreiser, has had as a writer options of quite another kind. To him—as a child of immigrants, as Jew, as one who came to age in the decade of the Great Depression, as part of a worldwide generation that must calibrate its sense of history not by Caporetto and the Huertgen Forest, but by Buchenwald, Gulag, and Hiroshima—the heroism of individual rebellion can hardly be other than a source of pathos and despair. One man on a cross at a time when death can be conceived as a salvation, a metamorphosis, a ritual passage out of disorder and injustice is certainly among the very great symbolic truths of man. Millions of crucifixions— senseless, unprovoked, unredeemable—are at best obscene sentimentalities and at worst statistics of successful criminal manipulation. In this essay I shall try to sketch the course that Bellow's art has taken in the development and presentation of a kind of protagonist capable of living with human decency within the restricted options of a post-World War II mentality. And what I shall be primarily concerned with is an investigation into Bellow's effort to develop the figure of the victim into that of the survivor.

Bellow has recently recalled that it was his ambition as a graduate student in anthropology "to investigate bands of Eskimos who were reported to have chosen to starve rather than eat foods that were abundant but under taboo. How much, I asked myself, did people yield to culture or to their lifelong preoccupations, and at what point would the animal need to survive break through the restraints of custom and belief?" If this question is reminiscent of Bellow's youthful reading of Conrad's *Heart of Darkness*, his own starving tribe of Arnewi, and the Humboldt-Citrine scenario, *Caldofreddo*, it suggests the persistence of the issue in his thinking. How much of his sense of selfhood can a man afford to sacrifice in order to survive without imperiling his sense of decency? In his first novel, *Dangling Man*, Bellow touches the problem obliquely as Joseph flounders, retreats into torpor and irritability, and finds himself finally unable to sustain his existence—his dignity and freedom—without the support of a predictable framework of routine occupations. Or, as Joseph declares, "The greatest cruelty is to curtail expectations without taking away life completely. A life term in prison is like that." It is difficult to take Joseph's plight very seriously, of course; he is not, after all, in a Siberian labor-camp. And yet the pertinence of his situation may be seen if we compare him with Artur Sammler hiding in a Polish cemetery during the war: "You have been summoned to be. Summoned out of matter. Therefore here you are. And though the vast overall design may be of the deepest interest . . . you yourself, a finite instance, are obliged to wait, painfully, anxiously, heartachingly, in this yellow despair. And why? But

you must!" Sammler in the Mezvinski tomb is in the same metaphysical
position as the young pampered Joseph in the Chicago winter of 1942-43.
And by extension, it seems to me, Bellow's other protagonists—Leventhal,
Augie, Tommy Wilhelm, Henderson, Herzog, and Charlie Citrine—are to
a greater or lesser extent in a similar situation of "yellow despair." Even
while they are moving, they wait under compulsion with minimal expectations. According to the degree to which they are able to preserve their
moral integrity without succumbing wholly to the compulsions that would
bend them, they are successful survivors rather than victims.

It was Hannah Arendt, I think, who pointed out that mankind's
first space-orbit had irradicably altered the terms of the human condition.
Earth was no more the encompassing womb and tomb of human kind; it
was now and henceforth a launching pad, a space-platform. And the
heady exhilaration of the first moonlander ("A small step for man, a giant
step for mankind") expresses the conquistador-enthusiasm of a sudden
vision of the universe as one of unlimited challenges and possibilities. In
his discussion with Govinda Lal and in his general response to lunar
exploration, Sammler appears to be speaking directly for Bellow: "I seem
to be a depth man rather than a height man. I do not personally care for
the illimitable. . . . I think I am an Oriental. . . . Jews, after all, are
Orientals. I am content to watch, and admire these gorgeous Faustian
departures for the other worlds. Personally, I require a ceiling, although a
high one." Bellow, to be sure, has had a lifelong fascination with Faustian
heroes, but he has usually given such characters a secondary and vaguely
corrupt place in his novels. His Faustian characters—his so-called "Reality
Instructors" (Grandma Lausch, Einhorn, Mintouchian, Basteshaw, Tamkin,
King Dahfu, Himmelstein, Simkin, Cantabile)—have more often than
not turned out to be self-deluding egotists, calculating Macchiavellians, or
lunatic con-artists against whom the Bellow protagonist must inevitably
protect himself.

But what mode of behavior, what kind of temperament can be
opposed to the Faustian? Let me suggest that the antithetical thrust to the
Faust archetype is the equally archetypal Christ figure. As is obvious, the
two character-types stand in an almost exact mirror-relationship and one
might guess that they are products of a single imaginative conception. The
God who chooses to become man and the man who strains to achieve
Godhead; the Christ that incarnates a total submission to the power of
love and the Faust who is the enfleshment of a lust for power. The victim
who vanquishes through his very abjuration of force and the rebel whose
defiance is annealed in the fire of his defeat; the masochist and the sadist;
the Word that becoming Flesh is the very spirit of an active Passion, and

the quite palpable flesh, so overweening in its attempt to metamorphose into the Word that it becomes in the process impersonalized into passivity. But although the Faustian role has been hesitantly assumed by some of Bellow's protagonists—we remember Joseph's intermittent outbursts of temper, Leventhal's sullen rebelliousness, Henderson's attempt to be the savior of the Arnewi, Herzog's futile assassination plan, Citrine's Steinerian rebellion against death—these quasi-Faustian endeavors are characteristically demeaned and burlesqued as inept and comic embarrassments. It is evident from even the most cursory reading of Bellow's novels that he has a deep and unrelenting suspicion of the effects of power on personality. Again Sammler can speak for Bellow: "Power certainly corrupts, but that statement is humanly incomplete . . . having power destroys the sanity of the powerful. It allows their irrationalities to leave the sphere of dreams and come into the real world." Indeed it would be no exaggeration to say that Bellow holds the Faustian impulse of man—its rejection of internal and external limitations—primarily responsible for the bloodbaths of history and the diminution and degradation of the private self.

But for the antithesis, the "Christian" accommodation, there is a similar reluctance in Bellow's work. A recurrent lesson that many of his protagonists learn is the ineffectuality of making a pact of mildness and docility between themselves and the encroaching fates. Herzog's self-ridiculing recital of the nursery rhyme, "I love little pussy / Her coat is so warm," is a characteristic belated realization on the part of the Bellow hero who represses or denies his own aggression in an attempt to placate potential hostility. Almost all of Bellow's heroes are visited by epiphanies of an underlying or overriding oneness of mankind ("a splash of God's own spirit" in every human being), but each learns also that the existence of such "psychic unity" is no defense against injustice, brutality, or the destructiveness of oneself or other human beings. Thus Leventhal must eventually guard himself against Allbee, Augie against Basteshaw, Herzog against Madeleine and Gersbach, and Sammler must deny the plea of a shared humanity from the disarmed German soldier whom he kills. In reference to his earlier work, Bellow has admitted a dissatisfaction with "realistic literature" which "from the first has been a victim literature." But even though Joseph, Leventhal, and Tommy Wilhelm are victimized personalities, each of them in different ways manages to assert an ultimate sense of self that resists mergence or psychic surrender.

Bellow has claimed that in the writing of his first two novels, he was cautiously following the Flaubertian standard of the well-made artifact; that is, a narrative structure closed rather than open, self-referential in texture, and one designed to minimize subjectivity and digressiveness. I think Bellow overestimates his adherence to such a standard, but it does seem true that his language, his handling of time-sequences, his characterizations, and his employment of narrative focus and structure change significantly after *The Victim*. He has explained this shift as a consequence of his greater confidence and his seeking a style that would be more closely consonant with his experience and talents. But a more useful way of regarding this change might be to see him developing a different kind of protagonist; or, more accurately, a protagonist cast under an archetypal model other than that of the Faust or the Christ. Or, to put it in different terms, having investigated the ambiguities of victimizing and victimization and rejecting the philosophic perspective inherent in these forms, Bellow found a more suitable model for his purposes than those of traditional victim or rebel. In short, he hit upon the conception of a hero who would be defined by his being in incessant motion. Let me stress the obvious here in order to make this point clear. Both the Christ and the Faust are necessarily static archetypes. The one suffers His agony on the cross to redeem mankind; the other sells his soul in a desperate bargain for total power. Each and every event in their fictional lives is subservient to the decisions to have them assume their respective fixed roles in a symbolically absolute mythic structure. And this structure, in turn, will tend to be ritualistic, morally didactic, and circular. Further, both archetypes are likely to realize themselves fictionally in protagonists who would fail Schlossberg's test in *The Victim*—protagonists, that is, who are faulty because they are either less or more than human; "more" in so far as they are godlike, "less" in their mechanical or animal responses to experience. "Good acting is what is exactly human," says Schlossberg. "More than human, can you have any use for life? Less than human, you don't either."

Arriving at Ludeyville after all his adventures are virtually concluded but shortly before the immense stock-taking which is to be the substance of the novel, Herzog says: "What a struggle I waged!—left-handed but fierce. But enough of that—here I am. *Hineni!*" The Hebrew word, *hineni*, provides a useful insight to Bellow's intentions. Abraham utters the word three times in Genesis 22: first when the Lord summons to sacrifice Isaac as a burnt offering; second when Isaac calls for his attention to question him about the sacrifice; and third when the angel of the Lord interrupts him before he can use his knife on his bound son. One would prefer not to be the kind of "deep" reader that Bellow has complained about, but it is hard to overlook the resonance of this famous Biblical word. *Hineni!* Here I am! In a sense, this is the climactic gesture that both punctuates and concludes the narrative action in all of Bellow's novels;

Joseph, no longer to be held accountable for himself; Leventhal, hurrying to return to the theater-seat for the third act; Augie declaring himself "a sort of Columbus of those near-at-hand," speeding toward Bruges and saying: "Look at me, going everywhere!"; Tommy Wilhelm above the open coffin of the stranger, submerged in the tears of "his heart's ultimate need"; Henderson prancing over the Newfoundland snow; Sammler at the corpse of Elya Gruner; and Charlie Citrine walking away from Humboldt's second burial. As Erich Auerbach has indicated, although *hineni* is usually translated "here I am," it means "only something like 'behold me,' and in any case is not meant to indicate the actual place where Abraham is, but a moral position in respect to God who has called to him—Here am I awaiting thy command." Similarly the Bellow protagonists are not announcing a geographical or psychological orientation. Like Abraham they are stating the primal moral identification of ethical Judaism. Accepting the limitations of their own creatureliness, they are merely reaffirming what they already know—namely, the contractual agreement between their souls and the object of their obligations. Striving to be neither less nor more than human, they are determined to act well. And being human—and hence, in motion rather than static—it is incumbent on them from time to time to call themselves present and ready to be accounted for. Thus I would suggest that Bellow's choice of narrative structure—the rambling, episodic, picaresque chronicle of jumbled sequential events—patterns itself loosely on the myth of the eternal journey or, better, the eternal wandering.

But here a necessary distinction must be drawn between that hero as quest-figure which has been such a rich character in the Western tradition—a hero who certainly seems to be in motion—and Bellow's wanderer or survivor. The hero with a thousand faces whom the Jungians have so well publicized is usually portrayed as a seeker or explorer with a fixed goal; he voyages to exotic places or descends into the underworld or the underconsciousness to discover or capture the Holy Grail, the Golden Fleece, a guarded princess, a new city, a blue flower, a white whale, or some other symbolic token to bring back to the world of time and mortality. Usually Faustian in his motivations, but obviously capable of Christian transformation, the quest-hero is a champion of mankind whose identity is realized in the process of his search and specifically in the mystical moment of embrace between himself and his goal. At no time is such a character likely to call *"Hineni!* Here I am!" because a substantial part of his efforts is directed toward denying boundaries, limitations, and definitions. His success is to demonstrate that *here is everywhere* and *I* is the exact and ecstatic equivalent of *All*. The traditional quest-hero, then, receives aesthetic validation in a dazzling transmogrification of self. Depending on the direction of his transcendence, he suffers or enjoys a supreme apotheosis as he throws off his guise of mortality and blends into the eternity of the damned or the glorified. Bellow's aims have been a good deal more modest, a good deal more earth-defined. Limited by mortality, his wanderer seeks no extra-terrestrial goals save the continuance of his sense of a morally connected life. "The spirit knows that its growth is the real aim of existence," argues Sammler; and the Bellow hero remains in the world of time and mortality, moving inexorably toward his death, a symbolic traveler who points less to the heroism of man than to the immeasurable grandeur of the gift bequeathed to man—life itself.

Here it might be useful to examine a little more closely the archetype that I think Bellow has been more or less indebted to in the gradual development of his fictional hero—this equally ancient, but much less commented-upon figure which dangles, as it were, between the Christ and the Faust—namely, the Wandering Jew or the Survivor. Rarely appearing in a pure unadulterated form but perceptible in such figures as Job and Odysseus, the Wandering Jew exerts its influence on that kind of hero who is engaged in aimless movement. The shaping force behind the *picaro*-hero and the personae of essayists like Montaigne, the Wandering Jew makes a lurid appearance as his own caricature in the Gothic novel and in Romantic poetry, emerging again in a form more compatible with Bellow's in characters like Joseph K. and Leopold Bloom. This is the archetypal hero who has tested his arms' breadth to their fullest reach, and touching the edges of reality on both sides—what Augie calls "the axial lines of life"—has neither suffered crucifixion nor been enabled to possess what he has grasped. Instead, his forehead has been seared with the mark of mortality; he has been denied entrance to heaven or hell and he has been sentenced to Mr. Sammler's planet—an eternal earth of endless and aimless ways. Forbidden damnation or glorification, his singular achievement is earthly survival. By definition he is consigned to eternal loneliness and eternal movement; he is prohibited from establishing permanent bonds between himself and anything else in the universe, nor can he cease in his wanderings for more than a moment to rest or take his pleasure. Bearing the history of the world on his stooped shoulders like some dreadful peddler's sack, serving ultimately and painfully as the world's conscience and memory, he can act in the present only as impotent witness. A strange figure for an archetypal hero, this Wandering Jew, this unwanted revenant, this almost obliterated importunate relic of time, but one which man's imagination seems to have been forced to add to the folklore of the race in order to complete the full round of human potentiality.

For if the Christ and Faust archetypes are extravagant personifications of man's capacities to surrender or assert the ego in their most resplendent and orgiastic extremes, the Wandering Jew may be an emblematic representation of man's naked consciousness. Despicable, isolate, possessing no power source of its own, separated from both its libidinal roots and its projected ideals, fated to be in irresolute motion as long as we have any experience of it, capable of registering precisely the pulses and throbs of frustration and desire while remaining itself neuter and unmoved, quintessentially sense-bound and sense-defined but without the possibilities of sensual gratification, the bare human consciousness is certainly an ambiguous blessing. And yet it exhibits an indubitable heroic quality in its consistency, the integrity of its performance under severe stress, its passive readiness to consider all possibilities, and its almost godlike detachment from hope and despair. For a writer like Bellow who obviously enjoys dramatizing the irrepressible cerebration of his protagonists there is a distinct advantage in projecting characters who are quasi-allegorical embodiments of mental energy. The artificiality of the novel-as-diary placed him under cramped restrictions in *Dangling Man*. *The Adventures of Augie March* showed Bellow how to loosen the formality of recording thought in narrative by interposing a voice between the thinker and the thought. Most brilliantly, in *Herzog*, Bellow was able to create the illusion of capturing thought as it flowed fresh from the mind, unmediated by the structures of journal-entries or conversation. And although this strategy of narration is surely grounded in the convention of the stream of consciousness, Bellow's articulate intellectuals rarely indulge themselves in free-floating reverie; in fact, they and he seem to regard the unconscious more as a dependable store of memory than a source of startling Freudian revelation.

Thus Bellow's choice of the picaresque form seems well-nigh inevitable as a frame within which to examine and exemplify the wanderings of man. Merging the picaresque at times with the related form of the Bildungsroman, and infusing both with the ironic style and tone of the Yiddish tale, Bellow's most consistent novelistic purpose has been to set a protagonist into burdened motion—not so much as an opportunity for social or psychological analysis as to italicize an unflinchingly moral view of the human obligation. In *Seize the Day*, perhaps his most concentrated and thoroughly successful work—the stripped poem, as it were, which resides at the center of his fiction—he describes Tommy Wilhelm, the bumbling agonized clown who is a kind of comic cartoon of the Bellow survivor: "The spirit, the peculiar burden of his existence lay upon him like an accretion, a load, a hump. In any moment of quiet, when sheer fatigue prevented him from struggling, he was apt to feel this mysterious weight, this growth or collection of nameless things which it was the business of his life to carry about." Like most of Bellow's heroes Tommy excites ambiguous responses in the people he encounters. His father feels both threatened and disgusted by him; to Tamkin he is an easy dupe. His wife regards him as self-indulgent and childish, while his mistress presumably pities him and decries the weakness that keeps him from arranging his affairs sensibly. Rubin behind the cigar stand and the manager of the brokerage try to look at him without seeing him because he projects blatant claims that most people cannot afford to honor. Struggling to survive in a world which ignores or feels contempt for the values he can scarcely articulate, Tommy exercises the same fascination on the reader who is simultaneously beguiled and repelled by him. He is an undesirable witness who forces us to regard what we are usually careful to be blind to. He would show us in the ludicrous contortions of his floundering that the web of relationships that sustains our lives—our friendships, loves, successes, family, occupation, social image—is, indeeed, thin and frangible. That we can take no security or succor in such impermanent support. And that, in spite of this, nihilism or hedonism are unacceptable solutions. That on a level beneath logic or remonstrance, even though we may profess no faith and admit no doctrine, we still hold ourselves responsible for the shape and momentum of our lives.

This is, of course, a difficult notion to discuss because Bellow's ironic techniques of narration make it easy for readers to dismiss the moral challenge, focusing instead on the undeniable elements of self-pity and deprecation that suffuse personalities like Tommy, Herzog, and Citrine. But because of the comic ambience that Bellow employs—Herzog saying: *"Lord I ran to fight in Thy holy cause, but kept tripping . . ."*—Bellow is able to express what might otherwise be inexpressible. It is true that the Bellow survivor is an irresistible target for manipulators and enthusiasts of all varieties and an unflagging source of irritation and affront to those who have made their accommodations with the bland empiricisms of the world. And it is probably true that his demands are so zanily immoderate that only a saint could abide him over prolonged periods of time. But Bellow succeeds in making his grotesquerie reinforce his serious role as Wandering Jew or Survivor. The typically askew protagonists of Bellow's novels—a blithe spirit like Augie, the manic Henderson, the middle-aged and aging dandies, Herzog and Citrine—moving awkwardly and out of step in the computerized traffic of modern conveniences, startle us into sudden perceptions of the bleak life-and-death seriousness which those very conveniences are designed to conceal. Thus it is no accident that in most of Bellow's novels there is a crucial confrontation with death; and to a large degree, the moral measure of the protagonist's character is revealed in his responsiveness to that finality. On this "bad literalness" are the symbols of civilization founded, and it is the function of Bellow's heroes to be more aware of this than most of us allow ourselves to be—to be aware of it without succumbing to it.

Bellow's protagonists manage to survive through a combination of restlessness, blind luck, cunning, egotism, and an erratic fortitude in holding themselves to the moral standard of their childhood pieties. Multi-married, familied, and befriended as they variously are, each is finally alone, "a prisoner of perception, a compulsory witness." Any individual's survival is a mutual or collective endeavor—man cannot exist except through the assistance of other men—but Bellow's survivors, ego-locked in the capsules of their own motion, tell us how it is with them and remind us of the pockets of forgetfulness in our own lives. Typically they own monsterlike memories of total recall—so much so that their friends use them as instant encyclopedias. Augie, Herzog, Citrine—they remember the precise gleam of light on the cast-iron kitchen stoves of their infancies, the names and physical characteristics of all their teachers, friends, and friends' friends, the specific shading of affection, wonder, and distaste that they felt in this or that situation. Perhaps because they are in perpetual transit—on trains and planes and taxis, from Chicago to New York, from America to Europe, from this wife to that mistress, from one consuming intellectual project to another—it is all the more incumbent upon them not to let any scrap of the past be lost.

They are, in addition, incorrigibly urban and one of the essential characteristics of the modern city, I suppose, is its protean acceleration—its unremitting self-demolition and reconstruction. No other American novelist except Dreiser has lavished such care and unillusioned affection on the modern city. Bellow has caught masterfully the urban texture of smells and heats, the striations of neighborhood, the humor, the indifference, the stimulation, the brutal movement of people in crowds, and the solipsistic frenzy of the individual alone in the middle of crowds. The Bellow hero tends to be cocky in his street-smart cynicism, sentimental at the loss of a remembered landmark, accepting as a matter of course new buildings on the sites of the old, neighborhoods lost to expressways, renewal projects, and urban blight, and the changing ethnic tides of settlement and exodus. Nor is it merely fortuitous that Bellow's wanderer happens to be perched in the city. Here he has a permanent impermanence, as it were, changing his address regularly while the city shifts its shape around and underneath him. Where else could the conditions of settled instability that define our problems of survival be so neatly represented? Cut off from the obsolete pastoral tradition that finds in natural cycles of recurrence a way of organizing life and absorbing death, Bellow's survivors must work out their own pragmatic accommodations on a daily basis in terms of rusting steel and cracked concrete. And thus memory has a special moral importance in the city novel. It is the only defense against the anonymous mutability of the city and its silent millions. For the Bellow survivor, each shard of life is unique and precious; if it is not remembered, it is the same as never having existed at all. In this respect one should recognize Bellow's deep indebtedness to Proust; the Bellow survivor struggles against the blurred diffusion of time by trying to respond to each instant fully and to hold it whole in his mind.

The city-settings may also partly explain Bellow's typical choice of plot materials. As the traditional country-novel coheres naturally around the seasonal cycle of family and rural community life, so the modern city with its insistent electric rhythms tends to be the fictional habitat of the footloose, the fragmented, and the flamboyant. The city-novel lends itself to treatments of art, business, crime, and romantic dalliance. Given Bellow's predisposition toward intellectuals who remain marginal to the established community, it is probably not surprising that an ample proportion of the plot incident in his fiction is concerned with the amorous couplings and uncouplings of his heros and their varied consorts. This, however, frequently causes a weakness in narrative tone because Bellow almost always treats the frets and fevers of romantic love as a symptom of immaturity. Thus there is an intermittently confused element in his handling of this romantic material—not because the material is intrinsically frivolous, but because his amorous narrators, becoming increasingly ironic and self-condemning as they chronicle their sexual exposures, seem to find their preoccupations frivolous. To be sure, one of Bellow's themes is the comic paradox of the devotee to the rational life who is duped by his own vanity and sensuality. And, after all, he has to give his protagonists something to do when they are not thinking heavy thoughts. But beyond this, it suggests that Bellow has significant trouble in finding plot circumstances that are strong enough to carry the intellectual burden of his concerns. As a comic writer and a moralist, he must establish a poised balance between the buffoonery of his heroes and the seriousness of what they represent. When the distance between the author and the protagonist is clearly fixed, as in *Seize the Day* and *Henderson the Rain King,* the result may be moral comedy of a consummate order.

But one final, possibly crucial element must be added to this rough sketch of the Bellow survivors—the element which saves them from being merely opportunists or *Luftmenschen* lucky enough to avoid the buffets of adversity. It is not through encasing themselves in defensive armor that Bellow's protagonists survive, but through remaining vulnerably responsive to a special claim of experience. Certainly they lavish a good deal of care upon themselves, but they also keep themselves open to others. Sammler rushing to arrive at Elya Gruner's bedside speaks not only for Bellow but also for the other Bellow heroes: ". . . compassionate utterance was a mortal necessity . . . About essentials, almost nothing could be said. Still, signs could be made, should be made, must be made." It is in their ungrudging readiness to feel and make the compassionate gesture that Bellow's protagonists transcend their grotesquerie and selfishness. Their instinctive compassion may very well be the manifestation of their "biological talent for life." "Signs" must be made or else the soul atrophies and life, individual and collective, is traduced and denied. For Bellow's Wandering Jews, death is not a challenge to be heroically mastered nor a negative judgment to be passively accepted; it is simply a destination, a definition. The survivor differs from the rebel and the victim by retaining his grip on the will-to-live (Henderson's "Grun-tu-molani"), by insisting on his obligation to keep alive within himself the sources of compassion (without which he is less than human), and by accepting the fact and finality of death. Such a character-type may seem drab and undramatic compared to the grand conceptions of overreaching and immolation that have been among the noblest creations of the Western mind. And yet in the intellectual wreckage of our past century, it may be such an imaginative concept of survival that we are most sorely in need of. Bellow's distinguished career as a novelist may finally be viewed as a series of his own compassionate utterances offered as signs of a mutual concern—a bonding—between himself and the world. And with this in mind, I think it not disrespectful to quote the words inscribed at the *Yad Vashem*, the Memorial to the Holocaust in Jerusalem: "I survived alone, to tell, to remind, and to demand . . ." Bellow's voice is a comic one, of course, but his passionate purpose is surely of the same moral tenor.

MALCOLM BRADBURY

Saul Bellow and
Changing History

Bellow's [Nobel Prize] acceptance
speech might indeed encourage us to see him as a writer concerned with
humanist and transcendental pieties, a writer urgent in pursuit of that
"broader, more flexible, fuller, more coherent, more comprehensive account of what we human beings are, who we are, and what this life is for,"
about which he spoke. Evidently, these concerns are central to Bellow,
but they are sometimes identified, by his more critical critics, with a
simplistic positivism and a taste for rhetorical afflatus—particularly visible
in the famous endings to his novels, which have not always been found
creditable or pleasing. What I want to argue is that we should not miss, in
Bellow's works, as in his statements, a vigorous and powerful sense of the
tensions involved, nor understanding of the dark places in which mind
and experience today are likely to take us. I want us to notice that note of
provisionality and resilience. If writers have any task to perform for us
critics today—and with the growing abstraction of modern criticism their
tasks seem to grow fewer and fewer; writers are steadily becoming something like heuristic devices to enable criticism to validate its own self-
generating functions—then it is surely to produce in us a sense of spiky
anguish and unease about what we make of them. In contemplating a
writer who has insisted on what could be crudely called his "message," but
also on his provisionality and his elusiveness, who has maintained a
proper doubt about the deductions made by the deep readers of the world,

From *Saul Bellow and His Work*, edited by Edmund Schraepen. Copyright © 1978 by
Centrum Voor Taal—En Literatuurwetenschap.

and who has a marked aversion to being plotted and fixed, we ought to pay our proper dues to that provisionality, to carry a due sense of the flexibility, variety and change of his career and his work. Bellow is indeed a writer who has sought the "true impression," those transcendentalist distillations that speak to vision, revelation, the worth of life that is greater than death. But he has always sought, as a writer best should, those affimations amid the paradoxes of life, amid time and history. His stories have sought coherence and comprehensiveness, but they have not done this by avoiding the historial and experiential continuum in which modern life is lived; each new novel is a new encounter with the shifting world of disorder and chaos, with a new hero, a new dilemma, a new milieu, a new culture-reading. This has shaped his style and his form, for both of these elements of writing are historical derivatives; Bellow has, I think, always understood as much, and this merits serious analysis.

And it may be that to that analysis a European perspective has much to give. Bellow has, indeed, long appealed to European readers, and some of the best criticism has come from this side of the Atlantic. I say this not to question or qualify the power of the excellent American criticism and scholarship his work has received, but to consider the reasons for his European appeal. Bellow is a writer who seriously inhabits a large tradition. His sources evidently go back deeply into American writing—both to Emerson and the transcendentalists, to whom he refers often, and to Dreiser and the naturalists, whom he has also praised—but he also reaches into the classic stock of European modernism. It is not hard to find the links with Dostoevsky's troubled heroes, caught in the fragmentations of a culture collapsing into political disorder, nor to Conrad's bleak world in which civilization is a thin veneer overlying anarchy, calling forth an "absurd" existential affirmation. Kafka and Camus lie behind him, as does Isaac Bashevis Singer, who carried the dark metaphysics of the Jewish tradition across the Atlantic; his novels touch on the pain and price of European history. In an essay of 1963, Bellow offered some ironic thoughts on the appeal of contemporary American writers for European intellectuals. Invoking Wylie Sypher's excellent book, *Loss of the Self in Modern Literature and Art,* he observed that a literature of the lost and inauthentic self had become a staple in modern writing, that this had arisen in Europe naturally, out of the crises of its contemporary history and thought, out of definitive theories of the human condition, but that it had also become an instinctive feature of modern American writing, giving it its modern appeal. "American writers," he said, "when they are moved by a similar spirit to reject and despise the Self, are seldom encumbered by such intellectual baggage, and this fact pleases their

European contemporaries, who find in them a natural, that is, a brutal and violent acceptance of the new universal truth by minds free from intellectual preconceptions." Bellow is indeed ironic about the phenomenon, and offers to stand, himself, outside it, challenging, as he does again in his attack on Robbe-Grillet in his acceptance speech, the novel of lost ego or privatized existence, the novel of a cybernetic or a post-anthropomorphic world. The alternative, evidently, is a humanist case, and this, indeed, is what Bellow offers at the end of this same essay ("Undeniably the human being is not what he was commonly thought a century ago. The question nevertheless remains. He is something. what is he? . . . The mystery increases, it does not grow less as types of literature wear out. It is, however, Symbolism or Realism or Sensibility wearing out, and not the mystery of mankind"). Bellow's writing is, indeed, humanist, but it is not the humanism of the past; if there runs through it a metaphysical intent, a desire to identify the weight and measure of the human mean, then the task can only be performed by a just registration of the power of a modern world where massified indifference exists, where the city and its hostile anonymity is truer than any message from nature, where war, holocaust and genocide are facts, where civilized cultural solutions must mediate with a world where Auschwitz has existed, and where men mechanize themselves to go to the moon, where individual experience is dwarfed by a commanding world of process and history. Bellow's books express an obsessively modern concern, a concern for finding his mean within a contemporary situation—a situation invested, as it is in the other great modern writers like Kafka and Camus, with whom we may worthily compare him, with crisis and loss. Bellow's attempt to reconstitute humanism—the classic seriousness of great fiction everywhere—within the context of such a vision seems to me essential to his contemporary appeal, and it does link him with modern European writing. It also leads to a very distinctive art form, to versions of the post-humanist humanist novel.

For the consequences of such an enterprise will be finally manifest as form, which I take to be a mode of grammar for relating figure to landscape, subject to object, self to society, in an historical context. Bellow apparently gestures toward the revival of the liberal novel, a form that has, as is well known, a strained history in our modern and modernist century. The liberal novel is, I take it, the novel of a Whiggish history, where there is a community of progress between self and society, where individuals reach outward into social community for civility, reality and maturity. Its character, then, is social and realistic, and it is attentive to history in individual and community, seen as a cooperative, onward, sequential process, so that chronology is growth, in man and society. Bellow's plots do have something like a liberal rhythm. They are hero-centred, to a degree unusual in modern fiction; the hero often gives his name to the novel. He is usually a man, often a Jew, cast in some representative role of seeking to acquire one; he is often very experienced in the life of the world, like the aged Sammler, or in its mental history, like Herzog; and is frequently a writer or an intellectual. He is anxious about Self, and is usually to be found exploring his solitude, establishing the inward claim, but experiencing loss of contact and connection. He is anxious about Mind, which may be our salvation or our highest source of suffering. And, irritably, he usually moves toward a social becoming, finding, if in ambiguous and often monetary forms, a bond of responsibility that ties him to others, relates him to the human structure, establishes a sense of man's measure ("He is something. What is he?") and the nature of his biological and mental tenure on earth. In this process, certain prime reminders are necessary; man is mortal, and the facts of death must be weighed; man is biologically in process, and his physical history drives him; man is consciousness, and the substance of awareness and thought are urgently on trial; man is urban, and can only take his measure from the social format he has evolved for himself; man is real, and so is the world, and the two substantialities have persistent trouble in coming into balance, so that we are tempted toward thoughts of extreme alienation, urgent romantic selfhood, intimations of apocalypse; man has an intelligence, which may destroy or redeem him; man is a performer in a conditioned and material universe, a post-romantic universe in historical evolution, so that his state is likely to be perceived by him as essentially ironic, a state of loss, comic or otherwise.

These are rhythms of stress, but they habitually press toward a characteristic Bellovian ending—the famous endings where something like a humanist reconciliation appears always to occur, life being seen in the view of death, self being seen in the view of the other. A balanced sense of reality is sought, though so is a transcendentalist composure. Involved in this is a reinvigorated sense of possible community, though it is not usually the community as given. The endings suggest composure following flux, but often they are ambiguous: because they are brief moments; because they are textually endings, with a rhetorical function; because they are not really firm stepping stones into a more transcendental tone in his next novel, which more commonly returns us to something like a beginning. For the rhythm involved is ceaseless, continuous, and very much in history, a history of perverting culture and misled consciousness in which, nonetheless, recoveries are possible. It is liberal insofar as

Bellow believes in the novel as a moral instrument for the large human questions: Keith Opdahl rightly stresses that Bellow's intentions have always remained "intensely moral," though he notes that the morality arises from unease and paradox: Bellow's heroes are, he says, "Ostensibly men of love, dependent on the world, but they are at bottom alienated." Bellow also understands the novel as a metaphysical or philosophical instrument, a mode for having and invigilating serious ideas: Nathan Scott identifies his work as "an essentially meditative enterprise" in which the character at the centre, transcending the immediate pressures of environment and the limitations of the social matrix, "asks himself some fundamental questions about the nature of his own humanity"—questions that, Scott says, are increasingly answered, as the sequence of novels develops, by a falling into peace, an acquiescent submission to the multilevelled mystery of existence. And, if Bellow's version of community or civility tends towards metaphysics and transcendence, so his version of history tends towards chaos. We do not live in an age of moral proportion or balanced sensibilities, which freely generates liberalism, a sense of relation with the natural world and the historical sequence; and we do not get such a world reflected back at us from Bellow's work. Rather we get a crisis of liberalism, a dark division between the domain of self and the reflection from the outward world. An awareness of isolation and inner madness in self, and void in the once reflecting universe, is crucial to this fiction. Thus, though his method moves toward reconciliation and realism, there is a systematic questioning of reality as a community or consensus. Bellow once remarked that no-one can will common reality and a communal world into existence by fiat; it is a crucial statement, and the attempt of the novels to open up an intercourse with the world—that large, transcendental aim that is present in much American literature, and produced many of its classically ambiguous texts, notably Moby-Dick—is challenged by it.

In Bellow's novels, world and consciousness are essentially at odds; the world is a substantially material and systematic process requiring a high cost of consciousness. If, as Bellow said, the theme of Herzog is "the imprisonment of the individual in a shameless and impotent privacy," then Herzog's faltering step onward is an equivocal progress. For the dominant realm of the book is the world of disintegration and madness that generates Herzog's fervent mental and social action, the wonderful letters, the incessant comedy of argument with the "reality instructors" and their five-cent versions of synthesis. The book is a comedy of the will to become, and it is becoming rather than being that is the main object of Bellow's attention; synthesis is itself a comic posture, a function of our metaphysical absurdity, and man is a "suffering joker" in whom self and community, reason and desire, constantly war. Bellow's heroes are modern men, formed by modern quandaries, living in a mental world deriving from the solipsistic vein in the romantic heritage, and a physical world naturalistically in process. History has its own massive social mechanisms; as Joseph, the ex-Marxist hero of *Dangling Man*, notes, the old metaphysical stage of good and evil has been reset in the secular world, and "under this revision, we have, instead, only history to answer to." With this, consciousness transacts on an evolutionary stage, much attended to in his story, "The Old System" and in *Mr. Sammler's Planet*. Consciousness thus is considerably a derivative of the times, is historically made. Bellow's transcendentalist questions thus occur within an historical continuum, in a world of determinants and processes, genetic and historical. An awareness of the changing history of consciousness has, traditionally, much to do with the evolution of the novel form, crucially concerned with the relation of individual to world. And this knowledge Bellow has in full measure; it sustains not only the pressure felt by his protagonists, but the pressure that history exercises over fictional form. In short, it has been an essential power in Bellow's artistic development.

II

The notion that Bellow's writing has developed and changed over the course of his career has not always appealed to his critics; some have seen one basic "type" of novel recurring right through his career, and others have found his writing "conservative" and singularly unresponsive to the historical pressures that have been held to have transformed the novel stylistically over the period during which he has been writing. Bellow's own comments about contemporary experiment (such as his criticism of Robbe-Grillet in the Nobel Prize speech) have encouraged the view that he has attempted to sustain beyond its time a mode of realism and civility that is now without full authority. In fact, of course, historical imperatives do not work so simply; a form authenticates itself by the forceful power of individual talents seriously creating it. But in any case the judgment seems wrong; indeed one of Bellow's strongest resources had been his artistic resilience and his power, through a very changeable period of history, to mediate the claims of form and the claims of time. Bellow first published in 1941, but he came seriously to notice as one of the new generation of novelists who came to prominence in the years after the war, when a distinct stylistic and aesthetic climate, which was also a political climate, was forming. This was a period of revived liberalism, invigorated by the reaction against totalitarianism that arose with the battle against and the defeat of Nazism, and then the cold war struggle with an imperialistic Communism in a volatile new balance of superpowers. The politics and aesthetics of liberalism were an important version of pluralism and democracy; yet at the same time the postwar social order, with its materialism, its pressure toward conformity, its move toward mass society, seemed also to threaten the liberal self. The reaction against totalitarian models also shaped aesthetic and formal choices. Both the lore of Modernism and the lore of Naturalism—especially in its thirties form as a politico-social realism—came under question. The 1950s seemed hungry for a post-political politics, a post-ideological ideology; in this process literature and culturist concern became centralized as foci of intellectual activity. Modern literature, with its sense of irony, scruple and moral ambiguity, with its dark report on modern angst and exposure, yet its hungry concern to identify an adequate modern image of man, provided a canon that, in many quarters, replaced more ideological texts, in particular the texts of 1930s Marxism, the god that had failed. In the new mood of political abeyance, when there was strong concern with a humanism that would recover morality from the holocaust, literature became a mode of anxious moral and metaphysical exploration. In particular it was Jewish writers, with their sense of traditional alienation and their profoundly relevant witness to the recent holocaust, who concentrated the spirit of the necessary imagination—what Lionel Trilling would call "the liberal imagination." And their novels, concerned both with the identity of solitude, and the hunger for community, became exemplary novels for the new season.

The liberal novel was, in fact, the appropriate form for a time that needed to identify itself afresh: to identify what it had lately passed through, and the character of the times now coming, times of mass and affluence, conformity and lonely crowd existence, intellectual unease and alienation. The result was a modernized liberal mode, one that related a sense of intellectual disablement to a feeling of oblique connection to a society which, for all its hostile indifference, its naturalist struggle, had remained pluralist. But it was, of course, a synthesis very clearly provisional in character: one that the new radical passions of the next decade, the Sixties, would rescind. For, with the Sixties, as Morris Dickstein has lately put it, "one of those deep-seated shifts of sensibility that alters the whole moral terrain" occurred: the cold war season that had put politics in abeyance ended; as young people reacted against the Vietnam war, a new politics of withdrawal from the social order evolved, and a much more

action-centred, kinetic and politically activist sensibility came to domi-
nate. In the arts, the moral containments of Fifties fiction weakened: a
new aesthetic of provisionality and counter-cultural action, an art of
irrationality and outrage grew to assault the mood of the Fifties. It was also
in part a reaction against the liberal synthesis of individual and communal
reality that brought the new post-modernist text, lexically complex but
moving toward a zero degree of meaning, an emphasis on its own fictionality;
so did confessional fiction, based on the subjectivity of narrators, and the
non-fiction novel, founded on the conviction that an extremist reality
and history was a relevant fiction in itself. The aesthetic change was
marked, and it clearly either restructured or disabled many careers. J.D.
Salinger, whose fragile moral and psychic redemptions seemed in the late
1950s and early 1960s to strike essential rhythms of possibility, followed
his Class family into an agonized and honourable silence. Norman Mailer
forewent an art of formalism for a fiction of risk-taking consciousness, a
self-advertising, hipsterish venture into the cannibalisms of contemporary
historical sensibility: an enterprise that, however, seems to have lost
latterly much of its original intensity. Philip Roth, who began writing a
fiction of Jamesian moralities, turned to a post-moral confessional, merging reason and desire, erotics and literature, and handing on the task of
judgement and order to the psychoanalysts who now populate his novels.
But of these writers Bellow has been the most enduring survivor, and
indeed survival has been one of his most lasting themes. He has not, of
course, become a post-modernist writer; he has not written the non-
fictional novel, and, though he has verged on the confessional mode,
most notably in *Herzog*, it has been within a highly contained framework. But he has paid a due attention to the changing historical world,
which resynthesizes forms and alters consciousness, and in each new novel
has presented us with a new world, a world conceived of as being in
historical motion and mutation.

Thus to go back to *Dangling Man* and *The Victim* is now to go back
a long way. These two first novels were fables of solitude and civility,
existential texts obliquely pulled back towards liberalism. *Dangling Man*
(1944), written in the then popular manner of absurdist diary literature,
inherited from existential writers like Sartre and Camus, set during the
war, takes its hero, bereft of employment and politics in the wartime
economy, off into a Kafka-esque solitude and absurdism, an irritable
enclosure, explicitly existential, for he is unable to find essence in existence. His military induction becomes the solution to the problem, a
moment of compulsory civility; the final cry, "Hurray for regular hours!
And for the supervision of the spirit! Long live regimentation!" is a

testament of loss, a testament of gain. *The Victim* (1947), written with the same closure and tightness, is also about social responsibility enforced: Asa Leventhal is required to recognize and respond to the oblique chain of connection that links him with the unemployment, poverty, and suffering of another man, a gentile, despite all the appropriate excuses—the impersonal naturalist struggle of the city, the general recognition of broken bonds, the open competition for place, the current philosophies of Darwinism that deny moral affiliation. Like *Dangling Man, The Victim* is set in the world of the modern hostile city, New York in the hot summer sun, a determinist, naturalist environment where bodies push against bodies and the world works through a process that—as in Dreiser's fatalistic writing—arbitrarily benefits some and sinks others. But both books, dependent as they are on absurdist or naturalist modes, use them to transcend the consequent syntheses; hence they generate a liberal metaphysic of connection, which he was to take yet further in his tight novella *Seize the Day*. Bellow took the tradition in order to amend it, to raise those questions about the measure of the human with which a central chapter in *The Victim* deals.

Then, however, his work moved into a new comic picaresque mode, the mode of *The Adventures of Augie March* (1953) and *Henderson the Rain King* (1959). The old naturalist and existential containments were relaxed, and the new novels were texts of expansion and flow, novels of character formation in which the heroes were large mental and moral travellers in quest through massive social, psychic and neo-mythic lanscapes to find the measure of their being, the nature of their human tenure. The new form released in Bellow a potential for mythic and fantastic writing we had not earlier seen; it also released a Bellovian metaphysical vernacular. Bellow himself reported a new prose manner in his work, though he would identify *Augie March* as "too effusive and uncritical." And in *Henderson* in particular the task became that of creating a modern method of fabulation, with an imaginary Africa providing an anthropological geography against which he could set a tale of psycho-mythic adventure. The claims of realism were amended; the aim was comic psychic progress through the kingdom of nature, where animals fabulously measure out the potential for realizing one's human characteristics. Henderson, moving from pig to lion to bear, falls into a rhythm of nature where there is biology but also a "becoming." Like Augie before him, like Herzog after him, Henderson, in the kingdom of process, finds it possible to become a self-creator.

But with the next novel, *Herzog* (1964), probably Bellow's best, one senses another essential change in his writing. The comic picaresque, releasing the hero to his adventures, will no longer serve: this is because Herzog's adventures are essentially those of the mind, but also because the mind is constrained, super-imposed upon, in interaction with, a universe at odds with it—the world of the modern city, which is an apocalyptic wilderness, corrupt, disintegrating, a place of assault and disorder. The novel's form is appropriately more elaborate: the extraordinary action of Herzog's well-funded but disordered mind is laid anti-chronologically over a plot that explores the outward world of reality and process, and brings him into contact with those who offer to speak for it, the "reality instructors" with their modern syntheses, their lives of contemporary boredom. Herzog's state is anguish, and it is an historical anguish as the text tells us:

> And why? Because he let the entire world press on him. For instance? Well, for instance, what it means to be a man. In a city. In a century. In transition. In a mass. Transformed by science. Under organized power. Subject to tremendous controls. In a condition caused by mechanization. After the late failure of radical hopes. In a society that was no community and devalued the person. Owing to the multiplied power of numbers that made the self negligible. Which spent military billions against foreign enemies but would not pay for order at home, which permitted savagery and barbarism in its own cities.

Herzog, through his intellectual sources and his surrounding world, inherits the appropriate agony, and turns his personal life "into a circus, into gladiatorial combat." In a world of perverted relations, where all guides, including one's women, are negative tutors, madness seems sense, and an outward violence, an act of retaliation against the city and the damaging boredoms that make up personal life, seems an answer. But the novel is comic; Herzog, "that suffering joker," recognizes that this is a farcical solution. History, massed in the city and in Herzog's own mind, where the old ideas of genius have become the canned goods of intellectuals ("Do we need *theories* of pain and anguish?"), is played as farce: "I fall upon the thorns of life; I bleed. And what next? I get laid, I take a short holiday . . ." Herzog, seeking to redistill history and our ideas of it, seeks "a new angle on the modern condition, showing how life could be lived by renewing universal connection, overturning the last of the Romantic errors about the uniqueness of the Self," does finally discard his violence and his madness, averts his "merely aesthetic critique of modern history," accepts the relation of self and world, and a balanced tenure of his own being.

Herzog is an apocalyptic novel about the defeat of florid apocalypse, a long mental battle with the advocates of an absurdist romanticism, of therapeutic syntheses, the life of alternated boredom and stimulation in the wasted city. The battle itself is Herzog's alternative therapy, and it is his vivid intellectual warfare that sustains the book. But if the confessional and therapeutic novel of the wasteland world has become an appropriate modern American form, this is the closest Bellow has come to it. Its achievement is to dismiss the obvious lore by which it might he interpreted, and to avoid the obvious solution: the psycho-verbal collapse and the sexual exposure of Roth's Portnoy, Tarnopol, or Kepesh, for example. Herzog finds his "new angle on the modern condition," recognizes a vividness and worth in the world, finds equilibrium without librium, accepts diurnality and contingency, making it whole. It is an ending we may doubt: the green rural world of Ludeyville, with its natural transcendence and its pleasure-principle associations, is a conventional pastoral outside the city where anguish is made; the surviving relationship with Ramona offers, too, an abeyance of the sexual warfare with which Bellow's later novels resound, but in the form of the complaisant, dreamlike woman who puts on no pressure. But the ending is within the comic contour of the book, and it is also provisional, a moment's step beyond solipsism and irrationality, but not a lasting answer. But what we should note is Bellow's comprehensive understanding of the lore of modern anguish, and his concern with the odds set against Herzog's momentary composure. If Bellow rejects the indulgent and spurious alienations that have come from the legacy of nineteenth-century romanticism and historicism, and have been fed into a late twentieth-century model of therapeutic and alienated man, he has also made his hero an alienated figure, living amid the intellectual social, political and psychological bewilderments of the modern urban world, and in a state of opposition.

Indeed it is these bleak apprehensions that pass on into *Mr. Sammler's Planet* (1970), Bellow's most anxious and apocalyptic novel, a crisis book for a crisis year, the year of high radical passions and moonshot. Again it is Bellow's evident assumption in the book that a dark history is once more in process; on earth, the cities decline, romantic and irrational passions run wild, and in the larger cosmos human consciousness seems to be in some moment of biological osmosis, adjusting to the move toward new planets. New York City is a Babelian waste, disorganized, crime-ridden, over-populated, lost, sexually barren; only evil appears to invigorate. Consciousness is overwhelmed by force, as in Henry Adams' model of the multiverse; only irony seems possible. Sammler is yet more displaced than Herzog, a survivor from elsewhere, a stranger, a man almost beyond life, twice born; he carries with him the dark ambiguity of inherited culture—which is both the civilized European intensities, and the dark underlying explosion of irrationality, disorder and holocaust in the concentration camps. Sammler is himself an apocalyptic figure, casting his one cold eye on the horsemen who pass by, gazing with his "kindly detachment, in farewell-detachment, in earth-departure-objectivity," from his own extra-territorial standpoint, that of the man who knows the death beyond life. He has seen the price both of repression and unmitigated selfhood, the well set free; trying to "live with a civil heart. With interested charity. With a sense of the mystic potency of mankind," he feels the powerlessness of his lesson, the uselessness of a liberal civility. But again the will to apocalypse seems the great enemy; and if to the modern world Sammler stands in muted resistance, he also stands in resistance to its most obvious solutions, is a figure for the death that in the end makes life worthy of more than purely biological or historical interpretation. Both of these novels are significant acts of restructuring, encounters with a dark time, and they both recognize and qualify the "florid apocalypse" of post-modern thought.

Sammler is not only Bellow's most apocalyptic but his most pessimistic novel, a book in which irony and a desire for human community are hardly sufficient to contain disgust. But in the event Bellow turned again, and moved richly away from the growing irony of mode, also visible in his short stories, toward comedy and picaresque. Humboldt's Gift not only replays some of Bellow's earlier resources; it also seems to secrete in itself a commentary on his whole development so far. It is a book about two writers, and the oblique inheritance that links them; about the space between two historical generations, two versions of culture; about a sort of literary history, and two versions of creative individual and process, between "we" and "it." Humboldt is the writer in the Fifties spirit, a man of the great Partisan Review age when it seemed mass society needed artistic intellectual saviours, Fisher Kings for the Waste Land; Citrine writes in a world where "culture" is furiously abundant, though not necessarily to culture's benefit. In a BBC interview with Melvyn Bragg, Bellow himself distinguished between Humboldt as the "modernist" writer (one could quibble with the term, but I take it the reference is to Humboldt's sense of artistic mission, his intensity, his fury) and Citrine the writer in a large age and a lowered season, making "a comic end run." We might take him to stand for Bellow himself, the anxious comedian writing amid a contemporary, confusing turmoil of style and ideology, expressing a struggle which makes inward life a strained farce and outward life an onerous technological process, though in fact Bellow evidently contains something of Humboldt too. Nonetheless the novel is seen from Citrine's point of view: the writer as survivor, sixty, with money in the bank, confused amid a difficult divorce, an anxious love-life, a sense of past obligations, an awareness of contemporary disorders. He lives in a new America where society rewards and demolishes its writers indiscriminately, playing a comic capitalist game with them, where art is affluent succour, supporting the display of the modern self; even the wives of *mafiosi* are doing Ph.D.'s in modern literature. It is, as in *Sammler,* a world of "hypercivilized Byzantine lunacy," and an exact contemporary culture reading. Notably its setting is Chicago, "a cultureless city pervaded nevertheless by Mind," a city of muggers and affluence, flamboyant selfhood and civic void, boom and boredom. The outward reality is so vast and fanciful that it seems useless to make sense of an inner one, but Charlie tries, hunting for some transcendental gesture, a vigorous tug from the realm of the mystical and the Platonic. Charlie's performance is a comic stumble, but it gets somewhere, finally to the graveyard, where, in a void modern necropolis, Humboldt is mechanically reburied, but Charlie inherits a legacy of survival, a myth of endurance.

Humboldt's Gift is a novel about the self in a world of mind, a world not only of history but versions of history, a world not only of psyches but of versions of psyche. "Around our heads we have a dome of thought as thick as the air we breathe," Augie March had reflected, ". . . there's too much of everything of this kind, *that's* come home to me, too much history and culture to keep track of, too many details, too much news, too much example, too much influence, too many guys to tell you to be as they are, and all this hugeness, abundance, turbulence, Niagara Falls torrent. Which who is supposed to interpret? Me?" Humboldt, attempting to master everything, from Verlaine, to the *Police Gazette,* writes himself large in such a world; and dies in a flophouse. Citrine, amidst an even more massive contingency, survives in the space that Humboldt leaves behind. And, as *Sammler* was a novel in and about the ironic spirit, *Humboldt's Gift* is a novel in and about the comic spirit. Citrine endures and survives, and so does his creator, making his own comic end run, not in the form of a high modernist text, but as a text in and about history, a metaphysical farce about contemporary consciousness in its turbulence. Like his heroes, the novelist is pushed himself into postures of resilience, strategies for survival. Bellow has thus been a novelist of conditional form; he has not become a post-modernist writer, concerned with the problems of fictionality or the redemption of text. Rather he has written of and within the cultural continuum, and written with, I think, Nietzsche's famous sixth sense: the capacity for historical insight, the *consciousness* of historicism.

III

In 1953, Philip Rahv, a friend of Bellow's, published an article, "The Myth and the Powerhouse," which had many cogent comments to make on what he called contemporary "mythomania": for this was the high season of mythic interpretation in American criticism. He remarked that, for many postwar critics, "the super-temporality of myth provides the ideal refuge from history," and added that "To them, as to Stephen Dedalus, history is a nightmare from which we are trying to awake. But to awake from history into myth is like escaping from a nightmare into permanent insomnia." It is perhaps not too far-fetched to suppose that when, in the opening chapter of *Humboldt's Gift*, Bellow is evoking the great mental and literary resources of Humboldt, "the Mozart of gab," and remarks:

> He had read many thousands of books. He said that history was a nightmare during which he was trying to get a good night's rest. Insomnia made him more learned. In the small hours he read thick books—Marx and Sombart, Toynbee, Rostovzeff, Freud . . .

He is recalling Rahv, his *Partisan Review* days, and the preoccupation with the struggle between the myth and the powerhouse of history. Humboldt, the great capitalizer of nouns—Poetry, Beauty, Love, History, the Waste Land, the Unconscious, Manic, Depressive—lives in Augie's Niagara Falls abundance. His joke, of course, goes back to *Ulysses*, and the classic answer Modernism gave to the nightmare of history was the move toward symbolism, toward the transcendent, spatial form; it was a move away from fiction as historiography and toward fiction as myth—the move that transliterates Homer's long historical tale of the founding of a nation through the return of a wanderer into Joyce's epic of consciousness, held within a single day. Modernist writing, in short, encouraged the mythic interpretation, but Rahv, a veteran of the Thirties, an editor of *Partisan Review*, where Bellow published, around which Humboldt so clearly functions, a voice of that movement from politics to cultural concern which marked the postwar years, was concerned with a necessary reminder. Bellow, I think, alludes to it, in his way of creating Humboldt; he also, I think, sufficiently shares it. The Nietzschean sixth sense, historicism, was not to be outrun; Bellow's own aesthetic and intellectual origins, his sense of the power of naturalism, his concern with sociology, his recognition of the weight of determinants, in short, his post-naturalist and post-Marxist synthesis, would dispose him to Rahv's view.

Rahv's challenge was serious because there has been a long disposition in American thought to suppose that history was a European phenomenon, Marx a European prophet. Mythic interpretations have long been important in discussion of, especially, American writing, just as mythic modes have been important in that writing itself. The intellectual results are familiar: but they have, as Rahv suggests, reached the proportions of an overemphasis, and especially in the post-political mood strong in the Fifties. The standpoint has been profitable; it has, for instance, helped us distinguish between the more social line of the European novel and the more metaphysical one of the American "romance." But it has ignored much, including the massive American investment in naturalism, and even misread the more mythic of the classic American novelists, who, while concerned with spatiality, pastoral, transcendence, have also been much concerned with history, historiography, historicism. Cooper may indeed be read, as R.W.B. Lewis reads him, as having created in Leatherstocking "a hero in space," lifted out of historical time, made romantically transcendent. But in fact Cooper is profoundly concerned with Leatherstocking's place in a socio-historical evolution, running through systematic stages; and Leatherstocking is, as Cooper says, the "borderer" figure of romantic historiography, clearly identifiable in Lukacs's typology of the bourgeois historical novel. Much the same can be said of Hawthorne and Melville. Hawthorne's *The House of the Seven Gables* is as pointed a fable as one could find of history in process, connecting past to present and future, displacing old patriciates, replacing them with new men—especially Holgrave, that realist of a modern history. Process is the name of the train that carries Clifford and Hepzibah from their old social retreat into a modern, secular democratic solitude—as it is the force that shifts Billy Budd from his eighteenth century yeoman pastoral world aboard the "Rights of Man" into the urban industrial economy of the nineteenth century warship. Seeking the timeless symbol, their writing also attends with care to the temporal process. It was, of course, with the coming of naturalism that American fiction found names for that process, forcefields to set against the life of individuals; the result was a turn to neo-scientific theories: biological theories of heredity and genetics, sociological theories of environmental conditioning. This let into American fiction a devotion to those realms of experience which see the modern world as a moving system: technologization, urbanization, corporate capitalism became systems demanding account in the structure of novels. The problem, which has perplexed much American writing ever since, was that of relating force to consciousness, process to the inward motions of being; it was, indeed, the problem of modernism, and Edmund Wilson, in *Axel's Castle*, valuably identifies the centre of modernist writing as lying in the attempt to synthesize naturalism and symbolism.

And indeed most of the great modern novelists—from Stephen Crane and Gertrude Stein and Henry James to Theodore Dreiser and Ernest Hemingway—perplexed themselves with the problem. A number of the major modern American novels—like Dos Passos's *U.S.A.*—are plotted both on historical-evolutionary and spatial-symbolist principles. Another form of attention lay in what one might call a therapeutic historicism: that is to say, the attempt to identify in the historical process the means by which we generate a self. Dick Diver, at the beginning of Scott Fitzgerald's *Tender Is the Night*, is an integral man; nonetheless he feels the urgent need to dive into a contemporary history which is a mixture of failed economic process and psychic trauma, in order to redeem and bless it. He fails, but in failing he attends to the secular clock by which we live; for, as Karl Mannheim says, in our post-teleological world we must tell by the cosmic clock of history what the time is. In a society, like the American, that worships as much to Freud as to Marx, history must be bonded, therapeutically or otherwise, onto consciousness. This has been a recurrent theme of postwar American fiction—in Mailer and Roth, for example—just as, in postwar American society, we have seen that "triumph of the therapeutic" of which Philip Rieff speaks: that model of post-cultural culture in which the cognate relation between interior understanding and the institutions of a society disappears, and a therapeutic model of the self as an historical performer is introduced. In a world where Freud and Marx must be synthesized, and history becomes manifest as a psychic condition, dramatized as a role in a process, displayed as style, fashion, or trend, where models of reality are accepted, donned, modified and lost, history becomes both the source of our despair and the means of our renewal: an alienating system that also feeds us new life-style, subjective revolution, in every boutique.

Bellow is, I think, essentially the novelist as invigilator of such a world, a world of historical, material and psychological abundance, an era of a Niagara Falls of history and culture under which self seems dwarfed, but to which it must react. For we are surrounded not just by History, but by thoughts about History: versions of liberation, images of provisional reality, notions of Alienation, Anomie, Plight. What we have now is a world in which there prevails both a nineteenth-century positivism and a twentieth-century relativism: Bellow knows both, as the writers and commentators of his generation, schooled in the Marxism of the 1930s, the rescinded historicism of the 1950s, so well did. His work contains as knowledge the proposition that environment and process may well determine man, as he shows us in *The Victim*; but equally that man may be a Columbus in such a world, that character may determine fate, as he suggests to us in *Augie March*. He knows that consciousness is a collective historical flow, as he shows us in *Mr. Sammler's Planet*; he proposes that mind may remodel all offered syntheses of reality and process, as he suggests in *Herzog*. But above all he is the novelist of ideas conserved or redeemed as consciousness in the universe of material and psychic abundance. It is ideas that offer Humboldt his answer to unmitigated process. "Maybe America didn't need art and inner miracles. The USA was a big operation, very big. The more it, *the less we*. So Humboldt behaved like an eccentric and a comic subject." Humboldt offers the large comedy, the picaresque synthesis; he fails and succeeds, leaving Citrine his gift. Citrine's role, as survivor, is a small comedy, in his later world which cannot become whole, where the merger of the material and the mental takes yet stranger forms, where life is populous with modern seekers, the new mental rabble of the wised-up world, where even "policemen take psychology courses, and have some feeling for the comedy of human life." In a world where everyone has internalized history, peace may be sought; a good night's rest would be nice but history, being consciousness too, is inside us, and we are glutted with it. Self is no longer freedom; history is no longer an outward politics, an independent process.

This is, I think, Bellow's abiding preoccupation, his continuing theme; and it is the word "comedy" that proposes the nature of his response. As early as *Dangling Man*, Joseph had observed comedy as the one power the self possesses: there is, he reflects, an "element of the comic or fantastic in everyone," and it is this element that cannot be brought under control. This is the transforming apprehension, the basis of a response to overwhelming mass that is inside as well as outside us. It is what releases the self into an attentive psycho-historical performance, the grounds for supposing that, between self and substance, it and we, we have an existence. It is the principle from which the actions of his heroes arise, which lets them be heroes: it is a recognition of man's absurd exposure in *Dangling Man*, a metaphysical acceptance of responsibility in *The Victim*, a euphoric mode of self-discovery in *Augie March*, a fantastic intercourse with the natural universe in *Henderson*. It is a self-compensating madness in *Herzog*, an ironic mode of survival in *Mr. Sammler's Planet*, the essence of the legacy in *Humboldt's Gift*. It is essentially both a self-realizing and mediating power, a form of due attention; it is the measure of an adequate mean for man in a world that seems, according to obvious logics of causality, to offer him none. It is the comedy of the mind in serious process, registering both its inventive splendours and its way of knowing its own confinements. It is, as form, the instrument that does not close the text up to its own formalism, but opens it to contingency, change, and process. Bellow seems to me the great modern novelist of the attempt to reconcile mind, in all its resource and confusion, its anguish but also its fantastic fertility, with a life that is absurd and extravagant, where not only material force but the ideas and forms of consciousness that surround it flow furiously, thrusting countervailing information at us, causing men to grope in boredom or despair for a version of reality, a right opinion, a therapeutic selfhood. We live in a world, then, when the measure of man can scarcely be taken, but where mind insists that we take it. The resulting perception is comedy, an observation of disparity—we are both grand and absurd, little and big—and also of freedom, for the mind, invigilating itself, has the power of discrimination, the gift to know. Absurdly, we have, amid all the powers, a vivid self-presence; of that curious presence Bellow is surely the great metaphysical comedian.

GILEAD MORAHG

The Art of Dr. Tamkin

Convinced that "The imagination is looking for new ways to express virtue," Saul Bellow argues for a fiction that achieves valuable didactic aims through effective imaginative means. He is a novelist who believes that "the moral function cannot be divorced from art" and who is profoundly concerned with "the connection between the understanding and the imagination and the future place of the intelligence in imaginative literature." Consequently, Bellow is repeatedly confronted with the problem of incorporating moral and intellectual concepts into his work in a manner that would prevent its reduction to the level of manifesto or sermon. Each of his novels involves a structural effort to communicate ideas and values without impinging upon the dramatic vitality and imaginative impact of the fiction. As Bellow himself has observed, ideas constitute a viable artistic element in fiction only if they are discovered, not merely asserted. Usually, he has said, such discovery can be made within the context of a vigorous and equally weighted clash of opposing philosophical viewpoints, maintained and expressed by characters of compelling intellectual substance. Bellow's fourth novel, *Seize the Day*, is problematic in that it does not provide such a context. A key to understanding both the value attributed by Bellow to the imaginative communication of ideas in fiction and his particular means of overcoming the problem of such communication in *Seize the Day* may be found in his creation of the elusive and enigmatic character of Dr. Tamkin.

"Here he is, here he is. If I could only figure this guy out," thinks Tommy Welhelm upon first encountering Dr. Tamkin on the morning of

From *Modern Fiction Studies* 1, vol. 25 (Spring 1979). Copyright © 1979 by *Modern Fiction Studies*.

his day of reckoning. Wilhelm's troubled perplexity concerning the true nature of Tamkin, his urgent need to figure the man out, and his inability to do so, are responses shared by many of the critics addressing themselves to *Seize the Day*. That the character of Tamkin plays a prominent role in the narrative development of the novel, as well as in the signification of its underlying meaning, has been generally confirmed by the critics. Yet he remains a most problematic and controversial figure. The problem and controversy arise, of course, from the apparent discrepancy between Tamkin's dubious and seemingly negative personality and his uncanny ability to communicate positive, healing ideas.

Critical assessments of Dr. Tamkin may be seen as falling into three broad categories. There are critics who attempt to resolve the problem by denying its existence. Theirs is a position maintaining that there is no discrepancy between Tamkin's ideas and personality, since both are regarded as being equally unreliable. Such a position amounts to a dismissal, usually inadvertent, of the validity of Saul Bellow's work as a whole, since, seen in its entirety, Tamkin's existential vision is strikingly similar to the vision emanating from Bellow's novels, previous and subsequent to *Seize the Day*.

A second critical position attempts to resolve the difficulty by regarding Tamkin as an unscrupulous sage. The claim of these critics is that although Tamkin does possess significant knowledge, he "specializes in the plausible misapplication of knowledge" [James Hall]. Or, in the words of another critic, although Tamkin has "knowledge and insight that seem breathtaking in their precision and perspicacity," he does not regard these attainments as a moral achievement but as a tool for the manipulation of others [William J. Handy]. Despite its apparent congruence with the surface action of the novel, this position is unsatisfying in its failure to account for what is probably the most significant aspect of the relationship between the dubious mentor and his reluctant disciple. It does not account for the fact that Tommy Wilhelm clearly benefits from his association with Dr. Tamkin, not as a speculator in commodities, but as a man. Tamkin is, indeed, in possession of significant knowledge. But he seeks not so much to use it on others as to communicate it to them. There can be little doubt that Tamkin is an unabashed liar and manipulator. Yet despite his deceptions and machinations, he is a source of authentic values and redeeming ideas that precipitate Wilhelm's transformation by providing him with a conceptual key for a truer vision of external reality, of the internal self, and of a morally satisfying relationship between them. Wilhelm emerges a better, freer, and more aware individual from his encounters with the protean psychologist. This is unquestionably a moral achievement on the psychologist's part. Tamkin considers it as such, and the novel as a whole bears him out.

Finally, there are the many critics who perceive the contradiction between Tamkin's personality and his ideas and take note of it without trying to resolve it. "Tamkin," writes Marcus Klein, "is an oddball and a crackpot, a jerk, an operator and a swindler, but he knows well what gives and the truth is in him." It is at this point that Klein's analysis comes to a halt. By merely identifying the two contradictory aspects of Tamkin's character, rather than exploring their possible significance, his discussion falls short of addressing itself to what appears to be a significant aspect of the novel. In dealing with a novelist of Bellow's ability and artistic awareness, one must assume that such a basic contradiction inherent in the character of a major fictional figure is no accidental or arbitrary matter. It should be approached as a structural device deliberately conceived for the dramatic expression of definite thematic preoccupations.

Despite Bellow's contention that a novel of ideas "becomes art when the views most opposite to the author's own are allowed to exist in full strength," he does not provide Tamkin with a worthy intellectual opponent with whom he can match wits and values while conducting a vigorous normative battle over the protagonist's soul. It is difficult to accept James Hall's view that Wilhelm's father, Dr. Adler, plays a part parallel and equal to that of Tamkin in generating the drama of Wilhelm's internal conflict and its ultimate resolution. He is a superficial and utterly distasteful person, who possesses nothing of the proselytizing drive and intellectual appeal of Dr. Tamkin. Since Tommy Wilhelm, Dr. Adler, and Dr. Tamkin are the only characters that actually come to life in the fictional world of *Seize the Day* and since neither of the former two is able, or inclined, to counter the intellectual thrust of the latter, Tamkin's ideas are expounded into something of an intellectual vacuum in which they encounter little, if any, effective opposition. Dramatically, this is a perilous situation.

In order to deflect the dangers of didactic preaching and retain the sense of discovery that is vital to a dramatic communication of ideas, Bellow has shifted the idea-generating locus in this novel from the dramatic dialectic of contradictory views to an equally dramatic conflict between character and vision. By endowing Tamkin with a personality that seems so much at odds with his convictions, Bellow has created a compelling fictional enigma that attracts the attention and demands the consideration of both protagonist and reader. Forcefully articulated, Tamkin's ideas are highly persuasive and have an unquestionable impact on Wilhelm. But Tamkin's personality casts such a dubious shadow over these ideas

that they cannot simply be regarded by Wilhelm as the benevolent teachings of a truly concerned benefactor or by the reader as obvious expressions of the author's convictions which may be accepted or rejected out of
hand. Both protagonist and reader, when confronted with such a character, must, of necessity, engage in a constant process of weighing the
import of the man's ideas against the aberrations of his personality. Thus,
any conclusion as to the validity of these ideas becomes a meaningful act
of evaluation and judgment, rather than a superficial gesture of acceptance
or rejection. The effectiveness of Tamkin as a viable artistic creation lies,
in part, in his being cast as a source of ideas that cannot be passively
acquired but must be actively pursued and discovered.

Tommy Wilhelm comes to accept the existential and moral vision
put forth by Tamkin despite his hesitations and suspicions concerning the
character of his mentor. But Wilhelm's acceptance is as much a result of
the *manner* in which the ideas are presented to him as it is of the
intellectual and moral matter they contain. The purpose served by casting
Tamkin as an ambivalent, contradictory character appears to extend beyond
the observance of the structural principle proclaiming dramatic ideological
conflict as an esthetically satisfying means of communicating ideas in
fiction. The character of Tamkin may also serve to reflect Bellow's general
conception of the essential relationship between knowledge of truth and
the art of fiction.

In his essays and lectures, Bellow has consistently maintained that
truth is one of man's most vital inner needs and the imagination is an
irreplaceable means of discovering and communicating truth. He regards
the literary artist as a person "invariably motivated by a desire for truth,"
who, through acts of imaginative creation, performs a moral function
which is inherent in all true art. The moral function of the novelist,
writes Bellow, is "to create scale, to order experience, to give value, to
make perspective and to carry us toward sources of life, toward life-giving
things." This function extends beyond the simple affirmation of life as a
definitive value. For, as Bellow has observed, "if we answer yes, we do
want it [life] to continue, we are liable to be asked how. In what form
shall life be justified? That is the essence of the moral question." Bellow
believes that "only the imagination by its acts can answer such questions." He regards the imagination as a "continually operative" mode of
knowledge, different from the ruling mode and capable, through the
discipline of literary art, of giving accounts of human existence that are
substantially more profound than those provided by modern intelligence.
Consequently, he takes the imagination "to be indispensable to truth."
The character of Tamkin is, of course, a specific manifestation of Bellow's

imaginative quest for essential truths. But in addition to being a fictional creation generating some of Bellow's most fundamental moral and existential convictions, Tamkin is also a creator of fictions by means of which he, much like the literary artist, seeks to communicate these convictions.

Following the rhythms of the novel's action, of Tamkin's ambivalent relationship with Wilhelm and of his unique method of presentation, Tamkin's ideas are communicated in fragmentary spurts. But seen in their entirety, these ideas constitute a cogent vision of human reality and of the place of the individual within it. The perceptions generating this vision are essentially analogous to those informing the constantly developing vision postulated in Bellow's later novels as necessary for the attainment of a humanly fulfilling mode of existence. Reflecting a position that has been consistently maintained by Bellow, Tamkin's vision combines an acute perception of humanity's present misery with a steadfast belief that true awareness and correct action may bring about future redemption. Humanity, Tamkin tells Wilhelm, is blind and sick. But "if it would only open its eyes it would be great." Clearly regarding Wilhelm as a representative of humanity's sickness and blindness as well as a sharer in its potential for greatness, Tamkin purports to diagnose the malady and to offer a cure that would induce the transformation of potential into actual.

Much like the character he has created, Bellow is dedicated to a cultural and spiritual mission which, he believes, may best be carried out through the medium of his art. He regards the profoundest level of present human misery as a spiritual agony caused by the estrangement of the individual from his innermost self. This estrangement is the result of a vast cultural failure to recognize the true needs of the essential self and to provide the individual with the normative means for the realization of these needs. From *Dangling Man* (1944) to *Humboldt's Gift* (1975), Bellow's novels constitute increasingly bold attempts to discover the essence of self-realization and determine the active means for eliminating the discrepancy between human pursuits and human fulfillment. Dr. Tamkin shares an affinity with a number of spiritually motivated characters who appear in later novels as manifestations of Bellow's dedication to his humanly beneficial mission.

Seeking to burst his spirit's sleep, Eugene Henderson, the protagonist of the novel immediately following *Seize the Day*, journeys to Africa in an attempt to "redeem the present and discover the future. . . . to find the wisdom of life." His repeatedly bungled quest is finally set on its true course through the teachings of the Wariri king, Dahfu, who bears a striking resemblance to Dr. Tamkin. Dahfu and Tamkin are similar not only in their medical backgrounds and self-proclaimed mission as healers, but also in their equivocal personalities, their unorthodox methods of instruction, and their effectiveness as spiritual guides. Dahfu consciously jeopardizes, and finally sacrifices, his life in his determination to practice what he preaches "because he hopes to benefit the whole world." Charlie Citrine, the protagonist of Bellow's latest novel, *Humboldt's Gift*, is also in pursuit of "a higher wakefulness" that would benefit humanity. Constantly seeking, and making, spiritual progress, Citrine struggles to transcend such culturally sanctioned but spiritually distracting preoccupations as the pursuit of wealth, power, and sexual conquests. He dedicates himself to his spiritual investigations with a missionary sense of having "business on behalf of the entire human race." Tamkin attests to similar motivation, dedication, and intention. Claiming that "the spiritual compensation" is all he looks for, Tamkin says that he pursues his "real calling" as a healer despite the suffering it causes him because, as he says, "I am only on loan to myself, so to speak, I belong to humanity." Tommy Wilhelm, his vehement protestations of disbelief notwithstanding, becomes a true beneficiary of Tamkin's humanitarian calling. The nature of Tamkin's affinity with such characters as King Dahfu and Charlie Citrine provides further confirmation of his role as the guiding spirit of *Seize the Day*.

Tamkin maintains that awareness of the distinction, made with increasing confidence and clarity in Bellow's later novels, between identity and ego is a primary prerequisite for the termination of man's spiritual agony. He reflects Bellow's conviction that human redemption must be pursued through an attempt to reject the misleading demands of the socially-conditioned ego and to realize the needs of the authentic self. Lecturing Wilhelm on the needs of the true self, Tamkin attributes humanity's sickness to its failure to fulfill the ostensibly contradictory, but substantially corresponding needs for genuine love and genuine identity. Like Henderson, who concludes that "love is a natural force. Irresistible," and Citrine, who states that "love is a power that can't be let alone . . . love is a standing debt of the soul," Tamkin regards love as a fundamental, ego-transcending need of the self. "Every man realizes he has to love something or somebody. He feels he must go outward."

Concomitantly with the need to love, the individual, according to Tamkin, is inherently instilled with an equally powerful drive to attain a sense of personal identity, a need "to be Something." But in the prevailing, socially sanctioned, conceptual context which equates identity with ego, the need for love and the need for identity are inevitably construed as two irreconcilably opposed impulses. For love, the epitome of emotional involvement with another, requires by its very nature the forfeiture of at least a measure of egocentric identity. However, for Tamkin, who regards liberation from the domination of the ego as a primary condition for the realization of authentic selfhood, the impulse towards love and the impulse towards identity are not only reconcilable but mutually dependent: fulfillment of the one is the essential condition for the attainment of the other. "If thou canst not love, what art thou?" he asks, and immediately supplies the answer to his rhetorical query: "What art thou? Nothing. In the heart of hearts—Nothing." But since in his heart of hearts every man needs to be Something, he must seek his identity through the liberating experience of love.

In maintaining this credo and attempting to instill it into Wilhelm's consciousness, Tamkin anticipates King Dahfu, who associates "perfect love" with the removal of the "ego-emphasis" and leads Henderson to an acceptance of both the validity of these two concepts and the connection between them. Similarly, Charlie Citrine comes to regard "the self-conscious ego" as "the seat of boredom" and "the only rival of the political and social powers" that run his life. He realizes that "there is far more to any experience, connection or relationship than ordinary consciousness, the daily life of the ego can grasp." Yet he does not "under any circumstances propose to do without love."

In the course of their explorative quest for human redemption, Bellow's novels reveal an increasing preoccupation with the transcendent dimension of man's inner being. His work reflects a growing conviction, most fully articulated in *Humboldt's Gift*, that the awakened soul constitutes the viable basis for both the reconciliation of the individual with his innermost self and the fulfillment of literature's role as a means of effecting this reconciliation. In an essay that appeared almost simultaneously with *Humboldt's Gift*, Bellow writes that "what can make a writer truly interesting is an inadmissible resource, something we all hesitate to mention although we all know it intimately—the soul." Tamkin does not hesitate to mention it and part of what makes him interesting is his being an early, and, consequently, rather rudimentary, manifestation of Bellow's developing perception of the transcendent soul as the essence of true selfhood.

According to Tamkin, man's inner being consists of many souls. "But there are two main ones, the real soul and a pretender soul." Much like Henderson, whose quest is a result of his refusal to agree to the death of his soul, and Citrine, who concludes that "the job, once and for all, was to burst from the fatal self-sufficiency of consciousness and put my remaining strength over to the Imaginative Soul," Tamkin defines salvation in terms of breaking the bonds of the egocentric pretender soul and attaining accord with the real soul. He describes the role of the real soul as directing the individual towards the experience of love which, in turn, will result in his attainment of authentic selfhood and thus lead to the consummation of his heart's ultimate needs. The pretender soul diverts the individual from his true course by substituting vanity for love and social success for genuine selfhood. Yet man in his blindness yields to the domination of the pretender soul. "This," says Tamkin, "is the main tragedy of human life."

The results of being dominated by the pretender soul are personally and socially devastating. The belief that the true value of the individual is the value attributed to him by his social surroundings deprives man of his freedom. It subordinates him completely to the values of the "social life," which he must obey "like a slave" if he is to obtain the social approval he yearns for. And, since primary among these values is the attainment of money, he must "work like a horse" in order to keep abreast of, let alone surpass, the multitudes of others similarly engaged. The defeat of the real soul subverts the love it embodies and transforms it into self-destructive hatred for the deceiving pretender soul. "Then you become dangerous," says Tamkin. "A killer. You have to kill the deceiver." As is so often the case, this urge to kill manifests itself on both sides of the psychologically blurred line of demarcation separating murder from suicide. "Whenever the slayer slays," Tamkin continues, "he wants to slay the soul in him which has gypped and deceived him. Who is his enemy? Him. And his lover? Also. Therefore, all suicide is murder and all murder is suicide. It's the one and identical phenomenon." Consequently, the widespread domination of the pretender soul creates an infectious social climate of homicidal aggression. Tamkin regards the obsessive pursuit of money as a life-negating sublimation of the homicidal tendencies resulting from the domination of the pretender soul and, thus, as the outstanding symptom of humanity's sickness. "People come to the market to kill," he says. "Only they haven't got the courage to kill, and they erect a symbol of it. The money."

The relentless pursuit of money, attended by the stultifying absence of genuine love, results in a state of terrifying isolation of the individual from his fellow men. It is a dehumanizing state in which, as Tamkin observes, "the lonely person begins to feel like an animal. When the night comes . . . he feels like howling from his window like a wolf." The most injurious result of the pretender soul's domination is its effect on the true soul. "The true soul," says Tamkin, "pays the price. It suffers and gets sick . . . Biologically, the pretender soul takes away the energy of the true soul and makes it feeble, like a parasite." Thus, by committing himself to the demeaning values of the social mechanism, the individual not only corrupts his life but progressively diminishes his chances of redeeming himself.

Appropriately cast as a self-proclaimed psychologist, Tamkin's declared mission is to provide insights into the inner workings of the soul and its relation to its social surroundings. He not only diagnoses the soul's sickness and describes its deadly symptoms, but professes to offer a way to cure the afflicted individual, reverse his orientation towards death, and lead him to an affirmation of life. Life, in *Seize the Day*, as in all of Bellow's novels, is the supreme value to be embraced by man if his existence is to be fulfilled. Love is likewise regarded as the vital emotional foundation upon which a life-affirming existential framework may be constructed. "Love," writes Bellow in a later novel, "is gratitude for being."

In his exceedingly bad but highly significant poem, "Mechanism vs. Functionalism," and in several subsequent utterances, Tamkin reiterates and expands his conviction that man can manifest his human greatness and exercise his capacity for choice and freedom by liberating the self from the destructive normative demands of the money-worshiping social context and dedicating it to the creative fulfillment of its authentic inner needs. He presents himself as a healer whose mission is to release men from the guilt-ridden burdens of their past mistakes, relieve the pressures of anxiety stemming from the terrifying knowledge of their inevitable demise in the future, and restore their capacity for love, affirmation, and fulfillment. This is what he seeks to accomplish by teaching people to concentrate their being upon the only reality which is truly beneficial, the reality of the immediate present. The mission, as he put it, is "bringing people into the here-and-now. The real universe. That's the present moment. The past is no good to us. The future is full of anxiety. Only the present is real—the here-and-now. Seize the day."

Tamkin's specific function as an enlightening moral agent in *Seize the Day* is significantly similar to the moral function attributed by Bellow to literary art in general. Moreover, Tamkin's success with Tommy Wilhelm may be seen as paralleling the success of the literary artist with his readers. The success of both depends not only on their ability to attain moral and existential truths, but also, perhaps especially, on their ability to communicate these truths in a social reality rife with conflict and distrust in which effective communication is difficult and rare. The effectiveness of Tamkin's means of communicating his ideas to Wilhelm merits consideration. For, if his function in the novel is a dramatic reflection of Bellow's conception of the function of literary art, his method, quite appropriately, is the method of the literary artist.

The parallels between Tamkin's relationship with Wilhelm and the relationship of the writer with his audience are numerous and striking. If Tamkin is, on the surface of things, an extravagant beguiler, so is the literary artist. Both appear willing deliberately to sacrifice facts to fancy in their efforts to communicate truth. For truth, as Bellow has repeatedly observed, is often best served by imaginative fiction. Even the greatest of the realists, Bellow argues, refused to limit their art to factual realities because they "always believed that they owed a special debt to truth." He observes that "the demands, editorial and public, for certified realities in fiction sometimes appear barbarous to the writer. Why this terrible insistence on factual accuracy?" The literary artist, says Bellow, should never allow himself to be bound and dominated by "the demon of first hand knowledge, documentation and naturalistic accuracy."

Although he claims to deal in facts, Tamkin appears far more interested in essential truths. He clearly subordinates factual accuracy to the demands of his imagination, substituting fiction for fact as the need arises, in order to produce the fanciful array of stories by means of which he seeks to convey his perceptions of truth. Like the creations of the true literary artist, Tamkin's fictions appear to be designed to serve a distinct moral purpose and to be motivated by a hopeful desire to communicate illuminating insights that would affect and imrpove the life of another. "In telling you this," Tamkin says to Wilhelm, after relating the fabulous story of old Rappaport's secret life, "I do have a motive. I want you to see how some people free themselves from morbid guilt feelings and follow their instincts." Tamkin's other stories appear to be motivated by a similar didactic intent and, to a large extent, prove to be effective means for carrying out this intent.

Listening to Tamkin's stories, Wilhelm finds himself repeatedly torn between a responsive acceptance of their moral and intellectual substance and a disbelieving rejection of their fantastic details. Although their veracity is forever held in doubt by Wilhelm, these stories have an undeniable impact on him. They continually compel him to ponder his own situation and gain insight into the nature of his difficulties, while intimating all along the direction in which deliverance may be sought. Wilhelm's attitude towards Tamkin remains ambivalent throughout the novel. "Was he a liar?" Wilhelm wonders. "That was a delicate question. Even a liar might be trustworthy in some ways. Could he trust Tamkin— could he? He feverishly, fruitlessly sought an answer." The question, to which Wilhelm never finds a completely satisfying answer, is ironic. For Tamkin, clearly a liar, does indeed prove to be trustworthy, but in a way

totally unanticipated by Wilhelm. Entirely unreliable as a financial ad-
viser, he emerges as a highly effective spiritual guide.

Having absorbed some of his teachings, Wilhelm is led to suppose
"that Tamkin, for all his peculiarities, spoke a kind of truth and did some
people a sort of good." The kind of truth Tamkin speaks and the sort of
good he does become clearer to Wilhelm later in the day. Still unable to
reconcile the psychologist's manner to the matter of which he speaks,
Wilhelm is, nevertheless, deeply affected by Tamkin's final pronounce-
ment on the supreme value of life:

> True, true, thought Wilhelm, profoundly moved by these revelations.
> How does he know these things? How can he be such a jerk, and even
> perhaps an operator, a swindler, and understand so well what gives? I
> believe what he says. It simplifies much—everything.

This is a considerable, if not completely conscious, tribute to Tamkin's
method. Bellow considers simplification and exaggeration as primary dramatic necessities for a writer. And Tamkin, combining a talent for
simplification through dramatic exaggeration with a capacity for manipulating others, much like an author manipulating his characters, into
dramatic situations that manifest, through experience, the substance of his
thought, enables Wilhelm, just as the author presumably hopes to enable
his reader, to attain a lucidity of vision that would have a positive effect
on his life.

The "treatment" which Dr. Tamkin administers to Wilhelm consists not only of using imaginative means for cognitive ends, but his
deceptions and manipulations are also highly instrumental in leading
Wilhelm through a sequence of experiences that impress upon him the
validity of Tamkin's views as a conceptual basis for possible redemption
and, at the same time, bring him to a state of psychological and circumstantial readiness to act upon these views. These experiences, culminating
in the liberating loss of Wilhelm's financial resources on the commodities
market and his equally liberating final encounters with his wife and father,
make Wilhelm's moral reorientation a viable possibility by terminating his
obsessive pursuit of financial success and irrevocably removing him from
the dehumanizing influence of the advocates of the money-getting gospel
as well as of money itself.

In a typical story-telling instance, Tamkin begins "to tell, or to
fabricate, the strange history of his father":

> "He was a great singer," he said. "He left us five kids because he fell in
> love with an opera soprano. I never held it against him, but admired the
> way he followed the life-principle. I wanted to do the same. Because of

unhappiness, at a certain age, the brain starts to die back." (True, true! thought Wilhelm.) "Twenty years later I was doing experiments in Eastman Kodak, Rochester, and I found the old fellow. He had five more children." (False, false!).

The story of a father who had left his wife for the love of another woman in his pursuit of the life-principle is aimed at reinforcing Wilhelm's awareness of the need to break his compulsive ties to his own father and wife and the life-negating values they represent. It is also intended to free him from the crippling guilt, which Tamkin regards as "a very special *destruct*," involved in making such a break and to suggest the direction in which Wilhelm should reorient his life after having made the break. And, indeed, despite the ambivalence of his response to the story, caused by the apparent conflict between its valid conceptual substance and dubious factual details, Wilhelm is led to affirm the life-principle and recognize the devastating effects of its denial. The story also stirs him to further ponder and understand the debilitating nature of his relationship with his father and wife as well as the true value of Olive's love. But it is only after the final fiasco on the commodities market that Wilhelm, now wholly dispossessed of his monetary hopes, finds the strength to disburden himself of his past and dedicate himself to the present. Literally and figuratively cleaned out, Wilhelm is finally able to break away from his father and wife and to commit himself to a new mode of existence based not on the pursuit of the respectability and financial success demanded by Dr. Adler and Margaret, but on the love offered by Olive.

Wilhelm's reaction to Tamkin's poem adds still another dimension to the parallel between Tamkin and literary artist. Having overcome the initial confusion and outrage the poem had aroused in him, Wilhelm concedes Tamkin's ability to surprise, excite, and move him. His subsequent observation that Tamkin had "picked up a lot of strange ideas" is attended by the suspicion that, although he voices them, the psychologist has not made these ideas his own. The question as to whether Tamkin has made the knowledge he seeks to communicate his own and is conducting his life in accordance with it addresses itself directly to the problem of the dichotomy between Tamkin's personality and his ideas. The parallels between Tamkin and the literary artist may provide an explanation of the dichotomy and suggest a resolution of the problem.

The works of many writers embody or imply a moral vision of human existence. But it is a rare literary artist whose life is conducted in full accord with the vision put forth in his work. This, Bellow seems to be saying, is not surprising, nor should it be. For the literary artist is only human; he shares the same human frailties as the people he writes about and is equally susceptible to circumstances and social conditioning. Gifted with perception and inclined towards introspection, the artist is often all the more aware of his inadequacy as a moral being and is prone to suffer from this condition more than others not similarly inclined. As often as not, his work is as much an inner-directed attempt at personal redemption as it is an outgoing effort to communicate his perceptions in the hope of redeeming others. Such motivation may be attributed to Dr. Tamkin as well. *Seize the Day* provides tantalizing suggestions indicating that the sources of the psychologist's penetrating insights into the nature of human anguish are intensely personal, and his profound preoccupation with the deeper matters of life, as well as the imaginative manner by which he seeks to communicate his vision, may very well be aimed not only at affecting others, but also towards redeeming his own degraded and tormented self. "Maybe," Wilhelm thinks, Tamkin "wished to do good, maybe give himself a lift to a higher level, maybe believe his own prophecies, maybe touch his own heart. Who could tell?"

An assessment of the work and vision of a writer should, of course, be carried out independently of the writer's personality and conduct. But when the man of vision is, as in the case of Dr. Tamkin, also a fictional figure in a novel, critical attention should clearly be focused on both facets of his characters. But in any such evaluation or analysis, the nature of the distinction between the two must be constantly kept in mind. As a morally motivated person who uses fiction in order to affect, and hopefully transform, the life of another, Tamkin is similar to the artist, the estimation of whose work is to be completely disassociated from any moral judgment concerning his personality and conduct. These should be reserved for a valuation of Tamkin as a socially involved man, of his relationship to himself and to others in the everyday reality of human interaction. The fact that in him the two levels of being are often in conflict, that his conduct often clashes with his vision, only serves to reinforce Tamkin's essential humanity, to authenticate him as a living person, and to establish him as a highly successful literary creation.

DAVID KERNER

The Incomplete Dialectic
Of "Humboldt's Gift"

The theme of all Bellow's work is the
possibility of resistance to the forces of victimization. In *Humboldt's Gift*
the source of that possibility is called the soul—Charlie Citrine, the
narrator, believes "that there's something in human beings beyond the
body and brain and that we have ways of knowing that go beyond the
organism and its senses." But what this apparently transcendental psychology and epistemology amount to, pragmatically, we see in Charlie's figures
of speech for Humboldt's last-minute reprieve: "it may have been as hard
for him [to break out of his case of hardened madness] as it might be for
someone—myself, for instance—to go from this world to the spirit
world . . . he made a Houdini escape." Since Charlie decides that no
one, not even Houdini, escapes from the grave and that "life on this earth
[is] actually everything else as well, provided that we [learn] how to
apprehend it," those figures of speech mean that Humboldt's miraculous
return to sanity—entering the story like a resurrection, seven years after
his death—identifies the immortal soul as man's capacity for spiritual
rebirth or self-determination: boxed in by prefabricated biology, chained
by conditioning and circumstance, all but buried, still the spirit breaks
out, like Houdini—"Where did Walt Whitman come from, and where did
he get what he had? It was W. Whitman, an irrepressible individual, that
had it and that did it." This irrepressibility establishes the "connection
between the self and the divine powers," so that the reprieved Humboldt
can claim we are "supernatural beings," but these "divine powers" are the

From *Dalhousie Review* 62 (Spring 1982). Copyright © 1982 by *Dalhousie Review*.

"inner powers of nature," which "art manifests": imagination, for Charlie Citrine, is "that Messiah, that savior faculty"—a metaphor amplified and clarified in *Henderson the Rain King* when Dahfu envisions the whole human race as having a natural ability to break out of its straitjacket of genes—successful mutations are not the product of chance: Dahfu teaches Henderson, "Imagination is a force of nature. . . . What Homo sapiens imagines, he may slowly convert himself to."

In school, of course, we are taught that Lamarck was wrong. Our "ruling premises," as Charlie calls them, tell us that we don't break out, not even as individuals—in *Dangling Man* an "untimely butterfly" seems "somehow alien to the whole condition of the century." Accordingly, the unreconstructed Humboldt, "overawed by rational orthodoxy," put his faith in the "*Merck Manual* . . . bound in black like the Bible," bowing to a century that teaches man he is a machine. But, says Charlie, those "ruling premises" of "mental" people, who have been "trained to resist what everyone is born knowing," are (by way of a pun) nothing more than a "mental coffin," for "It is not the world, it is my own head that is disenchanted": the mechanical universe is a depressive cognitive distortion, a Hotel Ritz Coffin (the ex-husband of Charlie's mistress, Renata, is a mausoleum salesman named Koffritz)—in *The Dean's December* Andrew Corde says, "The view we hold of the material world may put us into a case as heavy as lead, a sarcophagus." Thus Humboldt destroyed himself like Joe Christmas in Faulkner's *Light in August*, who, instead of seeing that he *was* whatever *he* chose to be, assumed he was black—and therefore doomed—because the myth of his time and place supported these ravings of his insane grandfather. As early as *Dangling Man*, in the conjunction of hypnosis and the auto-hypnosis of Christian Science, Bellow asserted this power of mind over body: what we believe we are decides what we are—man, says Charlie Citrine, is not programmed like the beaver. Therefore Schlossberg in *The Victim* advises, "Choose dignity. Nobody knows enough to turn it down": in *Henderson the Rain King*, when clouds come to the cloudless sky, so that Dahfu says, "Do you see, Mr. Henderson, the gods know us," these gods are the metamorphic "inner powers of nature" by which we ourselves bring the rain to our Newtonian Waste Land; and in *The Dean's December* a black heroin addict and hit-man abruptly and magically transforms himself into a savior. For Charlie Citrine, it is such resurrection that shows "what a human being is." The "irrepressible individual," outfoxing the century's "ruling premises," bursts out of nowhere like the universe itself, represented by the miraculous powers of the sun—Charlie says, "The sun like a bristling fox jumped beneath the horizon"; Henderson, "the sun was like the coat of a fox";

and Mr. Sammler, "Just then the sun ran up from the sea like a red fox."

All the same, Bellow recognizes that his salvationist art cannot simply wish away the strength of those "heavily fortified positions" built on our "Rationalistic, Naturalistic" premises. Twenty years ago he observed that in "The Grand Inquisitor" episode of *The Brothers Karamazov* Dostoevsky had in advance "all but devastated his own position. This, I think, is the greatest achievement possible in a novel of ideas. It becomes art when the views most opposite to the author's own are allowed to exist in full strength. Without this a novel of ideas is mere self-indulgence, and didacticism is simply axe-grinding." Yet the extent to which Bellow has lived up to this dialectical ideal, and the means he has used, have not been explored. *Humboldt's Gift* offers an especially interesting opportunity for that exploration. For example, the beliefs that "warmed the environment for" Charlie Citrine can seem delusions of benevolence paralleling Humboldt's delusions of persecution: Humboldt, who has no grounds for mistrusting docile Kathleen, builds fantasies of betrayal; Charlie, who has good grounds for mistrusting Renata (or Pierre Thaxter), builds romantic fantasies—for Renata (whose name may be taken as an anagram for "nature") remains Renata despite the enchantment in Charlie's head, twice she marries death; so Herzog can insert as a bookmark in a volume of Blake a psychiatrist's "list of the traits of paranoia." More important, while *Humboldt's Gift* keeps proclaiming our "connection [with] the divine [inner] powers," it also keeps reminding us of our connection with the infernal outer powers, such as we find in our sexuality—lust hounds us from adolescence to old age—and especially in our mortality: we wrinkle, sag, and thicken until we are pushed in wheelchairs, our memory fails, and we "put two socks on one foot and pee into the bathtub"; and no quasi-divine spirit breaks out of this biological box—only medical technology can do the trick. Thus, the moment Charlie Citrine feels the spirit world hovering near, he runs into Dr. Klosterman, the ophthalmologist who recommended surgery on Charlie's eye-bags; and when Charlie tries to "experience the sun . . . as a being, an entity with a life and meanings of its own" (a cosmic Houdini-fox), we are brought back to earth in the next line, which tells us that, "thanks to penicillin," little Roger Koffritz has recovered from the flu. Charlie's brother, Ulick, in late middle-age is still the glutton he was in boyhood—but Demmie Vonghel, Charlie's dead girl friend, who weighed "two hundred and eighty pounds at the age of fourteen," was made slender by "hormone injections and pills." A broken nose ruined Menashe Klinger's chances in opera—but Ulick's breathing "through the mouth" ended when "we could afford the nosejob." Behind

Renata's brilliant laugh—she is "a perfect Wenatchee, raised under scientific conditions"—lies the "fortune [her mother spent] on orthidontia"; and Charlie can see this mother's mind as a sewing machine ("nature, the seamstress," says Herzog) because veins from Ulick's leg are sewn into his heart, which the doctors shut "off like a small motor and [lay] . . . aside" while "by miraculous medical technology" "they circulate the blood by machine. . . . Poor humankind, we're all hurled down into the object world now"—"A heart can be fixed like a shoe," says Ulick. So the steward in the Mercedes body shop wears a "long white smock, like a dentist" and "charges like a brain surgeon" because the same technology works indifferently on teeth, cars, and brains as on shoes, hearts, and apples. If the Mercedes windshield can have "suffered a kind of crystalline internal hemorrhage," then, by reciprocity, "car-crazy" Humboldt must find at the end that his mental "gears are stripped," his "lining is shot."

But does all this witty jeering give us quite the Dostoevskyan dissonance the dialectic of *Humboldt's Gift* calls for? Mortality laughs at literal immortality; where is Bellow's ridicule of the metaphorical immortality that is his actual theme? Medical technology demonstrates that the *body* has been "hurled down into the object world"; from the engineering of teeth, nose, and heart, Bellow allows no inference about mind-technology, the engineering of the soul. The negation Bellow's theme calls for is the gross biological basis and limits of so-called "self-determination" (the limits of the credit mankind can give itself for the evolution Dahfu credits to man's imagination)—in other words, the evidence that there are only programmed outer powers in the brain (varying with the individual), no undetermined, magical "inner" ones (the caterpillar, after all, even if its metamorphosis is unseasonal, can do nothing but become a butterfly): Augie March's brother George, an imbecile, "was good at heeling and soling" but not "equal to making shoes by hand"; and the lives of the self-destructive poets *Humboldt* represents—Poe, Hart Crane, Jarrell, Berryman—and the life of Delmore Schwartz, on whom Humboldt is based—strongly suggest that these men were no more able to "choose dignity" (i.e., save themselves) than Georgie March was able to make a shoe. Such an apparently escape-proof naturalistic box—the "leprosy of soul" in Humboldt that repels Charlie Citrine at first ("It's no use going back to St. Julien or hugging lepers"),—Bellow has evaded by making Humboldt's "leprosy" a reversible, comparatively shallow and conscious, cognitive depression, much as if Faulkner had sent Joe Christmas to Norman Vincent Peale; and as a result, Bellow shows us Humboldt's box and chains from the outside only, as when a showman presenting an escape artist is afraid to let us examine the arrangements too closely—

Bellow himself evidently could not escape an uneasy awareness that his weakening of Delmore Schwartz's "case" or "coffin" betrays the Spartan complacency of the claim that consciousness is responsible for the health of the inherited constitution, rather than the other way round ("I'm not sick—why should you be?"). This flaw in the art of *Humboldt's Gift,* and the author's awareness of it, can be shown in two complementary ways.

The first necessitates some preliminary appreciation of the extent to which Humboldt *is* Delmore Schwartz, down to any number of details, like the scar on his forehead, his playing baseball with his childlike uncle in a long apartment-house hall, his cats, his fear of accepting an invitation to teach in West Berlin, his dropping in on Bellow at Tivoli just before the Bellevue episode, the glimpse Bellow had of Schwartz on West 46th Street in May 1966, etc., etc. If Ralph Ellison, who as a young man planned to write symphonies, "offered to light [Schwartz's wife's] cigarette" at a party in Princeton, why should Bellow, if he was writing fiction, need to keep Ellison in the incident, hardly disguised as "a Negro composer"? Was the implied comparison of Schwartz and Iago the "homosexual paranoiac" too good to pass up—like so many other things Bellow remembered? James Laughlin, who was Schwartz's publisher and friend for twenty years, says of Bellow's account of Humboldt, "It is *very* accurate. . . . it's very, very true"; and because the novel shows *Humboldt* punching his wife, William Barrett, who was Schwartz's best friend for almost twenty years, withdraws his own earlier statement that *Schwartz* was never physically violent—even though the violence does not appear in James Atlas's account of either occasion in question! No wonder there was a rumor in the late 60s that Bellow was writing a biography of Schwartz—he did, in fact, begin with a memoir. Once one recognizes the extent to which Humboldt is Schwartz, how is one to explain Bellow's deviation from those facts of Schwartz's medical history that, if dramatically developed, would have completed the book's dialectic?

At the very beginning of *Humboldt's Gift* we hear that "Insomnia made [Humboldt] more learned. In the small hours he read thick books"; and Humboldt says, after publishing his first book at twenty-two, "I have vertigo from success, Charlie. My ideas won't let me sleep. I go to bed without a drink and the room is whirling"—in other words, the insomnia is manic and comic. Although the opening pages flit back and forth over all of Humboldt's life, they make no other reference to his insomnia—it is not singled out as decisive, here or later. What Charlie at once emphasizes, instead, is Humboldt's drinking: "First he gave me black coffee, and then poured gin in the same cup." And that Bellow had nothing at all about Humboldt's insomnia in the first published version of the opening

(*Playboy*, Jan. 1974), where the subject is mentioned only parenthetically when Humboldt is awake at 3 a.m. the night of his death, further exposes Bellow's decision to evade what we may take as three facts about Schwartz's inability to sleep. First: its importance. William Barrett leaves us no doubt that without chronic insomnia, Schwartz would not have combined barbiturates, alcohol, and amphetamines and would not have suffered the paranoia and violence of amphetamine psychosis. In "The Hartford Innocents," the novella Schwartz placed last in the last book he published, sleep is called "that fountainhead of life"; and in a still later work, posthumously published, an all-night disc jockey celebrates "the magic and magnetism of sleep's divinity." Second: Schwartz's age at the onset of insomnia. Atlas, wary of Schwartz's "tireless [self-] mythologizing imagination," ignores the insomnia of the hero of Schwartz's autobiographical *Genesis* (New York: New Directions, 1943), which opens with Hershey Green at sixteen waking as soon as he falls asleep—"sleepless boy" he is called; we even hear that until Hershey was almost three he slept by day and cried by night, so that the family had to move out of one apartment after another. That at least such a *memory* was autobiographical would seem to be confirmed by its reappearance in a later story. Why should Schwartz have had such a memory? We know the autobiographical underpinning of the story that when Hershey Green was seven he would lie awake at night and his mother took him to a doctor to find out why—and may not Schwartz's remembered "wish not to sleep" when he was four (Atlas) suggest a pathological origin for what the boy took to be a wish, since the not-sleeping turned out to have an unalterable will of its own? Nothing of this appears in *Humboldt's Gift*. Third: the origin of Schwartz's drinking. According to Barrett, Schwartz at twenty-one—more than three years before the publication of his first book—had "brutal" insomnia (so "vertigo from success" had nothing to do with it) and "fought it bare-handed and toe-to-toe. . . . When he later took to sleeping tablets and liquor it wasn't for kicks, but out of grim need." "Jews don't drink," Schwartz used to say when he was young, and he was no exception—until 1942, when he was twenty-eight; and even then, the alcohol, as Barrett indicates, was as much a medication as the prescribed barbiturates Schwartz had begun taking in his early twenties. Since these "reliefs" (along with amphetamines) ruined Schwartz, his insomnia would seem to have been a symptom of mental chains beyond the power of "Houdini escape" and thus the perfect naturalistic challenge to Charlie Citrine's claims for the human spirit. Yet, close as Bellow hewed to the facts of Schwartz's life and character (not even the man's appreciation of Edith Wharton could be omitted), the central mystery of that life, the early insomnia, was rejected for the unchallenging stereotype of the bohemian alcoholic. The glimpse Bellow gives us of the young Humboldt is a tendentious extrapolation from the later Schwartz, whom Bellow knew, rather than the "magical" Schwartz of the first part of Barrett's memoir, whom Bellow did not know and did not choose to imagine.

The suppression strikes one as all the more unwarranted when investigation reveals that the pathology apparently underlying Schwartz's insomnia answers perfectly to the purpose of the organic dialectic of *Humboldt's Gift*. Charlie Citrine tells us (characteristically) that "[Humboldt] was a manic depressive (his own diagnosis)"—"I don't make diagnoses," says Charlie when asked, "You think Mr. Fleisher is off his nut?"; and not a line in Atlas's biography attempts to offer medical authority for Schwartz's "own diagnosis." But this pall of doubt inspired by Bellow is a red herring, for professional diagnosis would not impress him any more than it impresses Charlie. In any case, though Atlas cautiously and modishly steers clear of the clinical literature, he nevertheless identifies and documents Schwartz's "manic-depressive roller coaster"—Schwartz's moods had "vacillated wildly between elation and extreme depression for as long as he could remember." In addition (aside from the episodes of drug-induced paranoia), all accounts, including Bellow's, confirm Schwartz's paranoid personality, which is common in both mania and depression. And two of Schwartz's early works that cannot be attributed to "self-mythologizing" are transparent attempts to rationalize the disorder Schwartz only later came to believe he had: in both the story "The Statues" and the play *Dr. Bergen's Belief*—where the doctor founds a cult based on the revelation that the sky is "god's blue eye"—suicide is the price paid for the fleeting manic reenchantment of the world. By 1950, in *Vaudeville for a Princess* (New Directions), Schwartz could write, with unquestionable self-reference: "No one knows what the real causes of the manic-depressive disorder are, whether physical or mental or both. . . . You can have this gift or that disease, and no one understands why, no one is responsible, and no one can really alter matters, and yet no one can stop thinking that someone is to blame." This is why Schwartz could say, in a late poem, "I am a book I neither wrote nor read." His feeling that he (like Oedipus) was in the hands of a foreign power need not be regarded as a rationalization of what Charlie Citrine sees as a spiritual weakness in Humboldt. Ten years after Schwartz's death we could read:

> . . . in a number of families [some forms of manic and depressive illness occur] in association with such traits as color blindness and a specific blood group known to reside in the X chromosome. . . . When [this association] does occur, it follows a pattern so consistent that it cannot

be explained on a non-genetic basis. One is forced to reach the conclusion that . . . in a substantial number of manic-depressive illnesses,
genetic factors play a crucial causative role.

Another kind of support for this hypothesis is inferred from the mode of
action of the drugs with which severe mental disorders are now treated:
the "genetic factors" evidently express themselves as malfunctions in the
chemical transmissions of impulses across the synaptic gaps between neu-
rons in the brain. Among these drugs is lithium carbonate, whose value as
the one known means of unlocking the manic depressive box has been
demonstrated dramatically in the U.S. in the past ten years. By 1974 Dr.
Nathan S. Kline, the best-known practitioner in the field, could claim to
have "cleared up in about two months" the manic depression of a patient
who had been in psychoanalysis fifteen years. Of such cases, the most
publicized has been Josh Logan's; but by 1973, before Bellow had published any part of *Humboldt's Gift*, "more than 30,000 manic-depressive
patients [were] being treated with lithium. Now, if this treatment had
been known while Schwartz was a young man, and had been made
available to him (with proper safeguards) before he met Bellow, would
there have been a *Humboldt's Gift*? Here is a negation that might well
have "devastated" Bellow's thesis: that a salt might have done for Schwartz
what the Houdini spirit could not do—that technology at work among the
outer powers of nature can be as decisive for man's brain as for his teeth,
heart, and automobiles—is the dialectical opposition Bellow refused to
confront, thereby thwarting the organic development of his theme.

Recoiling as though we had discovered the human race to be less
human when we found that an iodine deficiency in the mother-to-be can
cause cretinism in the child, Bellow ridicules the challenge: a hundred
years ago, exclusive St. Petersburg doctors sampled Ivan Ilych's urine
(instead of seeing that the man's problem was an existential disease of the
spirit), and now NIMH biochemists working on manic depression trap
"neurotransmitter metabolites" in the spinal fluid—what a banal idea of
man (the canned naturalism of Claude Bernard that Tolstoy, like Dostoevsky,
was already laughing at when the one book he decided to show Ilych
reading is a new novel of Zola's)! Wasn't Josh Logan, born five years
before Schwartz, able to nourish his talent and to survive as a person until
the advent of lithium? and what about Lincoln, Schwartz's favorite manic
depressive? "A man's character is his fate," asserts Augie March, and
Bellow agrees: for Delmore Schwartz to claim he was suffering from an
uncontrollable hereditary disorder that absolved him of responsibility for
his fate was to demand from his friends a blank check—a metaphor that

Humboldt's Gift makes literal. For Charlie Citrine, Humboldt's madness was an "act," a "neurotic superdrama." But does this shifting of the blame dispose of the opposition? One traditional analyst concludes an exhaustive scholarly review of psychoanalytic theories of depression (which, in some genetic studies, seems a less severe form of manic depression), "It seems to me that the significant focus of new work on depression will continue to shift in a neurophysiological and psychopharmacological direction"—and he goes so far as to say:

> Especially after I have seen . . . the astonishing effectiveness of lithium carbonate on the modification not only of mood swings but of lifelong personality structures, I wonder more about the effect of neurophysiology on character. I refer, for example, to the sudden, dramatic transformation of an acting-out, promiscuous, unfeeling, "hysterical" personality into a stable, disciplined individual with a capacity for warmth and for lasting relationships following dramatically upon the administration of lithium carbonate, with relapses occurring in the early stages when the patient, unconvinced . . . , would discontinue her medication, only to change once more when she began to take her lithium regularly.

Thus the Newtonian Grand Inquisitor authorized by Humboldt's "Bible"— speaking with the "Naturalistic, Rationalistic" voice Bellow "borrowed" for Humboldt from Delmore Schwartz—makes deeper inroads into Charlie Citrine's Fort Dearborn. In other words, when we recognize that in Schwartz the neurophysiological insomnia of manic depression was aggravated by neurosis and failures of intelligence and character, we only uncover new sources of strength in the case Humboldt might have made for the outer powers. Whether this "Case"—"the beautiful version of one's sad life," mocks Charlie—is "bad art," warranting Bellow's dismissal of how Humboldt "saw it," the reader may decide by considering how Schwartz "saw it": without any attempt at posthumous psychoanalysis, we can hardly help appreciating the nature and potential victimizing force of neurosis—another kind of "case" that only drugs may be able to unlock— when we consider how Schwartz's insomnia led him to compare himself to both Oedipus and Kafka's Joseph K. in *The Trial.* "Why can't you sleep?" a landlady asked one summer when Schwartz, at 21 or 22, was trying to find a quiet rooming house; and Barrett comments, "Delmore would have given thousands then and in the years after to answer that question." Now, not to know why he couldn't sleep meant, for Schwartz, that he was under the control of forces he had no consciousness of: in other words, he did not know who he was. He felt like Joseph K., i.e., as though he were being punished for a crime he had no awareness of having committed. How are we to explain that the ancient Greek mind arrived at exactly

these terms in conceiving the legend of Oedipus—who did not know who
he was, who had no awareness of having committed the crimes he was
accused of, and who had lived under the control of forces he had no
consciousness of? In Schwartz's *Genesis* we find the explanation: "Like
Oedipus,/No one can go away from genesis,/From parents, early crime,
and character."

> . . . no man
> Escapes the Past, nothing is lost,
> —There in the ultimate pit, rising and falling,
> Lie all the deities which make our lives—

We appreciate the Freudian interpretation a good bit better when we
realize that no paranoiac could conceive a more fantastic, far-flung plot
against himself than the one the Oedipus legend assigns to the gods—the
implicit paranoia helps us see that the Oedipus legend, as much as *The
Trial*, is a paradigm of neurosis: the Greek gods, like Kafka's court, are a
projection of the neurotic feeling of being driven by an alien force; the
alien force is unconscious guilt—such guilt, on entering consciousness,
takes the shape of an external attacker; the inevitable working-out of the
gods' decree is a primordial metaphor for the inescapable power of the
unconscious mind; only this paranoid metaphor explains why the dual
crime that most haunts both the primitive and the neurotic mind should be
the one assigned to Oedipus. (And it is this metaphor that explains why
Kafka can be interpreted with equal cogency either theologically or psy-
choanalytically.) Similarly projecting, young Schwartz searched for a quiet
rooming house, as though other people were keeping him up; he would
later expose his unconscious guilt by resorting to "reliefs" that only
aggravated the punishment—he was really punishing himself, without
knowing what for. In this way, neurosis became decisive in Schwartz's
fate, since he turned his physiological insomnia into a confession of guilt.
We see the same self-punishment when Joseph K. accepts the court's
summons instead of ignoring it with a curse ("Let them go——themselves").
Because the unconscious mind's control feels like an external force, young
Schwartz could conceive of himself as Oedipus: in the autobiographical
"In Dreams Begin Responsibilities" (1937) he implies that he, like Oedipus, was doomed by his parents before he was born—his fate was irrevers-
ible; in the one-act play *Shenandoah* (1941), another autobiographical
fantasy, the infant's uncle predicts that "the boy will be handicapped" by
his *name* "as if he had a clubfoot," i.e., the swollen foot that gave Oedipus
his name. And we can see the same identification with Oedipus when
Schwartz at twenty-seven or twenty-eight claimed to feel like a "vessel of

wrath," a person whose fate (according to St. Paul) is, although predetermined, somehow also freely chosen (*The Truants*)—for Oedipus too *felt* free all the while he was under the complete control of the gods; and here is the climactic point of the legend. Because of the gods' utter control, we cannot blame Oedipus for the anger which drove him to kill the man who was sent to the crossroads at that moment for him to kill and who turned out to be Oedipus's father, any more than we can give Oedipus credit for the intelligence that solved the riddle planted in front of Thebes for him alone to solve: in part, at least, Oedipus blinds himself out of furious shame that he has lived blindly, thinking for so many years that *he* was master of his fate when, in fact, fate was leading him by the nose. What we are being told by the Greek genius behind the legend is that those who are under the control of unconscious forces lack responsibility for both their character and their intelligence: the sane are no more responsible than the mad when—like Oedipus—they do not know who they are and consequently *do not know what they are doing*.

To this, Bellow roars, What! ". . . no man/Escapes the Past"? Then where did Walt Whitman come from? This "case" of Schwartz's drives Bellow to parody—a parody that began in *The Last Analysis* (1964), where Bummidge's televised vision of his birth and conception mimics all three of the works in which Schwartz, like Sophocles' Oedipus, tries to find out who he is: in "In Dreams Begin Responsibilities," the narrator turning twenty-one dreams of his parents' courtship as a movie; the young man Shenandoah Fish imagines himself as a Greek chorus at his circumcision in infancy; and in *Genesis* Hershey Green obsessively searches for himself in the lives of his parents and grandparents, discovering such things as that he was conceived when a French bond "entered [his mother's] womb." Similarly, Schwartz's Shenandoah stands directly behind Charlie Citrine's "trying [like Oedipus] to solve the riddle of man" by looking through a window into the room where he was born—only to find a fat old woman in panties and be caught peeping by her husband; Cantabile emphasizes to Charlie, "When are you going to do something and *know what you're doing?*" Charlie comically laments, ". . . if, before I was born, you had submitted the tale of my own life to me and invited me to live with it, wouldn't I have turned you down flat?"; and Renata too asserts her "right to an identity problem" and is out "to solve the riddle of her birth." But in *Humboldt's Gift* the ridicule goes on to make a new point. The parallel between Oedipus at Colonus and Caldofreddo is explicit, and this self-exiled explorer is played by an actor whose resemblance to Humboldt is "uncanny"—and in Fenichel we learn why Caldofreddo's crime is cannibalism rather than incest and parricide: "The

manic depressive constitution [probably] consists in a relative predomi-
nance of oral eroticism"; "the unconscious ideas of depressed persons, and
frequently their conscious thoughts also, are filled with fantasies of persons
or parts of persons they may have eaten." As Bellow's Herzog reminds us,
in Freudian anthropology the "primal crime" was followed by the sons'
"eating [their father's] body"—but the motive for the murder was the wish
to return to the infant's feast on the *mother's* body; so the adult who
compulsively repeats his first despair—that oral-dependent response to
weaning (following the first long period of mania)—would like to, but
cannot, murder his father and go back to eating his mother. That Bellow
had in mind this "eating" of the mother, we see when four-year-old Roger
Koffritz, missing his mother, fills his mouth with a chocolate bar: "He
desired his Mama . . . feverish . . . beating all over with pulses—nothing
but a craving defenseless greedy heart." That is, Humboldt, unlike Henderson the Rain King, could not move his Mummah out of the way; and
when his wife disappears, Humboldt projects his own unconscious incest
onto her father. Nothing but Bellow's ridicule of manic depression as an
oral fixation can explain the rest of the book's pattern of ludicrous,
dreamlike displacements of the Oedipus legend and complex: Naomi
Lutz's son blasphemously demanding the word for "mother-fucker" in
Swahili and howling for milk in African villages ("It was easier to kick the
heroin habit than the milk"), the villages nesting among "giant anthills
like nipples all over the landscape; Ulick—who smells "Dirty work at the
crossroads"—"suck[ing]" on "breast-sized persimmons" and insatiably stuff-
ing his mouth with chicken breasts, the chocolate sauce on those breasts
tying him to little Roger Koffritz, whose mother goes to see *Deep Throat;*
and Charlie himself, who likes to sleep with his hands on Renata's breasts
and, his head lying on the "bib and bosom" of his 747 seat, "curl[s] his
forefinger over the top of the glass," like an infant feeding.

Instead of Humboldt's "horror, ideas of Fate," we see how Charlie
Citrine "saw it": Humboldt had "rushed into the territory of excess to
stake himself a claim"; "he was having a grand time being mad in New
York" "enacting 'The Agony of the American Artist' " "to "make [himself]
interesting"—now "merely the figure of a poet," "an actor" staging a
"melodrama" that wasn't even his own: "he couldn't find the next thing,
the necessary thing for poets to do. Instead he did a former thing. He got
himself a pistol, like Verlaine, and chased Magnasco"; Humboldt's "Agony" was "faked suffering"—his picket sign, "carried . . . as though it
were a cross," was written in mercurochrome, not blood. And this view of
Humboldt determines the book's structure, for the overriding picture of
the fraudulence of contemporary life is what unifies the book's two plots

and separate decades. For example, the lure of synthetic image-making—which prompts Charlie Citrine to compare Colonel McCormick, owner of the *Chicago Tribune,* to Circe—dictates Cantabile's maneuver to break into a Chicago gossip column, paralleling Humboldt's jealousy of Charlie's appearance in Leonard Lyons; the swings of Humboldt's manic depression as an "act" that makes demands on his friends are mimicked when Cantabile forces Charlie to attend him in a toilet stall (the dumps) and later manically drags him along the top girders of a skyscraper under construction—an "act" hard "to follow"; etc. And this multiply mirrored vision of Humboldt's madness as inauthentic, *Humboldt's Gift,* a defense of the imagination, implicitly offers as one of those "true impressions" that justify the claim of art to see "what is" more clearly and deeply than "the modern intelligence" can. "Reality didn't exist 'out there,' " thinks Corde in *The Dean's December.* "It began to be real only when the soul found its underlying truth. In generalities there was no coherence—none." A good novel, accordingly, "deal[s] with real or approximately real, human beings, not the zombies of a pamphleteer"—art, says Bellow, forced Tolstoy "to be fair to Karenin." "Truth, said Tolstoi at the conclusion of *Sebastopol,* was the hero of his novel."

But if Bellow's vision of Humboldt is the truth, why the tendentious distortions and omissions? Why do we not see Humboldt as a graduate student unable to sleep, moving from one rooming house to another, looking "ghastly, his face almost yellow-green with fatigue" —hardly an antic attempt to "make himself interesting"? Nor are we given Schwartz's hallucination that the Rockefellers were beaming voices and mind-destroying rays at him from the Empire State Building—a piece of pathology that would have blunted the comic axe Bellow was grinding. Mind-technology, representing the inescapable outer powers of nature, is missing from *Humboldt's Gift* because the watering-down of Delmore Schwartz's fate—and the consequent inorganic, Lysenko-ish double plot—could not have survived the challenge of the naturalistic tragedy in Schwartz's actual "leprosy"; Humboldt then could not have been resurrected from the Waste Land's "mental coffin," and the "Testament" forgiving the narrator (and author) would have been exposed as a wish-fulfilling fantasy. The disingenuousness of this "Testamant"—the authorial self-endorsement substituted for the self-subversion of "The Grand Inquisitor"—confirms our sense that we have been left with "axe-grinding," with deception in both the argument and the art. And, as is always the case with such evasion, Bellow's willful structure collapses—under the weight of the ghost that haunts the book, for so much of Humboldt is Schwartz that Bellow loses control of the character: the realities of Schwartz's

life manifest in the caricature (the photographed features under the cartoon moustache) break loose from Bellow's Procrustean zeal and repossess
what has been lopped off. Bellow's warning about the "coast of Bohemia"
does not protect the will that usurps the role of imagination: the maligned
and dismissed generalizing intelligence is justified in asking how Bellow's
"true impression" of Schwartz as the antic Humboldt can account for the
common ground of Schwartz's fate and the fates of two other twentieth-
century American literary men, Ring Lardner and Elliot Cohen, founder
of *Commentary*. Was prim Lardner (in whose crippling insomnia and
alcoholism Schwartz saw his own), was Lardner—while crusading against
double-entendre in popular songs that children could hear on the family
radio, and while telling a son, "No one, ever, wrote anything so well after
even one drink as he would have done without it"—also copying Verlaine,
enacting "The Agony of the American Artist"? When Elliot Cohen, after
ten years' success at *Commentary*, fell into a deep depression which was
unrelieved by treatment at the Payne-Whitney clinic (where, like Schwartz,
Cohen suffered "periods of delusion") and finally killed himself in 1959—was
he too taking literally the middle-class notion of the self-destructive poet?
Furthermore—since Bellow's caricature of Humboldt is meant to confirm
our responsibility for our fate—do we find Lionel Trilling, who considered
Cohen a genius as an editor and teacher ("the only great teacher I have
ever had"), surrendering belief in imagination and spirit when he finds
Cohen's fate teaching us our limitations:

> Perhaps he was licensed to give so much feeling to what in life is
> gratuitous—to what is finely free—because he had so much natural
> awareness of what in life binds us, whether for good or for bad.
>   . . . No one who knew Elliot as a friend through his mature life
> could be unaware that the pain of existence was darker for him than it is
> for most of us. I know of no response we can make to his pain other than
> that of our silent humility before it, and before the mystery of this great
> pain being bound up with so much delight in human life and with so
> much power. . . .

Very different is the tone Bellow's art dictates for Charlie Citrine's farewell: "Poor Humboldt! What a mistake! Well, perhaps he could have
another go at it. When? Oh, in a few hundred years his spirit might
return." Which version—Trilling's or Bellow's—gives more resonant support to Moses Herzog's claim that "human life is far subtler than any of its
models"? Bellow can make Charlie apologize—"I thought about Humboldt
with more seriousness and sorrow than may be apparent in this account"—
and have him reflect once, "I doubt that Humboldt had had a single

good day in all his life"; but such afterthoughts, or interpolations, do not change the book's structure or complete its dialectic.

In defense of his omission of Humboldt's "case," Bellow can be imagined as implicitly claiming that the banalities of determinist mythology could safely be left to any reader under its spell; but the claim would be untenable—a thousand Chernyshevskys could never have written "The Grand Inquisitor." And the fact is that Bellow, instead of making the imagined claim, has built into *Humboldt's Gift* an apology for his evasion of the determining forces in Delmore Schwartz's life: Charlie Citrine is blamed for the parallel evasion. After all, the picture of Humboldt is "how I saw it." And Charlie speaks of himself as having felt—one night in 1953—"entitled to my eight hours of oblivion and determined to have them"; twenty years later at fifty-five, he still speaks of his nightly period of sleep as "eight intervening clock hours." That is, Charlie is a normal sleeper, complacently unable to imagine Humboldt's insomnia. The point is reinforced when Charlie, practicing one of the exercises in an anthroposophic training manual, finds himself unable to "enter into" his daughter Mary's desire for a ten-speed bike: "To do this one had to remove all personal opinions, all interfering judgments. . . . But I couldn't do this. . . . If I couldn't know this kid's desire could I know any human being?" Such egocentric blinders shelter Charlie even when a missing piece of the picture falls within his line of vision: from Demmie's exophthalmic eyes, for example, he surmises that "it must have been thyroxine they put her on." Knowing such things, why does he bow out of all discussion of Humboldt's drugs? If Charlie knows "the symptoms of an overdose of caffeine," couldn't he have informed himself—and us—about amphetamine psychosis? Similarly, Charlie mentions Humboldt's "nutty old mother," he knows the "hereditary attainder rule" in horseracing, he can hear in his ex-wife's voice the voice of her grandfather and see his old girl friend Naomi Lutz in the "gums and teeth" of her daughter Maggie, and we learn Ulick's opinion that Charlie's memory was inherited from their father's father; but never do we hear of the genetics and biochemistry of manic depression, although Charlie must have heard of this from Humboldt. Twice Renata reminds Charlie that Humboldt "died nuts" —but Charlie grandly dismisses "the textbooks. I know what clinical psychologists say about manic depressives. But they didn't know Humboldt. . . . What does clinical psychology know about art and truth?" For all such self-imposed blinders and grandiosity in the narrator, distorting the characterization of Humboldt, how is the author to blame?

The answer is that Charlie's view of Humboldt's madness as an "act" is Mr. Sammler's view of the "theater" of the 60s—everyone imitatively dramatizing his "interest" instead of fulfilling "the terms of his contract" with God: Bellow has been reported as saying that "character [is] the single most important element in determining a writer's worth," and he has endorsed Charlie Citrine's interpretation of Humboldt's failure— "Humboldt is in some way following the pattern of the doomed poet . . . that banal pattern. . . . It was not self-definition." Further—despite the teasing of Charlie's quest for spirit, as in the suggestion of "paranoia in reverse"—Bellow shares Charlie's grandiosity: in 1972, while writing *Humboldt's Gift,* Bellow attacked André Malraux for seeming to say "that what a clinical psychologist learns about the human heart is far deeper and more curious than anything the greatest novelists can reveal"; Bellow reverses Malraux—"The accounts of human existence given by the modern intelligence are very shallow by comparison with those the imagination is capable of giving." As for biological psychiatry, in *The Adventures of Augie March* Bellow invented a mad "psycho-biophysicist," Basteshaw, a "Renaissance cardinal" type—like Dostoevsky's Inquisitor—who in the twentieth century expects to make his flock happy not by an iron theocracy but by a synthesis of protoplasm that will unlock the secret of depression. Allegorically, Basteshaw is fatally off course—and it is not Charlie Citrine who is stage-managing the allegory. Moreover, isn't the shadow of Delmore Schwartz visible behind Basteshaw? When Augie tells the madman, "No one will be a poet or saint because you fool with him," one can easily imagine that Bellow said something like this to Schwartz at Princeton in 1952 ("Dexedrine won't bring back your poetry"). And the past thirty years haven't changed Bellow's mind: in 1972 he drew our attention to Theodore Roszak's ridicule of the Brave New World that would reduce " 'the tragedies of our existence' " to " 'chemical imbalance within our neural circuitry' "; and in *The Dean's December,* although the new Basteshaw, Professor Beech, is made an eminent geophysicist, there can be no mistaking the caricature (counterpointing, belatedly, the anthroposophist Dr. Scheldt in *Humboldt's Gift*) when Beech attributes the fall of the Roman Empire to "the use of lead to prevent the souring of wine. Lead was the true source of the madness of the Caesars"—"human wickedness," mocks Dean Corde, "is absolutely a public health problem, and nothing but. No tragic density, no thickening of the substance of the soul, only chemistry and physiology. . . Pb is the Stalin of the elements, the boss," i.e., as much as the various forms of Soviet brutality, science under democracy is part of the Grand Inquisitor's "worldwide process of consolidation" reducing man to an object.

Finally, we cannot hold Charlie Citrine responsible for two inconsistent omissions dictated by Bellow's evasion of mind-technology. Since

Humboldt is the most complex character in the book (Charlie is more a mouthpiece than a character) and the narrator wants to explain the poet's fall, isn't our acquaintance with Humboldt's early life strangely meager? Philip Rahv found, after twenty-five years, that he remembered vividly Delmore Schwartz's talk "about his parents, his brother, and his early experiences." And isn't Charlie's omission of such talks surprisingly uncharacteristic of a professional biographer? True, Charlie is an ex-biographer: why bring up anybody's early life when Whitman came out of nowhere? But Charlie continues to have a fondness for "ontogeny and phylogeny." It is the author himself who wishes to avoid the question of why Schwartz had insomnia in childhood and youth, long before "vertigo from success." Also inconsistent is the omission of any attempt to display "the Mozart of conversation": not once does Charlie give us—directly reported, unparodied—a sustained example of Humboldt's conversation "in the days of his youth" when the poet was "covered in rainbows"; yet Charlie has a great memory, which he, unlike Ulick, attributes to love, and he claims to have loved Humboldt. Love would have given us Humboldt's arias; but Bellow had to exclude them, for any such attempt to give Humboldt stature would have made the author's caricature and the omission of Humboldt's own account of his fate so much the less acceptable.

As a scapegoat, then, the narrator is an ineffective mechanical device, exposing the author's attempt at a trick-escape from the dialectic his Dostoevskyan model imposed. And that Bellow felt the need of providing himself with such an escape-mechanism establishes his awareness of the deficiency in the characterization of Humboldt—a deficiency that may be attributed to the buoyancy of Bellow's temperament: there can be no "Grand Inquisitor" without the freighted ambivalence that could let D. H. Lawrence think the Inquisitor speaks for Dostoevsky.

ALVIN B. KERNAN

"Humboldt's Gift"

Poets have always, says Charles Cit-
rine, the narrative voice and center of consciousness of *Humboldt's Gift*,
had a difficult time of it in America:

> Edgar Allan Poe, picked out of the Baltimore gutter. And Hart Crane
> over the side of a ship. And poor John Berryman jumping from a bridge.
> For some reason this awfulness is peculiarly appreciated by business and
> technological America. The country is proud of its dead poets. It takes
> terrific satisfaction in the poets' testimony that the USA is too tough,
> too big, too much, too rugged, that American reality is overpowering.

Humboldt's Gift is the story of two more American writers who are
overpowered by the country in different ways. The first is the romantic
poet Von Humboldt Fleisher—named after a statue his mother saw in the
park, born on the IRT, and modeled closely on Delmore Schwartz, whose
combination of extraordinary talent and failure bid fair to make him *the*
representative poet of the 40's and 50's. The second is Humboldt's younger friend and admirer, Charles Citrine—a name suggesting a semi-precious
stone?—a successful writer of many kinds of work: a play, movie scripts,
essays, commissioned biographies, and historical studies. When Humboldt
"made it big" in the late 1930's with the publication of his slim volume of
poems *Harlequin Ballads* (Schwartz's *In Dreams Begin Responsibilities*), Citrine, then a student in love with literature at the University of Wisconsin,
took the bus to Greenwich Village to sit at the feet of this poetic idol, the
last remnant of the heroic age of pure visionary poetry—Wordsworth,
Keats, Verlaine, and Whitman are the figures most frequently mentioned—

From *The Imaginary Library: An Essay on Literature and Society.* Copyright © 1982 by
Princeton University Press.

living in a leaden age of prose and realism. But whatever the diminish-
ment, both the older poet and the younger writer are deeply committed to
a pure romantic conception of the nature and social value of poetry and
art.

Romanticism has always been in large part negatively determined,
and Humboldt and Citrine characteristically find the materialistic society
of the twentieth century completely unsatisfactory, an "awful tangle,"
"stale dirt," a "world of categories devoid of spirit" waiting "for life to
return," a place where "three-fourths of life . . . are obviously missing." In
this wasteland, the poet's divine mission as Humboldt conceives it is "to
join together the Art Sacrament and the Industrial USA as equal powers,"
by means of the "strength and sweetness of visionary words" enabling the
soul to flow "out into the universe and [look] back on the complete scene
of earthly suffering." Beyond this alien world we live in there is a
"home-world," and poetry is to be "the merciful Ellis Island where a host
of aliens began their naturalization." The poet is the instrument for
"ransoming the commonplace" and draping "the world in radiance." His
instruments are the usual orphic powers of imagination, love, the sentient
soul, enchantment, dream, madness, Platonic idealism, Blakeian excess,
Wordsworthian nature. The sacred words, always capitalized, are "Poetry,
Beauty, Love, Waste Land, Alienation, Politics, History, the Unconscious
. . . Manic and Depressive. . . ." Poetry through the visionary powers of
the poet will transform the world, showing the way to making the ugly
beautiful, the imperfect complete, the dark radiant, the microcosmic
macrocosmic, the commonplace wonderful, and the alien corn the world
of home. Citrine's poetic values are somewhat less grandiosely expressed
than Humboldt's, though at much greater length, but he too dreams of
works which will bring spirit into the world of flesh, explain mind and
substance to one another, bind past to present and future, and do some
great good to the suffering, confused world.

For all its other-worldliness and the vagueness of its terminology,
romanticism has usually had the social aim of transforming the immediate
given world into a new Jerusalem rather than escaping into a world of pure
beauty or perfect form. But, usually avoiding politics or social action, its
primary means of affecting the world have been the work of art itself and
the personality of the poet, both of which can, it has been hoped,
ultimately bring about the desired changes by giving concrete expression,
real substance, to poetic values and thereby making these values exist
objectively. Von Humboldt Fleisher attempts poetic transformation by
means more of his personality than of his work, for he publishes only the

few poems of *Harlequin Ballads* early in his career, and then writes no more, except for one brief poem on a postcard to Citrine,

> Mice hide when hawks are high;
> Hawks shy from airplanes:
> Planes dread the ack-ack-ack;
> Each one fears somebody.
> Only the heedless lions
> Under the Booloo tree
> Snooze in each other's arms
> After their lunch of blood—
> I call that living good!

But this is all, "Unwritten poems were killing him," and after his first success he spent his energy not in writing but in living out the role of a poet. And he has all the needed gifts to do so: a romantic family background, a great personal attractiveness, a noble nature, immense learning and splendid abilities in conversation, a voracious capacity for reading, and moments of high manic inspiration. He is, as Citrine says again and again, essentially a noble person, a man of spirit and great unused powers, but all the invention that "should have gone into his poetry," all that genius, went into his "personal arrangements," that is, to living out the traditional role of the romantic poet. After the success of *Harlequin Ballads* he becomes a personage in American letters. He writes critical essays for the *Partisan Review* and the *Southern Review*; he is praised by Conrad Aiken, T.S. Eliot, and, even, Yvor Winters; he is picked up and supported as an editorial consultant by Hildebrand, a wealthy playboy publisher and patron of the avant-garde; he teaches for a year at Princeton and nearly succeeds in conning a chair out of that university and the Belisha Foundation, headed by that mastermind of higher culture in America, Wilmore Longstaff, a thinly disguised version of Robert Hutchins; he marries and moves to a rural retreat in New Jersey, drives big cars, drinks heavily, takes pills, and chases girls. He is, as he himself memorably puts it, "the first poet in America with power brakes," and the reputation and money he acquires both brake and break his poetic powers.

But the period of success is short-lived. Always a manic-depressive with paranoid tendencies intensified, as they were in Schwartz's life, by pills and alcohol, Humboldt finds evil and enemies everywhere, breaks with and abominably maltreats his old friends, and, believing that his wife's father had sold her for a year to a Rockefeller, accuses her of infidelity with almost anyone she knows, beats her and tries to run her down with his four-hole Buick. When she leaves him out of fear for her life, he goes mad, tries to kill an imagined rival, and is at last carried off screaming and fighting to Bellevue in a straightjacket, fouling himself in his impotent fury on the way. Released by the effort of friends, he drinks and gets into further trouble, becoming particularly obnoxious about the success of a Broadway play, based partly on his character, by his old admirer Citrine. Through all this he maintains a certain high outrageous style—picketing Citrine's play, cashing a check on Citrine and buying a powerful Oldsmobile with the money, gathering a circle of acquaintances around him at the bar and amusing them with wicked stories about his former friends. But gradually he becomes what he most fears, a "farcical martyr," an artist who "by wishing to play a great role in the fate of mankind . . . becomes a bum and a joke." He lives his dreadful reality out to the end, growing old, fat, gray, and sodden in a cheap hotel, still reading and drinking. At last he dies of a heart attack in the elevator while taking his garbage out and is carried off to the morgue where he lies unidentified for days, until someone at the Belisha Foundation, which had reneged on funding his Princeton chair, pays for the maimed rites provided by an isolated New Jersey cemetery where the corpse is cramped into a grave without enough room for its knees to be straightened. This is deconstruction of the poet at the most fundamental level.

Although Bellow has rearranged the details, Humboldt is an extraordinarily accurate portrait of Delmore Schwartz as he appears in James Atlas' fine biography, *Delmore Schwartz, The Life of an American Poet* (1977), which remarks that Bellow in part wrote his novel to clear himself of persistent charges that he had used and betrayed Schwartz.

Humboldt's life is energized by the romantic desire to be "authentic," to recover mankind's imaginative powers, to express "living thought and real being," no longer to "accept these insults to the soul." But unable to live this life he is forced into a stereotypical role, that of "The Bohemian Artist," compounded of Coleridge's drugs, Pound's incarceration in an asylum, and Byron's non-conformity, which closely resembles such memorable Hollywood portrayals of the artist as John Garfield giving up his violin for the boxing ring, or José Ferrer drinking Toulouse-Lautrec to death at the Moulin Rouge. "Instead of being a poet he was merely the figure of a poet. He was enacting 'The Agony of the American Artist.' And it was not Humboldt, it was the USA that was making its point: 'Fellow Americans, listen. If you abandon materialism and the normal pursuits of life you wind up at Bellevue like this poor kook.'" Each of the stock components of the role of the romantic artist, alienation, poverty, turbulent mental activity, love, is transmuted from its original functions and made to serve as signs of weakness rather than vision and strength:

The weakness of the spiritual powers is proved in the childishness, madness, drunkenness, and despair of these martyrs. Orpheus moved stones and trees. But a poet can't perform a hysterectomy or send a vehicle out of the solar system. Miracle and power no longer belong to him. So poets are loved, but loved because they just can't make it here. They exist to light up the enormity of the awful tangle and justify the cynicism of those who say, "If I were not such a corrupt, unfeeling bastard, creep, thief, and vulture, I couldn't get through this either. Look at these good and tender and soft men, the best of us. They succumbed, poor loonies."

Humboldt has allowed himself to become merely a negative example in the American success story because his imagination has been overwhelmed by the enormous powers of the modern world. As the "first Americans were surrounded by thick forests," so modern man is "surrounded by things attainable," and the poet too desires these things and wants to become rich and famous. But when he does so his inspiration falters and he is unable "to fill up all the vacancy he felt around him" not simply because of his own greed but because as he becomes involved with the world he comes to know and ceases to be able to resist its awesome powers and a material reality too dense in its vulgarity to be successfully struggled with. "Humboldt wanted to drape the world in radiance, but he didn't have enough material. His attempt ended at the belly. Below hung the shaggy nudity we know so well." The poet once believed he had the power to affect the material world, to shape it and bend it to his ideas, but now that world has too much mass and power for him: it sends men to the moon, calculates the stars in heaven, covers the earth with factories, confers long life and endless goods on men, distributes a cornucopia of money, pleasure, benefits. And against this what can the poet, the man of spirit and ideas, oppose? Humboldt at least can offer nothing, and so he takes up the role the world has assigned him as "hero of wretchedness." "He consented to the monopoly of power and interest held by money, politics, law, rationality, technology because he couldn't find the next thing, the new thing, the necessary thing for poets to do. Instead he did a former thing. He got himself a pistol, like Verlaine. . . ."

America has tested "the pretensions of the esthetic by applying the dollar measure," and as a result the poet has dwindled into the clownish role created for him by society and manipulated for its own materialistic ends. Before he dies, however, Humboldt struggles back into a brief sanity, and his last Wordsworthian words to his friend Citrine, "remember: we are not natural beings but supernatural beings," assert the old values of the high romantic tradition. From these words Citrine extracts the comforting belief that despite his complete failure to affect the world with his almost nonexistent art, Humboldt was indeed "noble." He is the sad last of a line of titans, the great romantic poets who "wanted to be magically and cosmically expressive and articulate, able to say *anything;* . . . to prove that the imagination was just as potent as machinery, to free and bless humankind."

But Citrine is a poet too, Humboldt's pupil and successor, and after Humboldt's death he is left to try to find the necessary new thing that poets can be and do. He has always been quieter, less frenetic, less demonic, than Humboldt, as fits his "belatedness," but he too has the poetic vocation and all those marks by which the romantic tradition identified its poetic saints. He is the typical hero of Bellow's novels, innocent, sweet-natured, greatly desiring to do good and be helpful, cheerful, filled with a deep love for family and for the past. But he also has a "big time mental life," Wordsworthian intimations that he was singled out for some great work in the world and that his election will enable him and others to know "higher worlds" and to separate "consciousness from its biological foundation." As a child he had tuberculosis, that most poetic of diseases, and the isolation and awareness of death which his stay in the sanitorium gave him awakened his mind and sense of separateness from the objective world. As a child he also had his "own little Lake Country, the [Chicago] park where I wandered with my Modern Library Plato, Wordsworth, Swinburne, and *Un Cœur Simple,*" These experiences all combine to convince him that he

> had business on behalf of the entire human race—a responsibility not only to fulfill my own destiny but to carry on for certain failed friends like Von Humboldt Fleisher who had never been able to struggle through into higher wakefulness. My very fingertips rehearsed how they would work the keys of the trumpet, imagination's trumpet, when I got ready to blow it at last. The peals of that brass would be heard beyond the earth, out in space itself. When that Messiah, that saviour faculty the imagination was roused, finally we could look again with open eyes upon the whole shining earth.

But despite these high aspirations and noble words, Citrine's imagination has been subdued to the world, for as a writer he is always more a historian than a creative poet. He dreams of a great philosophical work, on the scale of Balzac's *Comédie Humaine,* on the "Intellectual Comedy of the modern mind," though he never quite manages to explain the nature of this work in any detail to himself or to others. He has written a successful Broadway play, *Von Trenck,* about the swashbuckling adventures of a hero somewhat like Humboldt. Though the play was a great hit and later became a movie which made Citrine a lot of money, it was really put together by the director, not the author. Citrine says of it, wryly, "I had the attention of the public for nearly a year, and I taught it nothing." Most of Citrine's writing, which has made him wealthy, has been, however, historical and political writing in which the facts, not the imagination, control the work: a book on Wilson and Tumulty which won a Pulitzer prize, a biography of Harry Hopkins, and a social history entitled *Some Americans, The Sense of Being in the USA*. He now proposes to write Volume II of this work, to the despair of his publishers, who offer to forgive a twenty-thousand dollar advance if he will forget the whole matter. He seems also to have ghosted biographies, perhaps for the Kennedys, and is planning a work on "Great Bores of the Modern World." This is not the œuvre of a poet or any great imaginative writer, but the marketplace-determined writing of a man who gives the world what it wants and will buy.

The world of fact has reduced his writing to history and biography of the most workaday kind, and this same world is at work on a more basic level in destroying his poetic vocation and absorbing him into itself in a way somewhat different from that in which it absorbed and changed Humboldt. Citrine is, as poets go—at least as romantic poets go—already a diminished thing, quiet, agreeable, willing to go along, aware of his own deficiencies, modest about his accomplishments, but still stubbornly nursing and protecting a conviction of his calling to make known to the world the reality of spirit and mind. He has deliberately chosen to try to preserve and nourish this spirit in the mythic center of American materialism, Chicago, where his mind and culture are a "Fort Dearborn deep in Indian (Materialistic) Territory."

The Indians of materialism whom Citrine encounters in Chicago are a most energetic and vital tribe. Bellow has always had a remarkable gift as a story-teller of the kind that flourishes in the bazaar or around the campfire, capable like Shahrazad of staying alive by telling stories for a thousand nights and a night. The essence of this kind of story-teller's art is the ability to make every object and person so powerful that it glows with its own force and shines with meaning. The knife is always the sharpest blade in the world passed on for many generations from noble fathers to brave sons, the gold paid as the bride price is heavier and yellower than any other that man has found deep in the earth, the villain glows with cruel energies violent beyond belief, the mother is more loving, the heroine more beautiful, and the hero more brave than man has ever seen. Citrine finds this same intensity of being in the bagels in the delicatessen around the corner, the softness of his Persian carpets, the speed and

beauty of his Mercedes 280SL coupe, the rich feminine smell given off by
his mistress, or the demonic delight of his gangsters in their strength and
riches. The elemental charge is particularly powerful in *Humboldt's Gift*,
where everything from the flavor of the chicken soup in the immigrant's
home to the smoothness of Citrine's Sea Island cotton underwear, is
brought to full sensuous life.

But it is the people who are truly extraordinary. All are comically,
unbelievably dreadful from a moral point of view, but each radiates his
own particular demonic energy, each is the best of his kind: the flashy
hoodlum Rinaldo Cantabile who destroys Citrine's Mercedes and forces
him publicly to humiliate himself over a gambling debt; Citrine's estranged wife, Denise, the granddaughter of an old police grafter, who is
out to break Citrine by raising the ante each time a divorce settlement is
proposed; the lawyers, who actually seem to become the sharks they are;
the endlessly malevolent judge, Urbanovich; the utterly charming and
unscrupulous aesthete Thaxter, who shamelessly uses Citrine to finance
his cultural institution and its proposed art publication, *The Ark*; and
Citrine's unbelievably lush and sexy mistress, Renata, who, with her
greedy old crone of a mother, the Señora, tries to force Citrine into a
January-May marriage. All these people are dreadful, a real world of
thieves, whores, and gangsters. But they are so wonderfully dreadful,
unbelievably self-confident, radiant with their own energies, violently
active, that they transcend moral categories and take on that kind of
being we have come to call archetypal or mythic.

There are mythic structures at the center of *Humboldt's Gift*, as in
all Bellow novels. When Rinaldo Cantabile wants to humiliate and frighten
Citrine, he takes him first into a modern version of the Vergilian and
Miltonic underworld, a fearsome underground public toilet where Citrine
is forced to enter a foul booth and stand there while Cantabile relieves
himself and fills the air with fecal stench. He is next taken to the heights
and shown the kingdoms of the world from the girders, fifty stories up, of
a skyscraper under construction, where in a freezing wind Cantabile makes
paper airplanes of Citrine's fifty-dollar bills and sails them off into the
gathering darkness. We are in the world of Petronius and Rabelais when
Citrine visits his older brother Julius, about to have a heart operation, and
finds him enormously fat, gorging his Gargantuan appetite on all the food,
all the land, all the money, and all the other things his overwhelming
orality can internalize: "The fish had been eaten. We sat with him under a
tree sucking at the breast-sized flame-colored fruit. The juice spurted over
his sport shirt, and . . . he wiped his fingers on it as well. His eyes had

shrunk, and moved back and forth rapidly in his head. He was not, just then, with us."

The story of Orpheus is the essential romantic myth of the poet, and it is this tale, alluded to several times in the narrative, of the Thracian poet who could charm even the animals and trees with his wonderous songs but could not rescue his wife nor save himself from death, which provides the deep structure for *Humboldt's Gift.* Although Citrine the modern writer, insecure in his powers and scarcely able to charm any audience, is only a pale reflection of Orpheus, his beloved, Demmie Vonghel, a teacher of Latin (a clue to her Ovidian status?), is taken from him by death in a plane crash in South America, and Citrine roams the jungles in search of her body, but is never able to bring her back. The Eurydice motif occurs again in connection with a later mistress, the unbelievably sexual and pneumatic Renata Koffritz, who abandons Citrine in favor of an undertaker, Flonzaly, who is said to have a "Plutonian" point of view, as well as enormous riches accumulated from the inevitability of death.

After Orpheus fails to rescue Eurydice from the underworld, he returns to earth to sing his beautiful songs, but is at last torn to pieces by a group of frenzied women, and Citrine after the loss of Demmie Vonghel becomes rich and famous from his writings, but as he says, "When you get money you go through a metamorphosis. And you have to contend with terrific powers inside and out." These "terrific powers" are the maddened people he now encounters—the most demonic of them are frenzied women—all of whom rip him apart, figuratively at least, in order to have their will and take his money. The furious ex-wife Denise, the gangster Contabile, the shark-toothed lawyers and judge, the gluttonous brother Julius, the sinister and implacable Señora with her Circean daughter Renata mad for marriage, the faun-like Thaxter, the Harvard Ph.D.-candidate wife of Cantabile, and even the insane romantic poet Humboldt, all want, as the modern idiom has it, to rip off a piece of Citrine. They are maddened by the smell of money, sex, power, like a school of sharks aroused by blood; they batter his car to pieces, threaten his life, forge checks on him, impound his money, steal from him, bully and insult him, and in general use him for their purposes. These are the demons, the Thracian women, of a completely materialistic world who tear the modern poet apart, and they are filled with an energy and power deriving from their absolute conviction that the only things that are real are those which can be experienced by the senses, be used to achieve desires, or be the means to make things happen. Renata, after she has married her "sure thing," the undertaker Flonzaly, speaks perfectly for all this world of the here and now which has no place for the poet nor any conception of his role:

> I don't want to get involved in all this spiritual, intellectual, universal stuff. As a beautiful woman and still young, I prefer to take things as billions of people have done throughout history. You work, you get bread, you lose a leg, kiss some fellows, have a baby, you live to be eighty and bug hell out of everybody, or you get hung or drowned. But you don't spend years trying to dope your way out of the human condition. To me that's boring.

These are mythic characters not because they merely correspond to the figures in the old story of Orpheus but because they are radiant with that energy, that remarkable power of being, which in Bellow is the true mark of the mythic rather than merely factual. Their excess, even their excess of cruelty, insensitivity, and selfishness, makes them wildly attractive in their awfulness. By so portraying them, Bellow gives full due to the materialistic world of get and take he is questioning and makes clear just why it is so difficult to believe that it is an illusion, or to continue to think that there is, or needs to be, anything else. And if there is no world of spirit, then there can be no poet.

Citrine, the writer-philosopher, the latter-day Orpheus of intellect and ideas, has few defenses of his art and his person. He believes tenaciously in, feels deep in himself, those values known only to thought and feeling which are, though totally undemonstrable and totally impractical in the world of fact and power, the roots of poetry and literature. He knows that his own vocation is to write some great work which will manifest the reality of mind and spirit, the awesome power of love, the pathos of things lost in the past, the continuity of human history and of families, the unity of body and soul, the existence of "higher worlds," and the real power of the poetic imagination. He has, in short, all the romantic Wordsworthian instincts, but his protection from the world which denies these values, and therefore denies any real value to poets and literature, are only the ludicrously weak defenses of the modern intellectual. Searching for reassurance, he reads occult works such as those of Rudolf Steiner, finds a guru, plays with anthroposophy, takes up yoga, dabbles in high culture, collects rare things, visits art museums and worships the paintings, backs a little intellectual magazine, *The Ark*, and as often as possible travels in Europe, that home-world of the soul for intellectual Americans. But his doubts are deeper than his defenses, for he can read "Five different epistemologies in an evening. Take your choice. They're all agreeable, and not one is binding or necessary or has true strength or speaks straight to the soul." His intellectual doubts about "this passing of highbrow currency" are only the signs, however, of deeper disturbances for, resist it as he may, he is in thrall to that merciless materialistic world he is trying to transcend. He loves its things—the cars, the rugs, the clothes, the food, the luxurious hotels and dark bars—and he is fascinated by the beautiful energy and lovely contentment in self of the sharks who tear away his flesh. Most of all he loves that flesh itself, his own aging but carefully bathed, clothed, and exercised body, but most particularly the warm, soft, generous flesh and rich smells of women. His most soaring passages celebrate the cicada-like rubbing together of the silken knees of his beloved Demmie, and the shining hair and teeth, the large breasts, and the happy gaiety of the blissful Renata. Since *Humboldt's Gift* is told entirely in the first person voice of the narrator, Charles Citrine, the style of the book is his style, and Bellow's marvelous ability to make the material world glow reveals Citrine's own fascination with the potency of material existence. The way he writes about the world constantly shows, that is, his own deep involvement in it and love of it as far more fundamental and consistent parts of his sentience than transcendental ideas. His style, as it were, overwhelms his thoughts, and reveals his helplessness.

This thralldom to the flesh finally betrays Citrine, to death. Because he loves the flesh so dearly, with equal intensity he fears the death which overtakes it, and is benumbed by terrible thoughts of the depth and coldness of the grave, the heaviness of the earth on the rotting body, and the absolute emptiness of death forever. Unable like Orpheus to go into the underworld and face death, he flees from it as he runs from a mugger who grabs him in a dark alley. He exercises furiously, has numerous affairs with young women to try to prove that he is not growing old, and on a terrible hot day in a New York smelling of mortality when he sees the death-marked Humboldt on the street, dirty, mad, decayed, he avoids him and takes the plane back to Chicago at once. Even when his last Eurydice, the divine Renata, is gathered to the arms of the Plutonian undertaker—"the course of nature itself was behind him. Cancers and aneurysms, coronaries and hemorrhages stood behind his wealth and guaranteed him bliss"—Citrine cannot bring himself to go into the underworld after her, but lingers in a Spanish pension, feeling sorry for himself and taking care of Renata's child by an earlier marriage.

Because of these deep ties to and fears of the world, the modern poet, Citrine, cannot bear witness to the values of poetry by enacting some flamboyant romantic poetic role, a Byron, a Baudelaire, or even a Humboldt. Caught between the powers of material existence and his own slight intimations of immortality—the contradiction is perfectly rendered by making him a *rich* writer, and a poet who writes history—Citrine takes for his model not a poet but the magician and escape artist, Harry Houdini, who was born in the same town as Citrine, Appleton, Wisconsin. Houdini escapes all the traps in which the world locks him: hanged in chains upside down from a flagpole, caged in the most secure prison, even buried in the grave, he somehow pops up again alive, free, and smiling. Citrine tries to achieve the same freedom by becoming a mental and social escape artist. Everyone lays traps for him, always using the same bait— "You can always make money, piles of it. Especially if you team up with me"—and always he escapes them by flying off in a jet, by smiling and paying off, by going to sleep for long periods, or by simply removing himself from the difficult and dangerous situation into his own reveries of higher things. But in the end, just as death finally does catch Houdini—an experimental punch in the belly by a medical student which causes peritonitis—so Citrine is unable to escape any longer. The sharks at last strip him of all his money, Renata leaves him for her undertaker, and he is left in a shabby Spanish pension, unable to break his ties to the world, dreadfully missing Renata's soft flesh, and forced to face his own failures and old age.

The last poet, however cunningly disguised and however clever at escapes and evasions, seems finally to have been caught by the world and utterly destroyed. But it is at this moment that Humboldt's gift is bestowed. Gifts are rare and startling in this world of taking everything and giving nothing, and the gift from Humboldt is both unexpected and of an unusual kind. Humboldt, in a period of lucidity and despair over his own lost genius, before he dies writes a letter to Citrine explaining and apologizing for his earlier anger, and leaving him as a final gesture a script for a movie or play, as well as a few words of good advice concluding with the words "remember: we are not natural beings but supernatural beings." In one way the letter itself, with its forgiveness and admission of past wrongs, is the gift of the poet, an act of noble generosity and concern in an otherwise selfish world, which greatly encourages the latter-day poet, Citrine, in his desperate but seemingly doomed efforts to continue to believe that men do have some supernatural quality. What Humboldt had never been able to achieve with his art or his life he now manages, in however attenuated form, by a generous act. But the gift is also a gift in the more practical sense that the world would understand, for Citrine is able to sell the script to a movie producer for a great deal of money and bail himself out of his financial difficulties, as well as being able to help

Humboldt's indigent uncle Waldemar to re-inter Humboldt in a more fitting manner beside his mad mother.

The gift has a more basic meaning, however. Citrine has continuously pondered the question of why the gifts of the artist seem never to achieve their promised end in America: "I meant to interpret the good and evil of Humboldt, understand his ruin, translate the sadness of his life, find out why such gifts produced negligible results, and so forth." The overhasty "and so forth," suggests Citrine's lack of desire or inability to get to the bottom of Humboldt's failure, but Humboldt's literal gift, the movie script, provides the answer. It is another parable of the artist—a comic *Künstlerroman within a Künstlerroman* in this multiple perspective of artistic selfconsciousness—which tells of a writer, Corcoran, loosely modeled on Citrine, who experiences ecstasy and fulfillment of soul on a trip to a magical tropical island with his mistress, Laverne. "The sensors open. Life is renewed. Dross and impurities evaporate." Upon his return he writes a novel about these experiences but cannot publish it because his wife, Hepzibah, would read it and realize that he has played her false. His agent, Zane Bigoulis, foreseeing a huge commission, proposes that the writer Corcoran take Hepzibah on exactly the same trip, on which the agent will precede them, bribing the natives to recreate exactly the same experiences that Corcoran had earlier enjoyed with Laverne. Corcoran is understandably reluctant, but he cannot bear not to publish the book, so he goes through the same experience again, but this time it has no magic, and every event is a parody and mockery of what had been. The book is published and is a huge success. Corcoran is inundated with money, but his wife leaves him when she realizes that she could not be "the heroine of these tender scenes," and Laverne abandons him too when she learns that he has re-enacted these sacred experiences with another woman.

The parable reveals that there is more than a little of the ridiculous in art, but it also wryly suggests that the inspiration of the artist and the source of his art are erotic, illicit, passionate, sensual, exotic, and profoundly personal. But the modern writer, like Citrine, in his anxiety for the public fame which comes from publication and his desire for social acceptance and respectability, the marriage to Hepzibah, covers up the original experience, and in so doing makes a clown out of himself "a bum and a joke," by trying to live over and legitimize the earlier visions. In the end he becomes rich and famous, but both his muses abandon him, the one that guides his experience of the forbidden dream world of romanticism, and the other that displaces the original eroticism and makes it respectable. The burlesque tone of the story makes it clear that the poet has become a joke in modern America, even though society pays him lavishly and makes movies seen by millions out of his ideas. Not only is the story of Corcoran bought by a film company, but they also pay handsomely for the rights to a movie they have already pirated from an earlier script collaborated on as a joke by Humboldt and Citrine while at Princeton. "Caldofreddo" tells the story of Nobile, an Italian arctic explorer, who tries to reach the North Pole by dirigible but crashes on the ice. The Norwegian explorer Amundsen starts to his rescue, though he despises Nobile, but his plane crashes on takeoff, and the survivors from the wreck of the dirigible turn to cannibalism before they are finally rescued. One of the survivors, Caldofreddo, returns home to become a *gelati* vendor in a small Italian town, where he is years later exposed as a cannibal but forgiven by the townspeople, who are moved by his story of the terrible effects of starvation and cold on a living creature.

The fact that both stories become the basis for movies, as the play *Von Trenck* earlier had, suggests that the primary function (of the) poet in modern society, for which he is amply rewarded, has become one of supplying the films with sensational plots. But both stories also tell of the extraordinary pressures that the material world exerts on men, and particularly on poets, wrecking their high enterprises and turning them into clowns and cannibals. The solution cannot be a return to the old romantic postures of Wordsworth tracing the growth of his poetic mind, or of Stephen Dedalus flying the broken world of Ireland to create the conscience of his race. The world has already transformed those attitudes and their gestures into a stock role bearing testimony to the power of the material world itself. Rebellion has become a demonstration of its opposite, and Humboldt, who had thought to be "the great American poet of the century," has lived out the role and found that he ultimately doesn't have the strength to impose his values on the world, "My gears are stripped. . . . The original fresh self isn't there any more."

If poets and poetry are not to die forever, then, Citrine sees, something new must be found, and for Humboldt that new thing is to be found not by trying to transcend the world and flaunting your own power as "a supernatural being," but by accepting the world in all *its* power:

> When the artist-agonist has learned to be sunk and shipwrecked, to embrace defeat and assert nothing, to subdue his will and accept his assignment to the hell of modern truth perhaps his Orphic powers will be restored, the stones will dance again when he plays. Then heaven and earth will be reunited. After long divorce. With what joy on both sides, Charlie! What joy!

The old romantic figure of the poet disappears into the grave with Humboldt, and Charles Citrine, the poet of the next generation, at last accepts that disappearance forever when he reburies Humboldt in a decent place, appropriately enough using the money the movie plot has earned. The machinery of the modern world, bulldozer and crane, bury the poet deep beneath "brown clay and lumps and pebbles," first placing a concrete slab on top of the concrete case for the casket. "But then," asks Citrine, the Houdini of poets, "how did one get out?" Then he fully realizes the answer, "One didn't, didn't! You stayed, you stayed!" The acceptance of the material world in its most potent and inescapable form of death is the ultimate admission of defeat for the great tradition of Petrarch, for poets who lived to tell us in their lives and poetry of realms of gold not subject to decay and death. *Humboldt's Gift* implies that in some other place and time, after the poet has learned again to live deep in the world and accept his thralldom to material fact, that the stones will dance once more with joy when the poet plays. But this is only a hope, and in the present the poet who had planned to drape America in radiance is gone. His successor Citrine, already only a pale image of his predecessors, though he triumphs in facing death in the most absolute of its many forms in the novel, cannot bring anyone back with him, and he settles in Europe to, he rather ambiguously tells us, "take up a different kind of life."

JEANNE BRAHAM

Reality Instructors

"He is arrived on a new continent; a modern society offers itself to his contemplation, different from what he had hitherto seen. The difficulty consists in the manner of viewing so extensive a scene."

—CREVECOEUR, "What Is an American,"
Letters from an American Farmer

"American history," writes James Baldwin in *Notes of a Native Son*, is "the history of the total, and willing, alienation of entire peoples from their forebears. What is overwhelmingly clear . . . is that this history has created an entirely unprecedented people, with a unique and individual past."

The alienation of which Bellow speaks is more than sociological and ideological: it flows into depths where the certainties of identity and value are wrought; it generates for the American a tradition of seeking the self as an individual, a member of a family, a participant in a larger social collectivity. Hawthorne, Whittier, and James all lamented the dearth of a "usable past" in America—a set of traditions and codified values against which one might measure his experience and certify its significance. It is a critical commonplace to talk of the American orphan, the Ishmael, the Huck Finn, the Leatherstocking, the Redburn, the Nick Adams—bereft of family and friends, cut off from supportive traditions and familiar ties—set adrift in an unknown and often hostile world. Yet the virtues of orphanhood have been insufficiently stressed. That American heroes exist

From *A Sort of Columbus: The American Voyages of Saul Bellow's Fiction.* Copyright © 1984 by University of Georgia Press.

unsupported by codified values opens meaning up to continual reexamination; since American heroes lack traditionally defined norms, each is the sole verifier of his or her own experience. To define oneself "by oneself," as Bellow writes, is both an American privilege and a hardship, both a frightening and an exhilarating process, which requires grappling squarely with the present while keeping a grip on the transiency of immediate time.

It is a terrifying task to discover America alone, as Augie puts it. To authenticate experience for oneself, by oneself, is an evolving process with many stages of development. Grounded in the conviction that dogmatic instructors in reality must be shucked off, the task of discovery demands that intermediaries, be they ideas or people, be discarded. Each person is both priest and novitiate of his or her own experience.

To borrow a phrase from *Herzog*, previous "reality instructors" for American protagonists have emerged from three sources: (1) the natural world, (2) intimate and familial relationships that form the basis of a sense of obligation, and (3) the understanding of history and culture.

Thoreau's *Walden*, Emerson's *Nature*, Whitman's *Song of Myself*, and Dickinson's poetry find "sanctity which shames our religions, and reality which discredits our heroes," as Emerson put it, in the "moral sensibility" of nature. Hawthorne's Hester Prynne, Melville's Ishmael, and Twain's Huck Finn find their definition within the "magnetic chain of humanity." Henry Adams's persona, in the *Education* and *Mont-Saint-Michel and Chartres*, and James's Daisy Miller seek to interpret and thereby integrate the worlds in which they move as self-conscious participants in history. While these sources of instruction are never wholly satisfactory in producing "lessons of the Real," they serve to define what the hero belongs to, as well as what body of experience he or she rejects.

Saul Bellow's heroes are peculiarly at home within this heritage. As Jews they possess instinctive holds on marginal "status," on the sense of being different, on the death of rural dreams, and on the press of cities. Further, as members of a group with powerful family ties, rigid requirements of fatherhood and sonship, and ancient cultural roots, they stand poised precariously on the tightrope stretched between the need to reestablish, comprehend, and ultimately honor the claims of family and the need to acknowledge that modern man is rootless, cut off, and that all he can be sure of is the "data of his own experience." While they feel these dilemmas with peculiar urgency, they eschew the expatriation of a Nick, the westward escape route of a Huck or a Leatherstocking, the "fugitivism" of a Compson. Instead, they remain *inside* the heart of American experience as special representatives of that experience, and are challenged to order it or else succumb to chaos.

Leaving his father's house is a particularly wrenching task for any of Bellow's heroes. Departure becomes a primary obligation for each male protagonist. The process involves a search for the father who is absent, or estranged, or uncaring. Moving toward atonement or reconciliation requires a rejection of false instructors—women temptresses particularly. It ends in beholding in the face of the father not only sonship, but the potentiality of the hero to be himself a father: a giver, not a receiver; a source, not a supplicant.

The search for the father in Bellow's novels does not become simply "the need of the Jew in America to make clear his relationship to his country," as Leslie Fiedler has claimed, nor is it merely a continuation of the need of the American Renaissance writer to find roots, to generate a culture against which the hero can define himself. Bellow's heroes, who have an abundant culture, search instead for "integrity" in the original Latin sense of *Integritas,* "the state of being whole, entire, undiminished." As Augie March insists, man can be "brought into focus" and can live in the fullness of his own experience. Bellow's heroes yearn to achieve an inviolate and expansive consciousness—humanity's true gift to humanity.

Seize the Day contains Bellow's most explicit treatment of this search. The very atmosphere breathes alienation. "The fathers were no fathers and the sons no sons," and money is the only medium of exchange among men. Communication is no longer possible under these circumstances. "Sons" like Wilhelm continue to behave like little boys searching for their fathers' approval, measuring themselves in capitalistic inches in order to ride the commercial roller coaster to success. "Fathers" like Dr. Adler selfishly clutch their own withered lives, offering advice rather than comfort. Olympian distance rather than intimacy measures relationships. Human rapport is brutally satirized in the Dickensian portrait of the retired chicken farmer, Rappaport, who sits day after day at the commodities exchange greedily waiting for a rise in rye or barley or lard. Wilhelm learns, however dimly, in the closing passages of the book, that his failure to achieve success in a commodities-exchange world is symptomatic of his opposition to these values, this inadequate avenue of exchange. His capacity to "seize the day" depends neither upon his aggressiveness nor upon his ability to excel in the expectation game. It depends upon his ability to see relationships, to view himself as kin to all other men and to act upon this perception.

It is Tamkin who articulates this view, a character who is both "right" and a fake, a resource and a charlatan, a false father. "You see," Tamkin tells Wilhelm, "I understand what it is when the lonely person begins to feel like an animal. When the night comes and he feels like howling from his window like a wolf." Wilhelm agrees with "this one last truth" but fails to see the phony package in which the truth is wrapped. Although skeptical of Tamkin's motives, he succumbs to the need for a surrogate father and clings childishly to the hope that he may yet be saved by efforts other than his own. In the capsule of Wilhelm's intense need for kinship and for the compassion of his father, the love of his wife, and the respect of his children, Bellow concentrates the message he will repeat in succeeding novels: an individual is obligated to redeem his or her own fate; he is the father of his own dignity. Wilhelm learns that reality instruction lies within consciousness, and that he can cease drowning in self-pity only when he ceases to view life as a malevolent conspiracy designed to foil him. It is a profound lesson rendered in stark terms and falling short of application into action. Nonetheless, it provides a clear diagram of Bellow's hero's search for the father as well as of the related capacity to reject "reality instructors" in favor of self-sufficiency.

Although Tamkin is the first clear-cut reality instructor, Joseph and Asa display crucial relationships with their fathers which hamper their self-regard and lead them to search for explanations beyond those they can generate for themselves. Their difficulty in relating to their fathers results in a confusion of values; a distrust of women (except the "safe," and for all purposes absent, wives they marry); and an inability or unwillingness to father their own children—in effect, an inability to exchange sonship for fatherhood.

The important emotional transactions are always between males: Joseph and Abt, Joseph and his brother, Joseph and his alter ego, Asa and Schlossberg, Asa and his brother, Asa and his brother's sons, Asa and Allbee. Recent critics complain that this is evidence of Bellow's inability to create a complex woman character; further, Leslie Fiedler suggests that this is yet another symptom of American literature's preoccupation with an exclusively male world.

More recently, John Clayton has argued that

Bellow's women . . . are tough bitches: Joan in "A Father-to-Be," Thea in *Augie March*, Mady in *Herzog*, Denise in *Humboldt's Gift* . . . these women are versions not of the mother but of the father image. Herzog plays "Grizelda" to Mady. He is "female," she "male." These women have financial as well as sexual power over the protagonist. Tommy, Herzog, Humboldt, acquiesce.

While these charges contain germs of truth, Bellow's primary concern is with self-discovery. He writes about the world he inhabits—a traditionally patriarchal world in which father-son relationships are pivotal. Sons recognize themselves in the mirrors of their father's pain, striving, achievement. Fathers see the reflection of themselves, their hopes, their inadequacies in the faces of their sons. It is the image of the self repeated in the faces of the male heirs with which Bellow's heroes must come to terms. Symbolically and perhaps even literally, the story of Joseph and his brothers informs Bellow's fiction with jealousy and disappointment, sibling rivalry, exile, symbolic death, and eventual reconciliation.

The appropriately named Joseph of *Dangling Man* is "dangling" precisely because he is waiting for an authoritative command to order his experience and certify its validity. He is looking for the ideal father, the patriarch who will provide a moral code to which he can anchor his own commitments. His family relationships have failed utterly to supply guiding principles. His own father is ineffectual; his father-in-law carries on a deliberate masquerade with a shrew of a wife; his profiteering brother Amos only patronizes him; his friend Abt has become cold-blooded and calculating. Joseph spends much of his life as a bachelor and wants his wife Iva to be subject to his strengths and weaknesses when and as they occur. He seems unready or unwilling to become a father; children are never mentioned. In an incident at his brother's house, he fights violently with his niece Etta, who closely resembles him; she is a vain teenager who has as many tantrums as he does, and who violates the sanctity of his Haydn record sessions by insisting on playing her Cugat records. In a violent outburst he spanks her, later interpreting his behavior as a thrashing of the immaturity he finds detestable in himself.

Beating the objectification of oneself and recognizing the face of the self in one's "attacker" are made vividly explicit in Asa's relationship to Allbee. Asa also suffers from a selfish and brutal father. "His father, who had owned a small drygoods store, was a turbulent man, harsh and selfish toward his sons." Their mother died in an insane asylum when Leventhal was eight and his brother six. At the time of her disappearance from the house, the elder Leventhal had answered their questions about her with an embittered "gone away," suggestive of desertion. "They were nearly full grown before they learned what had happened to her." Asa, after graduating from high school, had become the ward of Harkavy, a friend of an uncle, and had been encouraged to feel he never distinguished himself in anything, getting his jobs through a succession of favors from distant friends and their associates. His relationship with his wife he considers his single stroke of good fortune, though he thinks she is an unhealthy cross between mother and madonna, seeing to his every need, providing him with the emotional security he otherwise sadly lacks. Other women are perceived, if at all, as either insubstantial (Mrs. Harkavy), perverse (Allbee's whore), or directly threatening (his brother's wife Elena and her Italian mother). Asa's major confrontations, building to the climactic one with Allbee, are with males. Harkavy, who counsels him to grow up, instructs him:

> If you don't mind, Asa, there's one thing I have to point out that you haven't learned. We're not children. We're men of the world. It's almost a sin to be so innocent. Get next to yourself, boy, will you? You want the whole world to like you. There're bound to be some people who don't think well of you.

And Max insists that responsibility must exist distinct from Asa's "guilt." With Schlossberg, the Jewish patriarch who suggests that life is composed of choices and "no man knows enough" to reject "dignity," Asa also feels a certain rapport, which he manages eventually to understand at levels deeper than intellect.

With his nephew Philip, Asa feels a striking kinship that parallels Joseph's encounter with Etta. Asa recognizes, as he acts out the role of the surrogate father, how much he needs to rethink his relationship to his own father: his "payments," partial recognition of a debt owed, are not yet final.

> After all, you married and had children and there was a chain of con-sequences. It was impossible to tell, in starting out, what was going to happen. And it was unfair, perhaps, to have to account at forty for what was done at twenty. But unless one was more than human or less than human, as Mr. Schlossberg put it, the payments had to be met.

In all these instructive encounters, Asa comes to the conclusion that the "truth must be something we understand at once, without an introduction or explanation, but so common and familiar that we don't always realize it's around us." The truth is as close as the Narcissus image: Asa sees his face in Allbee's, his own cries of victimization in Allbee and Elena, his own evasions of responsibility in Max, and his yearning for sonship in Philip. In the reflection of these experiences, Asa sees, how-ever murkily, his own image. In recognizing this image, he makes peace with his heritage and, as the novel ends, begins a lineage of his own.

Augie's and Henderson's encounters with reality instructors hinge less on their relationships with their own physical fathers than on self-imposed blueprints of instruction. Both view life as a cornucopia of lessons spilling out in endless array for the eager novitiate. Both stress the importance of mobility, of independence, of continual reinstruction. If Joseph and Asa are capable finally of discerning their reflections in the pool of their collective experience, Augie and Henderson hit the road to multiply those reflections. Each searches for the ultimate verifier of his experience. Augie believes truth will emerge in the axial lines perceived in stillness. Henderson believes in the certainty of justice, its impact felt in blows. Each rejects a series of teachers' "versions of the real," yet each continues to believe in an ideal version, a harmonious way of living in concert with one's fellowman while still pursuing an "independent fate." This belief transforms Augie into a perpetual boy, an aging Peter Pan wandering about Europe alone, unable to right his experience but even less able to admit that it cannot, in its present terms, be righted. He continues to reject mythmakers and "destiny molders," yet he courts the belief that the axial lines will emerge to fire his imagination with hope. Henderson, unlike Augie, can return from exile to a New-found-land, reborn in the knowledge of the lion, schooled in the lessons of Dahfu and Queen Willatale. The land is barren, however. Henderson has found energy and joy, but he celebrates it on an unpeopled, icebound wasteland. On his way, he is not yet home.

Moses Herzog is. He puts reality instruction to its severest tests, asks of it the most complicated questions, and arrives at the most complex conclusions. Like Augie and Henderson, Herzog has been a romantic quester—a knight in search of the grand synthesis. Like Joseph's and Asa's, Herzog's need for self-authentication hinges on personal complications with his father. His legacy of doubt and guilt has been transferred, in turn, to his failed marriages. Herzog's "lessons" encompass the ideological configurations that literature, history, and philosophy have generated to explain human experience, as well as his personal, firsthand involvements with contradictory notions of equity, justice, and fidelity. His battleground is precisely at the nexus of historical justification and personal rationalization. He finds both wanting.

His looking glass is the wreckage of his life. He has abandoned teaching to reexamine the whole philosophical stance he once thought safely "synthesized." His first wife, Daisy, has custody of his son Marco, and his second wife, Madeleine, of his daughter June. His brothers don't understand him, and his closest friend, Valentine Gersbach, has become Madeleine's lover. His only real relationship is an affair with the forty-year-old Ramona, whom he can't help satirizing as a "priestess of Isis." He is, in short, required to rethink all his original premises, to meet life head on without the intermediary interpretations of "ideal constructions." In searching for a viable world view, Herzog collects, shuffles, and reorganizes the problems presented in Bellow's previous novels: the acceptance of human finitude, the incomprehensible complexity of truth, the need to believe in reason, the significance of choice in determining the direction and quality of one's life.

Herzog wishes to believe, as do all Bellow's heroes, that life has transcendent meaning. Yet the current systematic views of man, the "canned goods of the intellectuals," offend his sense of individual complexity and worth. Life is too complicated, too real, too mysterious to be reduced to a formula. He writes:

> We are talking about the whole life of mankind. The subject is too great, too deep for such weakness, cowardice. . . . A merely aesthetic critique of modern history! After the wars and mass killings! . . . As the dead go their way, you want to call to them, but they depart in a black cloud of faces, souls. They flow out in smoke from the extermination chimneys, and leave you in the clear light of historical success—the technical success of the West. Then you know with a crash of the blood that mankind is making it—making it in glory though deafened by the explosions of blood. Unified by the horrible wars, instructed in our brutal stupidity by revolutions, by engineered famines directed by "ideologists."

Even this "crisis instruction" known "in the blood" is too far removed from "ordinary experience" to suit Herzog. "No philosopher knows what the ordinary is, has not fallen into it deeply enough. . . . The strength of a man's virtue or spiritual capacity [is] measured by his ordinary life." All systems spun by theorists caught in crisis history Herzog calls "reality instructors. They want to teach you—to punish you with—the lessons of the Real." This view of life, which stresses the high value of suffering, "was becoming the up-to-date and almost conventional way of looking at any single life." Herzog's whole struggle is to free himself from this view. While he recognizes that he is still a "slave to Papa's pain," he believes that suffering is not the seat of wisdom, that "more commonly suffering breaks people, crushes them, and is simply unilluminating." Instead of hugging one's pain in the manner of a Tommy Wilhelm, Herzog believes that one must be forgiving, affirmative, even magnanimous. He attempts this in coming to peace with his father's memory on the abortive trip to Chicago, with Madeleine and Valentine, and even with little June: "Coming to offset the influence of Gersbach, and to give her the benefit of his own self—man and father, et cetera—what did he do but bang into a pole. . . . He seemed to have come to the end of that." Most important, he forgives Ramona and even himself.

Humanity's struggle, as seen through the lens of Herzog's experience, does not have to be given a systematic meaning: it is richer, more complex than any meaning man could assign to it. Reality instructors try to assign such a meaning because they fear endorsing "ordinary life"; they hope for official sanction because they fear living in the here and now. Their inflated models of life are caricatures of the real thing because "the soul lives freely, expansively, in modalities we may not know. Three thousand million human beings exist, each with *some* possessions, each a microcosmos, each infinitely precious, each with a peculiar treasure. There is a distant garden where curious objects grow, and there, in a lovely dusk of green, the heart of Moses E. Herzog hangs like a peach." Herzog discovers his own peculiar treasure by coming to terms with himself through his memory of his father, his divorces, and the courtroom drama at the end of the book.

In his trip to Chicago to avenge the Gersbach affair, Herzog visits his late father's house where his "very ancient stepmother" lives, "quite alone in this small museum of the Herzogs." In talking with the old woman, sitting amidst the painfully familiar photographs, Herzog recalls the day a year before his father's death when Papa threatened to shoot him. Moses had come for a loan and to commiserate about his failing first marriage, arriving "as a prodigal son, admitting the worst and asking the old man's mercy." His self-pity enraged the old man, who, in a burst of hidden strength, seized his pistol from his desk and waved it wildly at Herzog. In remembering the situation, Herzog concludes, "The old man in his near-demented way was trying to act out the manhood you should have had." Though he takes his father's pistol from his desk with vague promptings of revenge, he has in fact been reconciled to his memories, freed of his guilt. He recognizes that no one knows the extent and degree of his effect on another. "Who knows whether Moses shortened his [Papa's] life by the grief he gave him. Perhaps the stimulus of anger lengthened it." Freed from fearing he might have hastened his father's death, Herzog is able to see himself more clearly.

The divorce revelation is another moment of suspended guilt rendered in the shimmering flow of stream-of-consciousness:

> All this happened on a bright, keen fall day. He had been in the back yard putting in the storm windows. The first frost had already caught the tomatoes. The grass was dense and soft, with the peculiar beauty it gains when the cold days come and the gossamers lie on it in the morning; the dew is thick and lasting. The tomato vines had blackened and the red globes had burst.
>
> He had seen Madeleine at the back window upstairs, putting June down for her nap, and later he heard the bath being run. Now she was calling from the kitchen door. A gust from the lake made the framed

glass tremble in Herzog's arms. He propped it carefully against the porch and took off his canvas gloves but not his beret, as though he sensed that he would immediately go on a trip.

. . . What he was about to suffer, he deserved; he had sinned; sinned long and hard; he had earned it. This was it.

In the window on glass shelves there stood an ornamental collection of small glass bottles, Venetian and Swedish. They came with the house. The sun now caught them. They were pierced with the light. Herzog saw the waves, the threads of color, the spectral intersecting bars, and especially a great blot of flaming white on the center of the wall above Madeleine. She was saying, "We can't live together anymore."

In this brilliant scene Bellow uncovers Herzog's masochism. His remembrance of things past is a Proustian world where pain both gives rise to and is projected into images of piercing light, burst tomatoes, quivering panes of glass, spectral bars of color. Like Proust's protagonist, Herzog is the victim not only of a guilt he feels he "deserves," but also of an intense consciousness that feels every ripple from memory's reservoir. Wanted or not, painful images push through conscious barriers to instruct reality in the torment of loss.

From this pictorial consciousness we are ultimately carried to the fleshy, odorous courtroom, where on the sweltering day of Herzog's self-judgment he watches a parade of wretched men brought "before the bar." In each instance Herzog sees a reflection of himself. For example, the young homosexual's history comes painfully close to displaying his own disgust with female sexuality. The child abusers enact a scene that Herzog has fantasied as his own a hundred times while "writhing under the sharp heel" Madeleine grinds "into his groin." When the medical examiner reports that the bruises on the child were heaviest "on the belly, and especially the region of the genitals, where the boy seemed to have been beaten with something capable of breaking the skin, perhaps a metal buckle or the heel of a woman's shoe," Herzog runs from the courtroom with the acrid taste of recognition in his mouth. No longer can he project guilt; he must come to terms with it himself. "I willfully misread my contract. I never was the principal, but only on loan to myself."

Herzog has, by the end of the novel, sorted out the terms of his contract and reconciled himself to his father's disappointment, his ambivalence toward women, his agonizing love for his children. He has chosen to be, as Schlossberg would say, fully human.

I am willing without further exercise in pain to open my heart. And this needs no doctrine or theology of suffering. We love apocalypses too much, and crisis ethics and florid extremism with its thrilling language.

Excuse me, no. I've had all the monstrosity I want. We've reached an age in the history of mankind when we can ask about certain persons, "What is this Thing?" No more of that for me—no, no! I am simply a human being, more or less.

If Herzog's contract has been negotiated by the end of the novel, Sammler's is in evidence from the outset of his story. Sammler carries the notion of life's mystery to its furthest reaches. In more intellectual terms than Schlossberg perhaps intended, he explores Schlossberg's observation, "More than human, can you have any use for life? Less than human you don't either." The whole meaning of life derives from how we translate our own experience. The soul understands this truth intuitively, Sammler adds, for it "knows what it knows." No amount of intellection, no elaborate "Ideal Construction," no reality instruction can explain the terms of man's contract to himself.

Being right was largely a matter of explanations. Intellectual man had become an explaining creature. Fathers to children, wives to husbands, lecturers to listeners, experts to laymen, colleagues to colleagues, doctors to patients, man to his own soul, explained. The roots of this, the causes of the other, the source of events, the history, the structure, the reasons why. For the most part, in one ear out the other. The soul wanted what it wanted. It had its own natural knowledge. It sat unhappily on super-structures of explanation, poor bird, not knowing which way to fly.

Yet Sammler himself is filled with explanations. He has been cast into the pit and has escaped. He fights others' tendencies to see him as a reality instructor, a reigning intellectual, a survivor of the Holocaust, a Moses leading the chosen from one promised planet to another, "one of those kindly European uncles with whom the Margottes of this world could have daylong high-level discussions." While he, like Herzog, has had his "synthesis" (that is Maynard Keynes, Lytton Strachey, and H. G. Wells), he resists formulas as rigorously as Herzog and sees beyond them with greater scope and behind them with greater wisdom. To Sammler, an "important consideration was that life should recover its plentitude." This recovery is enacted when he chooses to "relax from rationality and calculation" and to allow the soul its knowledge. To further his spiritual evaluation, Sammler develops an abiding tolerance for all explanations: the lunacies of Shula-Slawa, the intimacies of Angela, the half-articulated consolations of Margotte, the academic pretensions of Feffer, the pathetic distortions of Wallace. In the cascade of words, the sad attempts at self-justification, the imploring gestures of self-analysis, he sees with "an intensification of vision" that man "does not know what he knows." This recognition sets him apart, rendering him a commentator both on his own experience and on the planet's. Particularly after the Columbia debacle, Sammler

> feels somewhat separated from the rest of his species, if not in some fashion severed—severed not so much by age as by preoccupations too different and remote, disproportionate on the side of the spiritual, Platonic, Augustinian, thirteenth-century. As the traffic poured, the wind poured, and the sun, relatively bright for Manhattan—shining and pouring through openings in his substance, through his gaps. As if he had been cast by Henry Moore. With holes, lacunae.

Sammler is thus both distanced from the society he perceives and cast as an intermediary through which its perceptions pass. He is a cultural vehicle, in a way, bearing the testimony of this planet's experience at the very moment it extends its reach to another planet. He has been instructed in "lessons of the Real"; but rather than making of them prescriptions for the future or even, tempting as it is, explanations of the past, Sammler insists that "all are the terms of our inmost heart."

Sammler's looking glass is the planet itself. He sees densely populated, teeming city streets, the looming specter of racial threat and sexual intimidation, the vacuity of "liberal" academic life, modern man's "peculiar longing for nonbeing." But he also experiences Margotte's care, Angela's pathetic attempts at communication, Shula's crazy regard, and Gruner's dignity. In the one long speech to Dr. Lal, when Sammler is pressed to present "his view," he admits bewilderment in the face of the desire for nonbeing: "People want to visit all other states of being in a diffused state of consciousness, not wishing to be any given thing but instead to become comprehensive, entering and leaving at will. Why should they be human?" Sammler argues that individual worth cannot be denied, the soul cannot be declared dead simply by assertion. "Inability to explain is no ground for disbelief." Man "has something in him that deserves to go on. . . . The spirit feels cheated, outraged, defiled, corrupted, fragmented, injured. Still it knows that its growth is the real aim of existence. . . . Besides, mankind cannot be something else."

Unlike Herzog, Sammler is not presiding over his own case history, an advocate at his own trial. "I am not life's examiner, or a connoisseur, and I have nothing to argue." His is a distanced view, a one-eyed squint at "our human fate" as it stands on the brink of "colonizing outer space."

While Sammler's thoughts are centrifugal, spinning away and outward from the planet, his actions are centripetal, directing him closer and closer to the center of the city, the center of his relationship with Gruner, the center of his consciousness about humanity. He is no wanderer on the outside of experience, but a borer from within. During the frantic taxi ride across the city, a vain attempt to reach Gruner before his death, Sammler passes through the layers of "the real" that compose this planet's experience. The brutal confrontation between the black pickpocket and the Israeli soldier Eisen, swinging his bag of heavy metal religious medallions, the ineffectiveness of the academic Feffer, the impotence of Sammler's age, the transfixed crowd serve to intensify his real destination. "It was Elya who needed him. It was only Elya he wanted to see." He arrives too late to be of comfort, but his words of benediction on Elya are words of benediction for himself and for the planet: "Remember, God, the soul of Elya Gruner, who, as willingly as possible and as well as he was able, and even to an intolerable point, and even in suffocation and even as death was coming was eager . . . to do what was required of him." Man's ability to do, as willingly as possible and as well as he is able, "what is required of him" is Sammler's message to this planet, the reconciliation of man to his society, the ultimate legacy from father to son to father to son ad infinitum, the only reality instruction that counts. These are the requirements of leaving the father's house, enduring the pit, meeting the forces that conspire to reduce personal significance.

Clearly Bellow sees the risks. But he is unwilling to grab at the preprogrammed explanations of "nihilism" or "absurdity" simply because, as he has noted, "modern writers suppose that they *know,* as they conceive that physics *knows* or that history knows." Man is not knowable, life is not knowable in any such way. "Undeniably the human being is not what he commonly thought a century ago. The question nevertheless remains. He is something. What is he?"

If Sammler, Bellow's deepest and most expansive intellectual, must learn to avoid reality instruction, Charles Citrine also worries about the intellectual's relationship to "ordinary life" in America. As Bruce Borrus contends, "Bellow's intellectual heroes are acutely aware of the reasons for their alienation from the rest of society, but they are unable to think their way through to an accommodation with it. Thinking leads only to more thinking—not to action."

Humboldt's fate is Charlie's lesson in the failure of intellection, for he "had it all." He was "an avant-garde writer, the first of a new generation, he was handsome, fair, large, serious, witty, he was learned." "He had read many thousands of books. He said that history was a nightmare during which he was trying to get a good night's rest." "Conrad Aiken praised him, T. S. Eliot took favorable notice of his poems, and even Yvor Winters had a good word to say for him." But as Charlie learns, despite this meteoric rise to attention and power, "all his thinking, writing, feeling counted for nothing, all the raids behind the lines to bring back beauty had no effect except to wear him out." Charlie must discover how to avoid Humboldt's fate by coming to value ordinary life, seeing the world as it really is.

Charlie also has a set of reality instructors who emerge from "Chicagoland." Embroiled in materialistic reality, they lure him from the snares of solitude. Rinaldo Cantabile throwing $50 bills off the steel girders of an unfinished skyscraper, Renata panting her way through an orgasm in the middle of the Palm Court of the Plaza, and the slick, modern, crowded restaurants of the "hog butcher of the world" are all tough and colorful "versions of the real." Both Cantabile and Humboldt are "fathers" to Charlie: the first schools him in the world of power and money; the latter represents the fate of the artist in America. Both are sources of guilt and confusion to Citrine, and both leave legacies that connect Charlie to salvation. Without Cantabile, Charlie would have an insufficient sense of the power of money, an insufficient materialistic drive. It might destroy him as surely as Tamkin argues it will destroy Tommy Wilhelm. Without Humboldt's "gift," Charlie would remain awash in guilt and paralyzed by a morbid fear of death. If Cantabile is the impetus to struggle successfully with the world of distraction, Humboldt is the spur Charlie needs to examine his guilt, confront his anxiety, and find in the world a spirit that transcends its boundaries.

Albert Corde encompasses both Sammler's sensitivity to human history and Citrine's dependence on human love to define the self. If Bucharest is cold and unrelenting, the United States is scarcely more rewarding. Underneath the veneer of respectable academic liberalism, Corde finds degradation and death. His brother-in-law swindles him out of part of his modest fortune, and his arrogant nephew joins a band of militants. When he returns to his home after the Christmas exile in Rumania, the first social event he attends is a lavish lakefront celebration for a wealthy couple's Great Dane.

Yet such symptoms of suffocation and decadence in both Communist and capitalist societies act as spurs to Corde. Perhaps he can prove, with Beech, that lead released into the atmosphere through centuries has been slowly poisoning the race. Perhaps his vitriolic articles on Chicago ghettos can help to alert people to the self-destruction he sees at work in American cities, if not entirely avert it. Certainly he has addressed this task at the conclusion, when he resigns his academic deanship and takes up his old job as journalist.

But for a fellow like me, the real temptation of abyssifying is to hope that the approach of the "last days" might be liberating, might compel us to reconsider deeply, earnestly. In these last days we have a right and even a duty to purge our understanding. . . . I personally think about virtue, about vice. I feel free to. Released, perhaps, by all the crashing. And in fact everybody has come under the spell of the "last days." Isn't that what the anarchy of Chicago means? Doesn't it have a philosophical character?

When Corde really examines the anger and hope that prompted his search for meaning, he discovers a need to assess cultural history and a need to honor human commitments. "What mood was this city? The experience, puzzle, torment of a lifetime demanded interpretation. At least he was beginning to understand why he had written those articles. Nobody much was affected by them, unless it was himself." That self, out of love for his sister, struggles to win the confidence of her radical son. That self, immobilized by Iron Curtain regulations, tries to support the dying Valeria whose daughter he reveres. That self, mired in several failed marriages, tries to create all the domestic comforts of a home to free Minna for her scientific endeavors. As she mounts the scaffolding to Mount Palomar's dome, she becomes "Corde's representative among those bright things so thick and close." He descends to the plane of human striving and activity to being his task once again. While a "higher consciousness" is the goal, Corde's ruminations are intensely human. While self-sufficiency is rewarded, an "independent fate" is impossible.

Asa and Tommy find their "lessons in the Real" by examining the outside world and discovering who they are not. Henderson and Herzog engage in personal quests where codified instructions must be discarded in favor of self-discovery and nourishment. Sammler, Citrine, and Corde register the historical and cultural convulsions of this planet. Yet their greatest sources of definition and renewal are found in compassion and love for others. Each is an initiate into an experience larger than he anticipated, a "sort of Columbus" exploring a New World that he as yet only partially understands. Each struggles to answer the question, "What is an American?" The answers are as diverse as the protagonist's perceptions. But none doubts that humanity is worthy of definition. If momentarily defeated by circumstance or temporarily exiled by choice, individuals can return to reclaim ties to Planet Earth. Human destiny matters. And the working out of its meaning is the mandate of life.

DANIEL FUCHS

Saul Bellow and the Example of Dostoevsky

It is no longer possible to say that all modern American literature comes from *Huckleberry Finn*. In a literal sense it was never possible, whatever *éclat* Hemingway's famous hyperbole has had. In view of recent developments in the novel, it sounds with the resonance of another era. True, Salinger is oblique witness to the life of a tradition that includes Anderson, Hemingway, Lardner, and Faulkner, but the figure of the innocent initiate cannot be the only iconographic center of a literature which is focused on the adult genital ego in culture, and on its corresponding mental sweat. It was once possible to think of a pure adolescent heart as symbolic of hidden virtue still resident in the young country, a natural, redeeming reality deeper than all worldly appearances. But the difference between Huck and Holden Caulfield is instructive: solitude has become isolation, traumatic experience full-blown neuroticism, lighting out for the territory retiring to the mental institution. Adolescence is no longer an example but a case. Salinger is on Mark Twain's side, on his far side—civilized life is scarcely worth living—but we no longer have the freedom of the asexual idyll; we have urban, claustral impotence. Holden's grey hair symbolizes the end of an American myth, a time when America comes of middle age.

There are, however, advantages to growing all the way up, fallen though that state may be: what is lost in innocence is gained in knowledge. Though this moral has often been full of possibility in American literature, the force of it is no longer widely considered to be dramatic in

From *Saul Bellow: Vision and Revision.* Copyright © 1984 by Duke University Press.

itself. America has moved closer to Europe, and much, not "all," contemporary American literature comes from Flaubert or the Russians if it "comes from" anywhere. We have seen what the Flaubert tradition affords.

Bellow, on the other hand, seems to be the leading contemporary exponent of the "Russian" way. The idea of a writer as teacher rather than martyr, citizen rather than artist, journalist rather than aesthetician: the idea of literature that is flexible enough to be tendentious and broad enough to be inspiring; a literature that refuses to adopt the pose of objectivity, detachment, and disenchantment with life in quest of the compensatory salvation of form and avoids comparing the artist with God—all this bears witness to the Russian influence. The Russians would never think of art as religion, yet moral feeling in their work is charged with an energy, a yearning, a hope, that may finally be described as religious. Their art respects, indeed thrives, on mental effort and expresses, as Irving Howe has remarked, "that 'mania for totality' which is to become characteristic of our time."

The postmodern Jewish writers have brought to American literature a dramatics of the mind which, generally speaking, recalls the Russians. V.S. Pritchett has suggested there is an affinity between the American writers of Yiddish background and the Slavs. They know what the western writers have long ago forgotten, says Pritchett, "the sense of looseness, timelessness and space." Pritchett's impressionistic remark acknowledges the essentialist affirmation, desperate though it may be, of irreducible moral truths that define a sort of rhythm of the ethical sphere. The artist-god comparison implies the need for a total subjective originality that denies the reality of this timelessness. These generalizations may be illustrated by a comparison between Bellow and the Russian master whose example is most instructive to him, Dostoevsky.

The central impetus in both writers, in periods marked by ideological confusion and in novels full of explainers, is the quest for what is morally real. Ivan Karamazov's "if there is no God everything is permitted" is the sort of immoralist proposition that they must refute. When Dostoevsky says of the "enthusiast," Belinsky, "He knew that the moral principle is at the root of everything," we have a statement in tune with Bellow's idea of "axial lines." To begin with a conventional illustration, both writers use the image of the child as the embodiment of innocence—sometimes offering it with an unabashed naiveté. We recall, for example, Augie's après vu of his fatherhood, or Myshkin's story of the peasant woman with a baby who says, "God has just such gladness every time he sees from heaven that a sinner is praying to Him with all his heart, as a mother has when she sees the first smile on her baby's face." While such an image may embarrass the properly jaded reader, we know that a character like Myshkin could not exist without such sentiment. The contemporary reader has, perhaps, less difficulty with Ivan's conception of the child as victim, as symbol of unspeakable injustice, as is seen in incidents of child beating so vividly represented that even Alyosha agrees that the sadistic perpetrator should be shot. Similarly, a courtroom re-enactment of child beating is a blow sufficient to turn the civilized Herzog to murderous thoughts. Of course, child abuse has a seductive force in Dostoevsky, who is sometimes called the Russian Sade; but its thematic effect inverts Sade in order to expose nihilism, not to promote it. The poetry of crime—fully orchestrated and directly dramatized in Dostoevsky, muted and usually the subject of a lyric polemic in Bellow—comes to serve as a last-ditch proof of the existence of God or, at least, of the existence of moral imperatives since, in modern literature, God typically enters through the back door. The creator of Raskolnikov might almost have written (though it was actually Bellow) that "there are friendships, affinities, natural feelings, rooted norms. People do on the whole agree, for instance, that it is wrong to murder. And even if they are unable to offer rational arguments for this, they are not necessarily driven to commit gratuitous acts of violence."

To be sure, the words of the Grand Inquisitor to Christ—"Dost Thou know that the ages will pass, and humanity will proclaim by the lips of their sages that there is no crime, and therefore no sin; there is only hunger?"—carry great force in an age of behavioral environmentalism. We are familiar with Brecht's paraphrase of "Feed men, and then ask of them virtue." And it develops into the argument of Mailer's "The White Negro" where he excuses the murder of a storekeeper by young killers. *Anomie* issuing in desperate boredom does link characters like Stavrogin and Mailer's Marion Faye. Stavrogin wishes to "put power under the four cor-ners of the earth and blow it all up"—as does Marion in similar words. The difference is that Dostoevsky, like Bellow, ultimately has a contempt for the immoralist Stavrogin, whereas Mailer's essential sympathy lies with the immoralist (now hipster) Faye.

Even greater is Dostoevsky's contempt for the radical Pytor Verkovensky, whose vision of the revolution come to pass is one of crime as the norm. Speaking to Stavrogin, he counts his troops: "The lawyer who defends an educated murderer because he is more cultured than his victims and could not help murdering them to get money is one of us. The schoolboys who murder a peasant for the sake of sensation are ours. The juries who acquit every criminal are ours. The prosecutor who trembles at a trial for fear he should seem advanced enough is ours, ours." Pytor concludes that "crime is no longer insanity, but simply common sense, almost a duty; a gallant protest." True, in Czarist Russia any protest was credible, but what we get in Pytor is a prefiguring of Stalinist manipulators. On his part, Bellow has always been mistrustful of the clairvoyance of radical solutions, but it is not until *Mr. Sammler's Planet* that he dramatizes a comparable political hysteria.

Dostoevsky's attack on nihilism, then, is political as well as ethical. Not confined to hysteria, the assault often expresses itself as comedy at the expense of ideology, which is seen to be utilitarian, socialist, individualist, western. The underground man is, perhaps, the most conspicuous illustration of the assault on the radicalism of the 1860s (as opposed to the more humanitarian radicalism of the 1840s with which he has some ambivalent sympathy, as did Dostoevsky himself), which is imaged as the wall, the piano key (determinism), the ant hill, the chicken coop (the urban mass and that utilitarian haven, the apartment house), and the Crystal Palace (the new cathedral of utilitarian perfection). As Ralph Matlaw says, Dostoevsky is attacking the utopia of Chernyshevsky, Fourier, and Saint-Simon, which tried to reconcile Hegel and Rousseau, the world historic process and the man of feeling, historical determinism and individual will.

In *Notes from Underground* and elsewhere Dostoevsky makes no distinction between ideology and utopia, which he uses in its pejorative sense. The uncensored version had intimations of Christian belief; however, the censor seems to have done well in deleting them if his aim was the dramatic coherence of the work. Despite the underground man's brilliance and authenticity, he is trapped in the atom of his ego, unable to love, unable to be more than a caricature of the "freedom" he claims to represent. But with *Notes from Underground* the genre of ideological comedy is established. The ruthless, loud honesty, the intellectual acuity, the comic dramatization of mental suffering—all these appear earlier in Diderot's *Rameau's Nephew*, but the full head of self-consciousness, historical awareness, and philosophical depth is Dostoevsky's addition. The underground man knows more than the nephew and enjoys less; he is isolated and, generally, impotent.

Ideological comedy—which is to have an impact on Bellow—is not confined to *Notes from Underground*. In *Crime and Punishment*, for example, there is the marvellous Lebeziatnikov, a rarely noticed character. After describing the "anaemic, scrofulous little man," the usually neutral narrator tells us that he was "really rather stupid; he attached himself to the cause of progress and 'our younger generation' from enthusiasm. He was one of the numerous and varied legion of dullards, of half-animate abortions, conceited half-educated coxcombs, who attach themselves to the idea most in fashion only to vulgarize it and who caricature every cause they serve, however sincerely." Lebeziatnikov is a theoretician and, in a wildly comic scene, expounds Fourier and Darwin to the smug bourgeois Luzhin who despises him as a man of no connections. Luzhin, ready for any praise, accepts Lebeziatnikov's commendations for being ready to contribute to the establishment of a new "commune," for abstaining from christening future children, for acquiescing "if Dounia were to take a lover a month after marriage, and so on." Luzhin, who is the most tyrannical, self-absorbed, money-mad character in the book!

When Luzhin asks to make certain that Sonia is a prostitute (later the sinister depth of this request is revealed), Lebeziatnikov says, in the tone of airy emancipation that Dostoevsky scorns, "What of it? I think, that is, it is my own personal conviction that this is the normal condition of women. Why not? I mean, *distinguons*. In our present society, it is not altogether normal, because it is compulsory, but in the future society it will be perfectly normal, because it will be voluntary. . . . I regard her actions as a vigorous protest against the organization of society." From Dostoevsky's point of view—and from her own—Sonia's life of prostitution is a martyrdom. This point of view is conservative, sympathetic to monogamy, privacy, Christianity, chastity. It is characteristic of Dostoevsky to scorn "advanced" ideas, to characterize them as utopian schemes masking the self-interest of the idea-monger. (Lebeziatnikov does "wait in hopes" of Sonia.) Dostoevsky, profoundly mistrusting meliorist realism, often sees the cause itself as the caricature. Lebeziatnikov says, "I should be the first to be ready to clean out any cesspool you like . . . it's simply work . . . much better than the work of a Raphael and a Pushkin, because it is more useful," and thus gives us the first statement of a theme which becomes major in *The Possessed*. Here, as elsewhere, Dostoevsky treats the ideologue as the buffoon. When, in his concern about the distraught Katerina, Lebeziatnikov tells Raskolnikov that "in Paris they have been conducting serious experiments as to the possibility of curing the insane, simply by logical argument," we have a delicious reduction of the excessive faith in rationalism which Dostoevsky condemns as western.

Dostoevsky's rare allusions to America suggest that he believes that the new land is about as western as you can get. In *The Possessed* it is for the fop Lebyadkin to sing its praises. He speaks glowingly of an American millionaire who "left all his vast fortune to factories and to the exact sciences, and his skeleton to the students of the academy there, and his skin to be made into a drum, so that the American national hymn might be beaten upon it day and night." The experience of Shatov and Kirillov in America gives this rationalist optimism the lie. America, with its capitalism, its science, its utilitarianism, is, in Dostoevsky's mind, a desperate place. He must sometimes have thought that Russian culture by comparison was concerned with the smiling aspects of life.

In Bellow and Dostoevsky the world that we know is in good measure a world of ideas, positions, solutions. The letters of Herzog are only the most celebrated instance of the endless interplay of explanation which strikes Bellow as the most salient characteristic of an anxious age. Some of the ideas are worthy of Lebeziatnikov—like the theory of the Bulgarian aesthetician Banowich, who believes that telling someone a joke means that you want to eat him, or, more seriously, the various Sadean theories of negative transcendence which espouse creative criminality. Basteshaw, Dahfu, Bummidge, Lal are among those heavy theoreticians in Bellow in whom ideology is open to the charge of utopianism. Dostoevsky's attack is centered on the utilitarian and the revolutionary; while not excluding these, Bellow's is directed at more recent utopian attitudinizing, including the psychoanalytic, the technocratic, the modernist visionary. The mold is the same but the material has changed somewhat, partly because Bellow has a common-sense sympathy for a number of the liberal utilitarian propositions which Dostoevsky burlesques. For Dostoevsky suffering is the mother of human consciousness; Bellow is willing to grant this, provided one holds, as he does, that pleasure is its father. Still, both writers reduce the Babel to a comic dimension from the point of view of a more traditional truth to be told. Both take confidence from older, "obsolete" truths, residues of a religious tradition.

II

Bellow's outlook is analogous to that of social theorists such as Raymond Aron and Edward Shils. A *précis* of their key arguments sheds a clearer light on his aims, and on those of writers like him.

Raymond Aron's *The Opium of the Intellectuals* implies in its title the reduced attraction of the Marxist ideology and revolutionism that had once greatly appealed to a number of the post-war liberal revisionist writers in America. Aron maintains that revolutionism had benefited from the prestige of aesthetic modernism, that the artist who denounced the philistines and the Marxist who denounced the bourgeoisie could consider themselves united in a battle against a single enemy. Aron notes, however, that none of the big literary movements was allied with the political left. Exceptions seem tangential and only prove the rule: "Sartre's itinerary toward quasi-Communism appears to be dialectical. Man being a 'vain passion,' one is inclined in the last analysis to judge the various 'projects' as all equally sterile. The radiant vision of the classless society follows on the description of the squalid society of today."

Bellow shares his view not only of high culture, but also of the mythicized proletariat, of whom Aron writes: "Servant of the machine, soldier of the Revolution, the proletariat as such is never either the symbol or the beneficiary or the leader of any régime whatsoever. . . . The common source of these errors is a kind of visionary optimism combined with a pessimistic view of reality." As for the justification of such pessimism, Aron points out that by comparing the division of wealth and the standards of government of a century ago with those of today, we can see that "the growth of collective resources makes societies more egalitarian and less tyrannical. They remain, nonetheless, subject to the old, blind necessities of work and of power and, *ipso facto,* in the eyes of the optimists, unacceptable."

This "doctrine of sustained tensions" with its emphasis on "the courage . . . to endure," as R. W. B. Lewis describes it, in a review of Lionel Trilling's *The Liberal Imagination,* gives us what Lewis calls "the new stoicism," which is analogous to the Burkean view of history. Though the word has little of its original meaning, there is a similarity between the "old" Stoic rejection of Platonism in favor of sense perception and the late forties' stoic rejection of Marxism in favor of a pragmatic sense of possibility. Both posit a dignified self-sufficiency in a world of failed illusion. In Aron's dichotomy the essentialists and the utopians are at odds. We have seen Professor Herzog lecturing in a similar vein on the modernist *"new utopian history, an idyll, comparing the present to an imaginary past, because we hate the world as it is."*

Along with Aron, perhaps the clearest exponent of the stoical view is Edward Shils, a student of Karl Mannheim, sociologist and Bellow's colleague at the University of Chicago. Bellow would seem to admire the tone that these men assume—totally unapologetic—in their critique of modernist utopianism. Like Aron, Shils must place the Marxist view in what he feels is its proper perspective. He points out that Trotsky thought "the average human type will rise to the heights of an Aristotle, a Goethe or a Marx. And above this ridge, new peaks will rise." But Shils feels that the working class, even where it is Communist, is uninterested in revolution, in the moral transformation of itself and the rest of the human race. Shils believes that all ideologues (e.g., Marxist, French monarchists, Southern agrarians) are hostile to human beings as they are. A revulsion against their own age makes intellectuals think of the elevated cultural life and dignified peasantry of a non-existent past (e.g., Tönnies, Simmel, Sombart, Marcuse). He denies the validity of the *Gemeinschaft/Gesellschaft* distinction, since it assumes a small-scale, perfectly consensual, theological society that never existed.

Shils does not believe that bourgeois individualism, urban society, and industrialism are an impoverishment of life. For him, as for Bellow since *Dangling Man*, the "fundamental problems of humanity are the same as in antiquity." He wants a pluralistic society rather than a completely integrated one, with a bow to British utilitarianism and Burke's critique of ideological politics, and with another to the British liberals, like Milton and Locke, who saw that society could be effective even if it had no uniformity of belief, no unifying ideology, and to Mill who, taking the next step, held that diversity of viewpoint was a necessity for a healthy society. Moreover, Shils believes that in mass society there is actually "more of a sense of attachment to the society as a whole, more sense of affinity with one's own fellows, more openness to understanding, and more reaching out of understanding among men than in any earlier society of our western history or in any of the great oriental societies of the past"; that is, "it is the most consensual."

Indeed, the "uniqueness" of mass society is its "incorporation of the mass into the moral order of its society." Since the mass means more to the elite than in other societies, we see an enhancement of the dignity of ordinary life. Again, with a bow to Weber, "the unique feature of the mass society is . . . the dispersion of charismatic quality more widely throughout the society" (e.g., working class, women, youth, ethnic groups previously disadvantaged). Shils does attribute some truth to the view which he is compelled to deny, saying that while there is alienation, there is another side to the conventional Marxist critique of mass society. The other side of alienation is disenchantment with authority; of egotism and hedonism, the growth of sensibility; of the decline of local autonomy, a more integrated society. Beyond all this dynamism the primordial attachments—kinship, locality, sexuality—will change but persist.

Shils attacks "ideology," a term that he defines with strict constructionist precision. Ideology is a highly systematized pattern of belief integrated around a few pre-eminent values—salvation, equality, ethnic purity. Political coherence overrides every other consideration, with supreme significance going to one group or class—the nation, the ethnic folk, the proletariat, the party leaders. It has a Manichean cast, positing uncompromisable distinctions between good and evil, sacred and profane, left and right, we and they; the source of evil is a foreign power, an ethnic group, or a class (e.g., bourgeois). There is a distrust of traditional institutions—family, church, economic organizations, schools, conventional political alignments. Shils distinguishes ideology from outlooks (e.g., Protestantism), which are pluralistic, containing creeds which shade off into ideology but do not take a sharply bounded and corporate form, and have much less orthodoxy. He also contrasts ideology with systems and movements of thought, which, like ideologies and unlike outlooks, are elaborate and internally integrated, but do not insist on total observance in behaviour, complete consensus among its adherents, or on closure vis-à-vis other intellectual constructions. Ideology, too, is distinct from programs, which involve specification of a particular limited objective, often in the form of a passionate rejection of one aspect of society.

Opposed to ideology is civility or civil politics; civility is the virtue of the citizen who shares responsibility in his own self-government. It is compatible with other attachments to class, to religion, to profession, but it regulates them out of a respect for tradition and out of an awareness of the complexity of virtue, an awareness that every virtue costs, that virtue is intertwined with vice. With characteristic benignity Shils, writing in 1958, says that "There is now in all strata, on the average, a higher civil sense than earlier phases of Western society have ever manifested." In the manner of civility Shils does not believe that ideology should be "completely dismissed"—the desire for greater equality, the distrust of authority, the need for heroism, all have "some validity." It is not the substance but the rigidity of ideological politics that does damage. Ideologies fail in their notions of global conquest because "normal" values assert themselves, compromises are made, and the world changes. As for the phrase "end of ideology," it applied only to a very specific time and in a very specific way; it did not mean that ideology could never exist. It was wrongly taken to mean that ideals, ethical standards, and general or comprehensive social views and policies were no longer either relevant or possible. Both sides failed, at times, to distinguish between ideology and outlook and between ideology and program. No society can exist without a cognitive, moral, and expressive culture; there can never be an end to outlooks and creeds, movements of thought and programs.

It is worth briefly noting objections to these views which, like the views themselves, bear on a comprehension of Bellow and Dostoevsky. Needless to say, historical events of the late sixties represented an anger, a sense of injustice, that does violence to the tonality of these remarks and to a number of the propositions themselves. This is not the place for a weighing of arguments. To an amateur observer, however, it appears that Americans now and in the past have often been passionate about what Shils defines as programs, and that ideology is a concept resonant with the struggles of *Mitteleuropa* from which a number of liberal and radical intellectuals derive perhaps too much of their vocabulary. Ideology, as Shils defines it, is as bad as he says it is. But it is difficult to gainsay Dennis Wrong's questioning of the total view: "If 'ideology' is by now, and perhaps with good reason, an irretrievably fallen word, is it necessary that 'utopia' suffer the same fate? . . . [Utopia] is the vision of a *possible* society, a vision that must deeply penetrate human consciousness before the question of how it might be fulfilled is seriously considered—and by that time we will already have advanced a long way towards its fulfillment."

The impatience or dislike shown by radical readers (adherents, say, of C. Wright Mills) for a book like *Mr. Sammler's Planet*, in which "ideology" is presented as brutality, or a book like *Herzog*, whose hero feels that the "occupation of a man is in duty, in use, in civility, in politics in the Aristotelian sense," not in ideology or politics in the Marxist sense, is another way of drawing the lines. One recalls Lenin's view of *The Possessed*: "great but repulsive." Bellow has his own personalist, novelist's point of view, but his explicit utterances about ideology, by which he means what Shils means, are in the manner of Aron and Shils: "Ideology is crippling to attention. It has no finite interests but makes a wholesale distribution of innumerable human facts. Its historical or biological schemes dispose of human beings by classification." In support of a deeper, contrary wisdom, he then quotes Dostoevsky, who writes in an accent Bellow comes to adopt: "We cannot exhaust a phenomenon, never can we trace its end or its beginning. We are familiar merely with the everyday, apparent and current, and this only insofar as it appears to us, whereas the ends and the beginnings still constitute to man a realm of the fantastic." The moral is then drawn by Bellow: "Ideology commands an end, imposes a law, speaks the first and last words and abolishes confusion. But it has no interest in the miracle of being which artists endlessly contemplate." This "mystery of mankind," as Bellow is later to call it, this inexhaustibility, is indicative of the personalist, anti-ideological view.

Even more so are Dostoevsky's critical remarks on *Anna Karenina*. Addressing himself to the question of Anna's guilt, Dostoevsky repudiates the "physician-socialists," saying that, for the Russian author, "no anthill, no triumph of the 'fourth estate,' no elimination of poverty, no organization of labour will save mankind from abnormality, and therefore— from guilt and criminality . . . that in no organization of society can evil be eliminated, that the human soul will remain identical; that abnormality and sin emanate from the soul itself, and finally, that the laws of the human spirit are so unknown to science, so obscure, so indeterminate and mysterious, that, as yet, there can neither be physicians nor *final* judges, but there is only He who saith: 'Vengeance belongeth unto me; I will recompense.' " (the epigraph to the novel). This is deeper than environmentalism, which says, "inasmuch as society is abnormally organized, it is impossible to make the human entity responsible for its consequences. Therefore, the criminal is irresponsible and at present crime does not exist." But, Dostoevsky continues, Tolstoy, knowing in this case the consequences of adultery and equal "crimes," expresses his older wisdom in an "analysis of the human soul." Though Bellow is far more sympathetic than Dostoevsky to the environmentalists, he gives us in Alexander Corde of *The Dean's December,* a man who does not want to see crime go unpunished. And Corde is sorry that in the murder of a white woman by a black psychopath, "Nobody actually said, 'An evil has been done.' "

One of the truisms of Dostoevsky criticism is that the writer who excoriated the ideology of political radicalism himself embraced the ideology of pan-Slavism with its belief in the messianic mission of the God-bearing Russian people, the truth of Russian orthodoxy and the falsehood of western Roman Catholicism, the sanctity of the Russian soil, and the even more sacred quality of the Russian peasant; here we have the we-they, sacred-profane dichotomy, which Shils says characterized the ideologist. But Dostoevsky scarcely knew the peasants he idealized. And, as Philip Rahv has said, the manner in which he embraced orthodoxy was so apocalyptic as to undermine orthodoxy, subvert dogma, shatter the notion of institutionalized religion itself. If, in *The Possessed,* he saw the failure of revolutionary ideology, he was too honest not to portray the nihilistic vacuum which revolution must fill. Perhaps anyone viewing political reality in Czarist Russia with a clear eye would see a chaos beyond the politics of civility to set right. Dostoevsky dreaded the Antichrist whose arrival he intuited, which accounts for the gloom behind the comic balance of the book. As for his belief, does he ever really convince us of anything more than Shatov's "I—I will believe in God"? And for all his sweet clairvoyance, the final point about Myshkin is that he fails.

III

Above all, the dramatic force of Dostoevsky's art often works against his didactic intention with a brilliance that illustrates the subtle uniqueness of literature—the exposition, in action, of ambivalence, the complex of feelings in the face of which any idea must be a simplification. The underground man, Raskolnikov, Ivan—all characters whom Dostoevsky fundamentally rejects—are creations of a child of light who saw best in darkness. But the metaphor should not confuse. Dostoevsky was nothing if not a personalist. In saying of him that "nobody was less preoccupied with the empirical world. . . . His art is completely immersed in the profound realities of the spiritual universe," Nicholas Berdyaev gives us what is, at best, a half-truth. How can one be a non-empirical psychological genius? More to the point is the description by Strakhov, who knew Dostoevsky intimately: "All his attention was upon people, and all his efforts were directed towards understanding their nature and character. People, their temperament, way of living, feelings, thoughts, these were his sole preoccupation."

This personalism is consonant with the intellectual depth of his work; for he is, as Arnold Hauser puts it, "a romantic in the world of thought" in that "the movement of thought has the same motive power and the same emotional, not to say pathological, impetus in him as the flood and stress of the feelings had in the romantics." In this lyricism of ideas combined with a centrist conception of character Bellow finds Dostoevsky the acknowledged master. Typically, in a Bellow novel, an essentially urban man—usually "cracked," often intellectual, portrayed in his solitude or isolation, usually unemployed in one way or another, whose business turns out to be personal relationships—is thrust forward at the moment of intense subjective crisis. Everyday apprehension is shattered by a welling up of the demonic. What George Steiner says of Dostoevsky also applies to Bellow: his "characters—even the neediest among them—always have leisure for chaos or an unpremeditated total involvement." Virtuosi in mental suffering, these characters embody the heady balance of disequilibrium. When Dostoevsky, in his famous letter to Strakhov, wrote, "I have my own view of art, and that which the majority call fantastic and exceptional is for me the very essence of reality," he was a pioneer, not aware that he was writing a motto for much of the literature of the future. It is this merging of realism and fantasy in a context of pained, obsessive, often funny subjectivity—this art, as Philip Rahv has it, of psychic distortion, moral agitation, and resentment, the way of Gogol rather than the "objective" way of Pushkin—that Dostoevsky and Bellow take as their aesthetic norm. Herbert Gold called the author of *Henderson the Rain King* the "funniest sufferer since Gogol," to which one can only add, with the possible exception of the creator of *The Double*, *Notes from Underground*, and *The Eternal Husband*.

"All Dostoevsky's heroes are really himself," says Berdyaev, offering a version of the distinction between Dostoevsky, a writer of subjectivity and obsession, and Tolstoy, one of objectivity and proportion. This is a distinction of convenience, but it is a contrast that can tell us something about Bellow as well. Both present a theater of self-realization where the heart is laid bare in the act of defining what is real. In this personal quest sociological categories are secondary to the spiritual. If this implies a distance between object and subject, society and self, action and tempera-ment, it is a distance which both writers feel must be bridged. In both, brotherhood is a refrain whose melody they are trying—and often failing—to recapture. Both attempt to break out of what Edward Wasiolek has called *"the circle of hurt-and-be-hurt,"* the network of sado-masochism, which appears to be a governing principle in Sammler's era. But, in both, meekness or mildness is largely its own reward. *Caritas* is typically con-founded by *Eros* in a scenario where man-woman relationships testify to the potency of moral tenuousness or disintegration. In Dostoevsky, as Berdyaev says, "The mystery of marriage is not consummated," and in Bellow the marriage is consummated, but the mystery is not dispelled. For both, in Berdyaev's phrase, "love serves only as an index of . . . inner division."

Yet the delineation of similarities points significantly to differences, for Dostoevsky presents us with a drama of extremes, a moral *chiaroscuro*, an acting out in fact of what in Bellow often remains fantasy or sugges-tion. Raskolnikov commits the murder; Herzog does not. Herzog thinks of and, in some ways, embodies the strength of mildness; Myshkin is its apotheosis; hit by a block of wood and his senses clarified, Henderson says that truth comes in blows, but when Dmitri Karamazov says, "I under-stand now that such men as I need a blow," he has been condemned for a parricide he wished for. The self-willed in Dostoevsky are pathological, the meek incredibly self-effacing. And sometimes both extremes inhabit the same soul. Corde skeptically, reluctantly admits that he cannot accept such paradoxes: "It was foreign, bookish—it was Dostoevsky stuff that the vices of Sodom coexisted with the adoration of Holy Sophia." When a "murderer-saviour" type appears in *The Dean's December* in the person of Toby Winthrop, Bellow does not do much more than include him as part of the grim local color. Respecting his male-nurse qualities, he nonethe-less considers him a "case," part of abstract modern consciousness rather than Christian miracle. Still, in his articles, Corde finds it necessary to mention the Antichrist.

Czarist Russia had a way of rendering fantasy literal, making for a dramatic, even operatic, quality which in a kindred contemporary spirit more usually comes out as *opéra bouffe*. Dostoevsky's ideological prefer-ences lent substance to an often Manichean opposition of forces. The outcome in Dostoevsky is typically tragic in overtone, a Dionysian coming to grips with the demonic, leaving one with a sense of waste nobler than the hidden cause. In Bellow even the Dionysian inspiration—e.g., Henderson, Herzog—is ultimately comic in that the painful, headlong quest is inseparable from knowledge that constitutes the self—the western, Dostoevsky-doubted ego, the last court of appeals; the self that, in its constant exposure, cannot be taken as seriously as it once was, yet is most of what we have to take seriously. Where Dostoevsky dramatically records the disintegration of the self, Bellow tentatively assumes it, and the tragic is converted into the comic. In Bellow, accordingly, more often than in Dostoevsky, the soul is finally restored to a firm outline.

The one point at which the two writers would seem to differ most is the apprehension of the self in its full sensual regalia. Here Bellow appears to be positively Tolstoyan. A character like Stiva Oblonsky, in *Anna Karenina*, lives in the literary love of an author whose judgment is otherwise morally proscriptive of him. Many of Bellow's characters exist in this way. Ramona, for example, illustrates the delights of inner division. The observation of sensuousness implies the "normal" world, but the dramatic situation implies the Dostoevskian "extreme." It is precisely this integration of opposites which describes a good part of the course of the current literary *zeitgeist*, for what we see in Bellow, and in other recent writers, is the normalization of the extreme—making it comfortable, cozy, charming. "If I'm out of my mind, it's all right with me," says Herzog and any reader of the book would understand him.

IV

Bellow's work offers some extended illustrations of the Dostoevskian influence—unconscious or otherwise. It has not been noticed, for example, that the dialogue between Joseph and the Spirit of Alternatives in *Dangling Man* is a low-keyed recasting of the apparition of the devil to the hallucinated consciousness of Ivan Karamazov. Ivan recognizes that the devil is his double: "You are the incarnation of myself, but only one side of me . . . of my thoughts and feelings, but only the nastiest and stupidest of them." The devil appears as a shabby genteel Russian, whom Dostoevsky sees as a type. They "have a distinct aversion for any duties that may be forced upon them, are usually solitary creatures, either bachelors or widowers. Sometimes they have children . . . brought up at a distance, at some aunt's. . . . They gradually lose sight of their children altogether." That is, the devil is worldly self-absorption divorced from the essential ties. Child abandonment, while not quite the equivalent of child abuse, is closely related. Yet this prince of darkness is a gentleman, "accommodating, and ready to assume any amiable expression," possessing, in Dostoevsky's view, the complete western veneer and the basic western wisdom. He does not know if there is a god; he knows only *je pense, donc je suis* and, Descartes's "proof" of the existence of God to the contrary notwithstanding, its attendant solipsism (a sort of fantasy extension, in Dostoevsky's view, of the rationalistic, ego-oriented west): "Does all that exist of itself, or is it only an emanation of myself, a logical development of my ego which alone has existed for ever."

Goethe was enough of a traditional humanist to create a Mephistopheles who desired evil but did only good; Dostoevsky's Mephistopheles, however, operating in a universe much more attuned to the modern saturation of alienated consciousness, sees that he desires good but does only evil—which perfectly describes Ivan's predicament (culminating in his harrowing scenes with Smerdyakov, whose suicide he hears of immediately after the apparition vanishes). Ivan realizes at the outset that the devil embodies his "stupidest" thoughts, yet so attractive are they that they threaten to destroy his "intelligent" ones. "God is dead," "the man-god," "will," "science," "all things are lawful," " the old slave man," parade so tantalizingly before his hallucinated view that Ivan can dispel them only in the way Luther with his inkstand set the devil to rout—he throws his glass at him. If this is a breakthrough for Ivan, the devil himself remains *déclassé*. Konstantin Mochulsky notes that "in his *Legend* Ivan represented the devil in the majestic image of the terrible and wise spirit, and here he has proved to be a vulgar hanger-on. . . . The spirit of non-being is an imposter: this is not Lucifer with singed wings, but . . . the incarnation of world boredom and world vulgarity."

Precisely. And it is this note of boredom and vulgarity that Bellow strikes in his ostensibly reasonable, genteel representative of non-being, the Spirit of Alternatives. There is no nightmare, no sickness here—at least in the first meeting. Consistent with the meandering movement of the work itself, the encounter is "relaxed." So reasonable is the Spirit, so plausible to the dangling man are his alternatives, that he is also called "On the Other Hand" and *"Tu As Raison Aussi."* Yet it is clear that in his equivocal manner, his indeterminacy, his inevitable drift to the negative, the alienative, his flirtation with ideology, his attitudinizing in a vacuum of conviction, and above all, in his compulsion to the center of indifference, to death, he is the dangling man's devil-double in the same sense that the apparition is Ivan's—a representation of his own worst, his own "stupidest" ideas and tendencies. (Joseph, we recall, is already separated from the older, benevolent, rational, Enlightenment Joseph.) This apparition is even quieter than Joseph; his point must be elicited, but when it is seen to be "alienation," Joseph retorts that "it's a fool's plea." Not that there is no alienation, but "that we should not make a doctrine" of it.

Trying another route, the Spirit suggests "changing existence" through politics, but Joseph rejects the revolutionary and even politics per se. He does, however, admit the value of "a plan, a program, perhaps an obsession." When the Spirit converts this typically American ad hoc impulse into "an ideal construction," Joseph notes the "German phrase," and wonders about the ideological exemplar or type. He concedes that an "obsessive device" may be "the only possible way to meet chaos" and sees the apparent "need to give ourselves some exclusive focus, passionate and engulfing," but the essentialist in him asserts itself: "what of the gap between the ideal construction and the real world, the truth? . . . Then, there's this: the obsession exhausts the man. It can become his enemy. It often does." When the Spirit has no answer to this, apparently having no real convictions to defend, Joseph drives him out, flinging "a handful of orange peel" at him.

Like Ivan, Joseph seeks that which "unlocks the imprisoning self," and in order to escape being "self-fastened" he himself is willing to entertain the "highest 'ideal construction,' " though, more or less, as a passing fancy. Still, he feels that *Tu As Raison Aussi* stands refuted; Joseph has confidence that the "final end" of everyone is "the desire for pure freedom," which he defines in Dostoevskian fashion, not simply as free will but as will defining itself as spirit, "to know what we are and what we are for, to know our purpose, to seek grace." This is as far as Joseph will go towards religion. But the resolution is offhand and represents only a moment of equilibrium.

Joseph's depression worsens, and in the next encounter the Spirit appears as an almost old-style Mephistopheles, the Spirit that Denies, tempting Joseph to "give up," to succumb to indifference, to die, to "worship the anti-life," Joseph recognizes his "inability to be free," and this is the cause of his "weariness of life." Unmistakably, and despite his noble wish to share the pain of his generation, Joseph joins the army in the same way one joins the Grand Inquisitor's church: "We soon want to give up our freedom . . . we choose a master, roll over on our backs, and ask for the leash." When Joseph utters the hollow cry, "Long live regimentation!" he is aware that he is "relieved of self-determination, freedom cancelled." This conclusion has little of the ambiguity sometimes attributed to it. In the end Bellow's devil-double emerges as one who ascertains one's doubt of selfhood, uniqueness, "separate destiny." Joseph is rendered almost as pale, sickly, chilled, and enervated at the end of his encounter with the double as Ivan is with his.

The dramatization of guilt leading to confrontation with the double becomes conspicuous in comparing Bellow's *The Victim* with Dostoevsky's *The Eternal Husband*. This comparison has not gone unnoticed, but the context of extended comparison here affords us a wider view of its meaning. Actually, Dostoevsky's *The Double* is the precursor of both. A solitary spirit in a dreary urban landscape is the necessary beginning to each crisis of subjectivity. In *The Double* "the damp autumn day, muggy and dirty, peeped into the room through the dingy window pane with such a hostile, sour grimace that Mr. Golyadkin could not possibly doubt that he was not in the land of Nod, but in the city of Petersburg, in his own flat on the fourth story of a huge block of buildings in Shestilavotchny Street." If his living is compartmentalized, so is his job, for Golyadkin is a result of the dehumanizing Russian bureaucracy. The crisis in his life breaks out when the moral qualities that the system exacts of its lesser lights—bootlicking, toadying, a fidgety, manipulative quality, a nastiness masking as playfulness, a choreographed self-interest—appears in the shape of Golyadkin Junior who, like Ivan's devil-double, is the embodiment of Senior's worst self.

As the story begins, we see Golyadkin "satisfied" with the "insignificant" face and bald head he views in the morning mirror. He feels so good that he counts his money. Beware!—a sure sign of anal-retentive meanness in Dostoevsky is viewed here as a sign of life in the bureaucracy. A volatile mixture of self-esteem and self-abasement (before his superiors, or any other male authority figure), this isolated, hostile, sado-masochistic urban bachelor is Dostoevsky's first underground man. "Sick," he goes to see a physician, palpitating before the meeting but greeting him with a schizoid "figuratively crushing" glare. He is suffering from "the perfumed compliment," the "masquerade," and a sense of his own unimportance; this feeling of insignificance is intensified when a rival in love, with better bureaucratic connections, wins out. In one of those scenes of comic humiliation of which Dostoevsky is in a class by himself, Golyadkin is rebuffed at the entrance to an important party only to stand in an obscure corner near the garbage—for three hours! Attempting to crash the party and dance with his beloved Klara, he is thrown out. Shaken, even his "secure" office life seems to be disintegrating. At this point the doppelgänger appears, full of Schilleresque sentiment. Raggedly clothed, he tells a three-hour story which makes Golyadkin sob, "even though his visitor's story was the paltriest story." Senior, on his part, confesses his personal torment, saying, "It's from love for you that I speak, from brotherly love." But the very next day Junior is formal, official, self-important, a hypocritical mask-wearer who usurps Senior's place and wipes his hand from Senior's handshake; later he condescendingly pinches Senior's cheek and finally has him committed. His attempt at *Bruderschaft* and all the worthy emotions a failure, it is no wonder that Senior goes crazy.

The Eternal Husband presents us with another comedy of self-exposure, another crisis in the life of an ostensibly well-ordered existence, another confrontation with the double. Where Golyadkin represented the harassed little bureaucrat out of Gogol, Velchaninov is the smug bourgeois; in Wasiolek's terms, where Golyadkin was the "mouse," the underground man, the sexual loser, Velchaninov is the "bull," the sort who abuses him, the sexual winner. He is confident, muscle- and ego-bound, apparently immune to suffering or guilt. Mysteriously, he is smitten by an attack of "higher ideas." For a long time he had felt a vague malaise, a nervousness, a hypochondria; for an equal time solitude has replaced his social life. The "higher ideas" are the kind "he could not laugh at in his heart," but are forgotten the next day.

Aware that his night thoughts are radically different from his day thoughts, Velchaninov consults a doctor friend about his sleeplessness and is informed that being "too conscious of the double nature of [his] feelings" is a symptom of approaching illness. Why is it that he forgets the recent past but remembers things that happened fifteen years ago? "Why did some things he remembered strike him now as positive crimes?" His vulnerability to conscience, among other things, distinguishes him from unfeeling characters like Luzhin or Totsky. Like Ivan, like Golyadkin, he is pursued by the embodiment of his worst thoughts. This embodiment takes the elusive form of Pavel Pavlovitch Trusotsky, whom Velchaninov finally confronts, recognizing in his changed man the cuckold of nine years ago. Attempting to redeem his idle life, Velchaninov is genuinely moved to do what he can for his natural daughter.

Pavel is the buffoon, the mouse, the sado-masochist, who had been cruel to the child—though his cruelty once took the oddly reflexive form of hanging himself before her—out of resentment. *Ressentiment* is the key to his character, explaining his alternate wallowing in bland *Bruderschaft* and intimations of revenge. As with Golyadkin and the underground man, he is seized by a compulsion to humiliate the humiliator. But between the guilty and the shamed there is some question about who the real predator is. Pavel tells the story of Livtsov, the best man at Golubenko's wedding, who was insulted by Golubenko and who lost out in love to him; he stabs Golubenko (but does not kill him) at the wedding, saying, "Ach! What have I done!" When Pavel says, "he got his own back," Velchaninov roars "Go to Hell!" and their understanding is clear.

Pavel invites Velchaninov to meet what he hopes will be his fifteen-year-old bride-to-be, and the situation threatens to be a repeat of their original one. Velchaninov pulls back: "We are both vicious, under-ground loathesome people," he tells Pavel, recognizing a grim mutual dependency. Pavel later appreciates Velchaninov's not telling him about the girl's true feelings for him and nurses him with tea and compresses when he, exhausted and suffering from chest pains, seems to have a constitutional breakdown. "You are better than I am! I understand it all, all," says Velchaninov shortly before embarking on a sleep from which he nearly never awakens. Pavel attempts to murder Velchaninov with a razor in a not precisely premeditated act: he "wanted to kill him, but didn't know he wanted to kill him." Velchaninov sees that "it was from hatred that he loved me; that's the strongest of all loves."

Though Bellow's *The Victim* is strikingly similar in certain respects, the emphasis is almost as much metaphysical as it is psychological. Whereas, for example, the child-victim of *The Eternal Husband* dies as a result of humiliation derived from the guilt of both men, the child-victim in *The Victim* dies from a fated physical disease. Accordingly, the double here is not so much a projection of a particular guilt as it is a conception of suffering. In *The Eternal Husband* Velchaninov is clearly at fault; his subconscious wells up for release. With Bellow's Leventhal it is much more a question of obligation or responsibility, in that disillusioned, late-forties sense. An illustration of the end-of-innocence stoicism of liberal ex-radicals—like Trilling's *The Middle of the Journey* and Mary McCarthy's *The Groves of Academe*— *The Victim* gives us a picture of the victim as victimizer, the tyranny of the disadvantaged and outcast. To complicate the tough-mindedness, *The Victim* also subverts the image of the benevolent Jew of popular fiction dealing with anti-Semitism.

The general scene of *The Victim* can fairly be called Dostoevskian: the hallucinatory, nocturnal, numinous quality; the unpromising urban backdrop; the steps, the room, the heat; the hide-and-seek beginning; the protagonist wishing to be decent but caught up in a petty bureaucracy which is a temptation to the contrary; the urban "bachelor" (Leventhal is married, but his good wife is necessarily out of town). But there are differences: where Velchaninov was directly guilty, Leventhal's real guilt is in unfeeling. His eyes are indifferent, not "sullen but rather unaccommodating, impassive." Physically large, he has none of the *amour-propre* of the Dostoevskian bull for, unlike him, he has not had a privileged life. On the contrary, it is not the softness but the "harshness of his life [which] had disfigured him." Meeting with the modest success of a respectable job and marriage, he tells his wife, "I was lucky. I got away with it," having avoided "the part that did not get away with it—the lost, the outcast, the overcome, the effaced, the ruined."

Allbee represents precisely this reality, as Leventhal comes to realize, but in a way that makes it very difficult for one to accept responsibility, even if direct in an attenuated way. Allbee is a victim of his own inadequacies and circumstances rather than any malicious action on Leventhal's part. Since Allbee is a determinist, his claim on Leventhal is more a gesture of revenge on conditions than it is an argument for individual agency: "The day of succeeding by your own efforts is past. Now it's all blind movement, vast movement, and the individual is shuttled back and forth. . . . Groups, organizations succeed or fail, but not individuals any longer . . . people have a destiny forced upon them." Determinism is the cuckoldry of thought, but we are far from the direct guilt of *The Eternal Husband.* (And even there one can argue that Pavel needs Velchaninov and feels a sexual attraction to the man who brings him such masochistic undoing.) For his part, Leventhal will accept responsibility. (Allbee was fired as an indirect result of a scene between Leventhal and his boss.) But Allbee plays so heavily on the sentiment of guilt that it comes out as self-righteousness, despite the fact that he is not so much Leventhal's psychological double as he is, so to speak, a metaphysical one; for, as the story develops, he comes to represent, in Leventhal's mind, a necessary allegiance to those who are not lucky, the ruined. This is the meaning of the two epigraphs to the novel. Responsible or not, we are responsible. There are, after all, these faces in a sea of suffering.

Allbee claims an ideal relationship with his ex-wife, but the more we know about it, the more sentimental it seems to be. He cries when he sees the picture of Leventhal's wife because she reminds him of his own. It seems that their relationship was so good that she left him, because, he claims, he could not get a job. True love? Did Leventhal then break up his marriage as well? It turns out that Allbee had been fired at a number of places before and that his drinking really is something like the problem that the excessively restrained Leventhal thinks it is. His alleged depth of feeling for his wife is refuted by his not attending her funeral. (Pavel did not attend the funeral of his "daughter.") They were separated; it was hot; he would have had to see her family. Surely this is one of those instances, common in Bellow and Dostoevsky, where fine sentiment is travestied by contrary action. For both writers it is a *spécialité de la maison.* In *The Eternal Husband* Pavel attempts to kill Velchaninov after effusiveness, tea, and hot compresses: "it's just with a Schiller like that, in the outer form of a Quasimodo, that such a thing could happen," says Velchaninov. "The most monstrous monster is the monster with noble feelings." Velchaninov might just as well be speaking of Allbee.

Part of Allbee's "nobility" is hereditary. The depth of his *ressentiment* stems from his being the dispossessed Wasp, a *ressentiment* from above, deeper socially than Pavel's is from below. It explains his gloomy determinism, his excessive drinking, his difficulty in performing well at a job. When Allbee accuses Leventhal of ruining him "out of pure hate," we see an instance of pathology. Even more pathological is Allbee's virulent anti-Semitism; in New York "the children of Caliban" run everything, whereas "one of my ancestors was Governor Winthrop." He asserts that his "honor" tells him not to ask Leventhal for damages—though this is what he is doing, and then some—because he does not want to act like a "New York type." If things were not bad enough, books on Emerson and Thoreau are written by people with names like Lipschitz. Later Leventhal finds Allbee in his own bed with another woman, and the degradation of the sentimental widower proceeds apace. Ousted, the resentful Allbee sets the gas jet in Levental's apartment. He "tried a kind of suicide pact without getting my permission first," thinks Leventhal; and in a rare judgmental remark, never quoted by those critics making a case for Allbee, the narrator says, "He might have added, fairly, 'without intending to die himself.' "

Leventhal does err on the side of suspicion—though Allbee shows that this is sometimes impossible to do. Leventhal has none of the charm and little of the energetic temperament of later Bellow central characters. *The Victim* is the only longer work of Bellow with no comic element to speak of. There is a scrupulous meanness in the description of the milieu— between father and son, brother and brother—which goes with the Flaubertian-Joycean texture of the whole. Leventhal notices that the lights over the Manhattan building are "akin to the yellow revealed in the slit of the eye of a wild animal, say a lion, something inhuman that didn't care about anything human and yet was implanted in every human being too, one speck of it." If this is the aura of sinister New York, it is also an intimation that the sympathetic heart is in danger of being lost.

Allbee is the double of Leventhal's impassivity—both are finally overcome, exorcised by Leventhal. When Leventhal finds out that—because of the office dispute (his boss "made [him] out to be a nothing," something he could ill afford to hear)—he was indirectly responsible for Allbee's losing his job, he wonders if he unconsciously wanted to get back at Allbee for some of his anti-Semitic jibes. Leventhal dreams of missing a train and of trying to catch the second section of it, from which men divert his path. His face is covered with tears. On awakening, "he experienced a rare, pure feeling of happiness. He was convinced that he knew the truth . . . [that] everything without exception took place as if within a single soul or person." Yet "he knew that tomorrow this would be untenable." Still, he recalls the recognition in Allbee's eyes, which "he could not doubt was the double of something in his own," a natural sympathy. Bellow, like Dostoevsky, does not end with a tearful wallowing in *Bruderschaft*. Despite the occasional closeness, even physical intimacy of a sort, the gain for Leventhal is in consciousness, not in a new relationship.

Like *The Eternal Husband*, *The Victim* ends with a coda which affirms the dubious character of the double. In a scene which takes place a few years after the main action Allbee, like M. Trusotsky, seems to be reincarnated—fancy clothes, wealthy woman, and all. Cantankerous, accusing, Jew-baiting by habit, pushing his lady around but speaking of her in ideal terms, denying any guilt in the murder attempt—he is changed only in circumstance, and Leventhal notices an underlying decay. Unlike Leventhal, Velchaninov does not seem to have changed: money, good food, and other creature comforts once again define his life. Pavel remains the eternal husband, subservient, harassed by infidelity, resentful of Velchaninov.

In a well-known speech in *The Victim*, which has no counterpart in *The Eternal Husband* but does in Dostoevsky's general outlook, wise old Schlossberg says, "It's bad to be less than human and it's bad to be more than human . . . I say choose dignity. Nobody knows enough to turn it down." These are sentiments to which the creator of Raskolnikov, the underground man, and Dmitri Karamazov would say "Amen." "More than human" is like that "sense of Personal Destiny" leading to "ideal constructions" for wisdom, bravery, cruelty, and art, which the dangling man thinks about. The man Leventhal meets in the men's room during a Karloff movie comprehends the type: "He really understands what a mastermind is, a law unto himself." Similarly, Caesar in Schlossberg's illustration of "more than human" in his idealized bravery (self-overcoming, casting out any human weakness) and his aspiration "to be like a god."

There is an attraction-repulsion in both writers to the "ideal construction," the "obsession [which] exhausts the man," superman transcendence, as there is to underground-man envy, self-laceration, and unfeeling (e.g., Golyadkin and Pavel, Joseph and Allbee). Leventhal, Bellow writes, "disagreed about 'less than human.' Since it was done by so many, what was it but human?" He adds: "he liked to think 'human' meant accountable in spite of many weaknesses—at the last moment, tough enough to hold." A nice touch this, recognizing as it does the common denominator of secular selfhood and its attendant anxiety, it establishes more-than-human/less-than-human as a continuum of gain and loss, up and down, in the struggle for subjective freedom. This is something of what Nietzsche meant when, in a remark attributed to him, he claimed that Dostoevsky's underman and his overman were the same. But this famous admirer of Dostoevsky's psychology misconstrued the Russian's relation to his character, for his transvaluation of morals, unlike that of Dostoevsky or of Bellow, was not related to Judeo-Christian roots. Did Nietzsche understand the anguished cry of the underground man—"They won't let me—I can't be good"?

CYNTHIA OZICK

Farcical Combat in a Busy World

A concordance, a reprise, a sum-
mary, all the old themes and obsessions hauled up by a single tough
rope—does there come a time when, out of the blue, a writer offers to
decode himself? Not simply to divert, or paraphrase, or lead around a
corner, or leave clues, or set out decoys (familiar apparatus, art-as-usual),
but to kick aside the maze, spill wine all over the figure in the carpet, bury
the grand metaphor, and disclose the thing itself? To let loose, in fact, the
secret? And at an hour no one could have predicted? And in a modestly
unlikely form? The cumulative art concentrated, so to speak, in a vial?

For Saul Bellow, at age 68, and with his Nobel speech eight years
behind him, the moment for decoding is now, and the decoding itself
turns up unexpectedly in the shape of a volume of five stories, awesome
yet imperfect, at least one of them overtly a fragment, and none malleable
enough to achieve a real "ending." Not that these high-pressure stories are
inconclusive. With all their brilliant wiliness of predicament and brainy
language shocked into originality, they are magisterially the opposite.
They tell us, in the clarified tight compass Bellow has not been so at
home in since "Seize the Day," what drives Bellow.

What drives Bellow. The inquiry is seductive because Bellow is
Bellow, one of three living American Nobel laureates (the only one,
curiously, whose natural language is English), a writer for whom great
fame has become a sort of obscuring nimbus, intruding on the cleanly
literary. When "The Dean's December" was published in 1982, it was not
so much reviewed as scrutinized like sacred entrails: Had this idiosyncrati-

From *The New York Times Book Review* (May 20, 1984). Copyright © 1984 by *The New York Times*.

cally independent writer turned "conservative"? Had he soured on Augiesque America? Was his hero, Albert Corde, a lightly masked Saul Bellow? Can a writer born into the Jewish condition successfully imagine and inhabit a WASP protagonist? In short, it seemed impossible to rid Bellow's novel of Bellow's presence, to free it as fiction.

In consequence of which, one is obliged to put a riddle: If you found "Him with His Foot In His Mouth and Other Stories" at the foot of your bed one morning, with the title page torn away and the author's name concealed, would you know it, after all, to be Bellow? Set aside, for the interim, the ruckus of advertised "models"—that Victor Wulpy of "What Kind of Day Did You Have?" has already been identified as the art critic Harold Rosenberg, Bellow's late colleague at the University of Chicago's Committee on Social Thought; that the prodigy-hero of "Zetland: By A Character Witness" is fingered as the double of Isaac Rosenfeld, Bellow's boyhood friend, a writer and Reichian who died at 38. There are always anti-readers, resenters or recanters of the poetry side of life, mean distrusters of the force and turbulence of the free imagination, who are ready to demote fiction to the one-on-one flatness of photojournalism. Omitting, then, extraterritorial interests not subject to the tractable laws of fiction—omitting gossip—would you recognize Bellow's muscle, his swift and glorious eye?

Yes, absolutely; a thousand times yes. It is Bellow's Chicago, Bellow's portraiture—these faces, these heads!—above all, Bellow's motor. That he himself may acknowledge a handful of biographical sources—"germs," textured shells—does not excite. The life on the page resists the dust of flesh, and is indifferent to external origins. Victor Wulpy is who he is as Bellow's invention; and certainly Zetland is. These inventions take us not to Bellow as man, eminence, and friend of eminences (why should I care whom Bellow knows?), but to the private clamor in the writing. And it is this clamor, this sound of a thrashing soul—comic because metaphysical, metaphysical because aware of itself as a farcical combatant on a busy planet—that is unequivocally distinguishable as the pure Bellovian note. "The clever, lucky old Berlin Jew, whose head was like a round sourdough loaf, all uneven and dusted with flour, had asked the right questions." If this canny sentence came floating to us over the waves, all alone on a dry scrap inside a bottle, who would not instantly identify it as Bellow's voice?

It is a voice demonized by the right (or possibly the right) questions. The characters it engenders are dazed by what may be called the principle of plentitude. Often they appear to take startled credit for the wild ingenuity of the world's abundance, as if they had themselves brought it into being. It isn't that they fiddle with the old freshman philosophy-course conundrum, why is there everything instead of nothing? They ask rather: What is this everything composed of? What is it preoccupied with? They are knocked out by the volcanic multiplicity of human thought, they want to count up all the ideas that have ever accumulated in at least our part of the universe, they roil, burn, quake with cosmic hunger. This makes them sometimes, jesters, and sometimes only sublime fools.

"What Kind of Day Did You Have?," the novella that is the centerpiece of this volume, also its masterpiece, gives us a day in the life of "one of the intellectual captains of the modern world"—Victor Wulpy, who, if love is sublime and lovers foolish, qualifies as a reacher both high and absurd. Reaching for the telephone in a Buffalo hotel, Victor calls his lover, Katrina Goliger, in suburban Chicago, and invites—commands—her to fly in zero weather from Chicago to Buffalo solely in order to keep him company on his flight from Buffalo to Chicago. "With Victor refusal was not one of her options," so Trina, sourly divorced, the mother of two unresponsive young daughters, acquiesces. Victor's egotism and self-indulgence, the by-blows of a nearly fatal recent illness and of a powerfully-centered arrogance are as alluring as his fame, his dependency, his brilliance, his stiff game leg "extended like one of Admiral Nelson's cannon under wraps," his size-16 shoes that waft out "a human warmth" when Trina tenderly pulls them off.

Victor is a cultural lion who exacts, Trina surmises, $10,000 per lecture. In Buffalo his exasperating daughter, a rabbinical school dropout who once advised her decorous mother to read a manual on homosexual foreplay as a means of recapturing Victor's sexual interest, hands him her violin to lug to Chicago for repairs; it is Trina who does the lugging. Victor is headed for Chicago to address the Executives Association, "National Security Council types," but really to be with Trina. Trina suffers from a carping angry sister, a doting hanger-on named Krieggstein who carries guns and may or may not be a real cop, and the aftermath of a divorce complicated by psychiatric appointments, custody wrangling, greed. She is also wrestling with the perplexities of a children's story she hopes to write, if only she can figure out how to extricate her elephant from his crisis on the top floor of a department store, with no way down or out. At the same time Victor is being pursued, in two cities, by Wrangel, a white-furred Hollywood plot-concocter, celebrated maker of "Star Wars"-style films, a man hot with ideas who is impelled to tell Victor that "ideas are trivial" and Trina that Victor is a "promoter."

Meanwhile, planes rise and land, or don't take off at all; there is a bad-weather detour to Detroit and a chance for serendipitous sex in an airport hotel, and finally a perilous flight in a Cessna, where, seemingly facing death in a storm, Trina asks Victor to say he loves her. He refuses, they touch down safely at O'Hare Airport, the story stops but doesn't exactly end. Wrangel has helped Trina dope out what to do about the trapped elephant, but Trina herself is left tangled in her troubles, submissively energetic and calculating, and with no way up or out.

What emerges from these fluid events, with all their cacophonous espousal of passion, is a mind at the pitch of majesty. The agitated, untamable, yet flagging figure of the dying Victor Wulpy, a giant in the last days of his greatness, seizes us not so much for the skein of shrewd sympathy and small pathos in which he is bound and exposed, as for the claims of these furious moments of insatiable connection: "Katrina had tried to keep track of the subjects covered between Seventy-Sixth Street and Washington Square: the politics of modern Germany from the Holy Roman Empire through the Molotov-Ribbentrop Pact; what surrealist communism had *really* been about; Kiesler's architecture; Hans Hofmann's influence; what limits were set by liberal democracy for the development of the arts. . . . Various views on the crises in economics, cold war, metaphysics, sexaphysics."

Not that particular "subjects" appear fundamentally to matter to Bellow, though they thrillingly engage him. The young Zetland, discovering "Moby-Dick," cries out to his wife: "There really is no human life without this poetry. Ah, Lottie, I've been starving on symbolic logic." In fact he has been thriving on it and on every other kind of knowledge. "What were we here for, of all strange beings and creatures the strangest? Clear colloid eyes to see with, for a while, and see so finely, and a palpitating universe to see, and so many human messages to give and receive. And the bony box for thinking and for the storage of thought, and a cloudy heart for feelings."

It is the hound of heaven living in the bony box of intelligence that dogs Bellow, and has always dogged him. If the soul is the mind at its purest, best, clearest, busiest, profoundest, then Bellow's charge has been to restore the soul to American literature.

The five stories in "Him with His Foot in His Mouth" are the distillation of that charge. Their method is to leave nothing unobserved and unremarked, to give way to the unprogrammed pressure of language and intellect, never to retreat while imagination goes off like kites.

These innovative sentences, famous for pumping street smarts into literary blood vessels, are alive and snaky, though hot; and Bellow's quick-witted lives of near-poets, as recklessly confident in the play and intricacy of ideas as those of the grand Russians, are Russian also in the gusts of natural force that sweep through them—unpredictable cadences, instances where the senses appear to fuse ("A hoarse sun rolled up"), single adjectives that stamp whole portraits, portraits that stamp whole lives (hair from which "the kink of high vigor had gone out"), the knowing hand on the ropes of how-things-work, the stunning catalogues of worldliness ("commodity brokers, politicians, personal-injury lawyers, bagmen and fixers, salesmen and promoters"), the boiling presence of Chicago, with its "private recesses for seduction and skulduggery."

A light flavoring of Jewish social history dusts through it all: Victor Wulpy reading the Pentateuch in Hebrew in a cheder on the Lower East Side in 1912; or Zetland's immigrant father, who, in a Chicago neighborhood "largely Polish and Ukrainian, Swedish, Catholic, Orthodox, and Evengelical Lutheran," "preferred the company of musical people and artists, bohemian garment workers, Tolstoyans, followers of Emma Goldman and of Isadora Duncan, revolutionaries who wore pince-nez, Russian blouses, Lenin or Trotsky beards."

What this profane and holy comedy of dazzling, beating, multiform profusion hints at, paradoxically, is that Bellow is as notable for what isn't in his pages as for what is. No preciousness, of the ventriloquist kind or any other; no carelessness either (formidably the opposite); no romantic aping of archaisms or nostalgias; no restraints born out of theories of form or faddish tenets of experimentalism or ideological crypticness; no Neanderthal flatness in the name of cleanliness of prose; no gods of nihilism; no gods of subjectivity; no philosophy of parody. As a consequence of these and other salubrious omissions and insouciant dismissals, Bellow's detractors have accused him of being "old-fashioned," "conventional," of continuing to write a last-gasp American version of the 19th-century European novel; his omnivorous "Russianness" is held against him, and at the same time he is suspected of expressing the deadly middle class.

The grain of truth in these disparagements takes note, I think, not of regression or lagging behind, but of the condition of local fiction, which has more and more closeted itself monkishly away in worship of its own liturgies—of its own literariness. Whereas Bellow, seeing American writing in isolation from America itself, remembered Whitman and Whitman's cornucopia, in homage to which he fabricated a new American sentence. All this, of course, has been copiously remarked ever since Augie March; but these five stories say something else. What Bellow is up to here is nothing short of a reprise of Western intellectual civilization. His immigrants and children of immigrants, blinking their foetal eyes in the New World, seem to be cracking open the head of Athena to get themselves born, in eager thirst for the milk of Enlightenment. To put it fortissimo: Bellow has brain on the brain, which may cast him as *the* dissident among American writers.

But even this is not the decoding or revelation I spoke of earlier. It has not been enough for Bellow simply to have restored attention to society—the density and entanglements of its urban textures, as in "A Silver Dish": "He maintained the bungalow—this took in roofing, painting, wiring, insulation, air-conditioning—and he paid for heat and light and food, and dressed them all out of Sears, Roebuck and Wieboldt's, and bought them a TV which they watched as devoutly as they prayed." Nor has it been enough for Bellow to have restored attention to the overriding bliss of learning: "Scholem and I [of "Cousins"], growing up on neighboring streets, attending the same schools, had traded books, and since Scholem had no trivial interests, it was Kant and Schelling all the way, it was Darwin and Nietzsche, Dostoyevsky and Tolstoy, and in our senior year it was Oswald Spengler. A whole year was invested in 'The Decline of the West.' "

To this thickness of community and these passions of mind Bellow has added a distinctive ingredient, not new on any landscape, but shamelessly daring just now in American imaginative prose. Let the narrator of "Cousins" reveal it: "We enter the world without prior notice, we are manifested before we can be aware of manifestation. An original self exists, or, if you prefer, an original soul. . . . I was invoking my own fundamental perspective, that of a person who takes for granted distortion in the ordinary way of seeing but has never given us the habit of referring all truly important observations to that original self or soul." Bellow, it seems, has risked mentioning—who can admit to this without literary embarrassment?—the Eye of God.

And that is perhaps what his intellectual fevers have always pointed to. "Cousins" speaks of it explicitly: "As a man is, so he sees. As the Eye is formed, such are its powers." Yet "Cousins" is overtly about "the observation of cousins," and moves from cousin Tanky of the rackets to cousin Seckel whose "talent was for picking up strange languages" to cousin Motty, who, "approaching ninety, still latched on to people to tell them funny things." All this reflects a powerfully recognizable Jewish family feeling—call it, in fact, family love, though it is love typically mixed with amazement and disorder.

The professor-narrator of "Him with His Foot in His Mouth"—the title story—like cousin Motty is also a funny fellow, the author of a long letter conscientiously recording his compulsion to make jokes that humiliate and destroy, put-downs recollected in tranquillity. But the inescapable drive to insult through wit is equated with "seizure, rapture, demonic possession, frenzy, *Fatum,* divine madness, or even solar storm," so this lambent set of comic needlings is somehow more than a joke, and may touch on the Eye of Dionysus.

"A Silver Dish," with its upside-down echo of the Biblical tale of Joseph's silver cup, concerns the companionable trials of Woody Selbst and his rogue father, the two of them inextricably entwined although the father has abandoned his family; all the rest, mother, sisters, aunt and ludicrous, immigrant uncle, are Jewish converts to evangelicalism. Woody, like Joseph in Egypt, supports them all. The Eye of God gazes through this story too, not in the bathetic converts but in the scampish father, "always, always something up his sleeve." "Pop had made Woody promise to bury him among Jews"—neglected old connections being what's up that raffish sleeve. It is Woody's "clumsy intuition" that "the goal set for this earth was that it should be filled with good, saturated with it." All the same, the commanding image in this narrative is that of a buffalo calf snatched and devoured in the waters of the Nile, in that alien country where Joseph footed the family bills and his father, Jacob, kept his wish to be buried among Jews up his sleeve almost to the end.

The commanding image of this volume—the concordance, so to speak, to Bellow's work—turns up in the reflections of one of the cousins, Ijah Brodsky: " 'To long for the best that ever was': this was not an abstract project. I did not learn it over a seminar table. It was a constitutional necessity, physiological, temperamental, based on sympathies which could not be acquired. Human absorption in faces, deeds, bodies, drew me toward metaphysical grounds. I had these peculiar metaphysics as flying creatures have their radar."

This metaphysical radar (suspiciously akin to the Eye of God) "decodes" Saul Bellow; and these five ravishing stories honor and augment his genius.

Chronology

1915	Born July 10 in Montreal, Canada, the fourth child of Abraham Bellow and Liza Gordon Bellow.
1924	Family moves to Chicago.
1933	Graduates from Tuley High School and enters University of Chicago.
1935	Transfers to Northwestern University.
1937	B.A. from Northwestern.
1941	"Two Morning Monologues," first publication.
1942	"The Mexican General."
1944	*Dangling Man*, first novel.
1947	*The Victim*.
1948	Guggenheim Fellowship.
1949	"Sermon of Dr. Pep."
1951	"Looking for Mr. Green"; "By the Rock Wall"; "Address by Gooley MacDowell to the Hasbeens Club of Chicago."
1952	National Institute of Arts and Letters Award.
1953	*The Adventures of Augie March*; National Book Award; translates Isaac Bashevis Singer's "Gimpel the Fool" from the Yiddish.
1955	"A Father-to-Be"; Guggenheim Fellowship.
1956	*Seize the Day*; "The Gonzaga Manuscripts."
1958	"Leaving the Yellow House"; Ford Foundation grant.
1959	*Henderson the Rain King*.
1960–62	Co-edits *The Noble Savage*; Friends of Literature Fiction Award.
1962	Honorary Doctor of Letters, Northwestern University; joins Committee on Social Thought at the University of Chicago.
1963	Edits *Great Jewish Short Stories*; Honorary Doctor of Letters, Bard College.
1964	*Herzog*; James L. Dow Award; National Book Award; Fomentor Award; *The Last Analysis* opens on Broadway.
1965	International Prize for *Herzog*; three one-act plays: "Out from Under," "Orange Souffle," "A Wen."
1967	"The Old System"; reports on the Six-Day War for Newsday magazine.

1968   *Mosby's Memoirs and Other Stories*; Jewish Heritage Award from B'nai B'rith; French *Croix de Chevalier des Arts et Lettres*.

1970   *Mr. Sammler's Planet*.

1971   National Book Award for *Mr. Sammler's Planet*.

1974   "Zetland: By a Character Witness."

1975   *Humboldt's Gift*.

1976   *To Jerusalem and Back: A Personal Account*; Nobel Prize for Literature.

1978   "A Silver Dish."

1982   *The Dean's December*.

1984   *Him with His Foot in His Mouth and Other Stories*.

Contributors

HAROLD BLOOM, Sterling Professor of the Humanities at Yale University, is the author of *The Anxiety of Influence, Poetry and Repression* and many other volumes of literary criticism. His forthcoming study, *Freud: Transference and Authority*, attempts a full-scale reading of all of Freud's major writings. He is the general editor of *The Chelsea House Library of Literary Criticism*.

ROBERT PENN WARREN is our most distinguished living man-of-letters. His best known novels are *All the King's Men* and *World Enough and Time*. His other crucial books include *Selected Poems* and *Selected Essays*.

RICHARD CHASE was professor of American Literature at Columbia University. His books include *The American Novel and Its Tradition* and studies of Walt Whitman and Emily Dickinson.

DANIEL HUGHES is Professor of English at Wayne State University. He is the author of a book of poems, *Waking in a Tree*, and of articles on Shelley, Blake and John Berryman.

IRVING HOWE is Distinguished Professor of English at Hunter College. His best-known book is *World of Our Fathers*. He is also known for his studies of Faulkner, Hardy and Sherwood Anderson.

TONY TANNER is a Lecturer in English at Cambridge University. His books include *The Reign of Wonder* and *City of Words*.

JOHN JACOB CLAYTON is Professor of English at the University of Massachusetts, Amherst, and the author of *Saul Bellow: In Defense of Man*.

JOHN BAYLEY is Warton Professor of English Literature at Oxford University. His books include *The Uses of Division, Selected Essays* and *The Romantic Survival*.

JOHN HOLLANDER is Professor of English at Yale University. His most recent books include *The Figure of Echo* and *Powers of Thirteen*, a poetic sequence.

FRANK McCONNELL is Professor of English at the University of California, Santa Barbara. His books include studies of Wordsworth and H. G. Wells, as well as works on the relationship between film and literature.

EARL ROVIT is Professor of English at City College of the City University of New York. Among his books are *Herald to Chaos* and *The Player King.*

MALCOLM BRADBURY is Professor of American Literature at the University of East Anglia and the author of many articles on contemporary literature.

GILEAD MORAHG is Associate Professor of Hebrew and Semitic Studies at the University of Wisconsin, Madison, and the author of the critical afterword to the Hebrew version of *Henderson the Rain King.*

DAVID KERNER is Professor Emeritus of American Literature at Pennsylvania State University. He has published many stories and critical articles on American prose fiction.

ALVIN B. KERNAN is A. W. Mellon Professor of Humanities at Princeton University. His books include critical studies of Shakespeare and of the genre of literary satire.

JEANNE BRAHAM, Associate Professor of English at Allegheny College, is the author of *A Sort of Columbus: The American Voyages of Saul Bellow's Fiction.*

DANIEL FUCHS is Professor of English at the College of Staten Island, City University of New York. He is the author of *The Comic Spirit of Wallace Stevens* and *Saul Bellow: Vision and Revision.*

CYNTHIA OZICK'S most recent books are a novel, *Cannibal Galaxy* and *Art and Ardor,* a collection of essays.

Bibliography

Bellow, Saul. *Dangling Man.* New York: Vanguard Press, 1944.

————. *The Victim.* New York: Vanguard Press, 1947.

————. *The Adventures of Augie March.* New York: Viking Press, 1953.

————. *Seize the Day.* New York: Viking Press, 1956.

————. *Henderson the Rain King.* New York: Viking Press, 1959.

————. *Herzog.* New York: Viking Press, 1964.

————. *The Last Analysis, A Play.* New York: Viking Press, 1965.

————. *Mosby's Memoirs and Other Stories.* New York: Viking Press, 1968.

————. *Mr. Sammler's Planet.* New York: Viking Press, 1970.

————. *Humboldt's Gift.* New York: Viking Press, 1975.

————. *To Jerusalem and Back: A Personal Account.* New York: Viking Press, 1976.

————. *Nobel Lecture.* New York: Targ Editions, 1979.

————. *The Dean's December: A Novel.* New York: Harper and Row, 1982.

————. *Him With His Foot in His Mouth, and Other Stories.* New York: Harper and Row, 1984.

Bradbury, Malcolm. *Saul Bellow.* New York: Methuen, 1982.

Clayton, John Jacob. *In Defense of Man.* Bloomington: Indiana University Press, 1968.

Cohen, Sarah Blacher. *Saul Bellow's Enigmatic Laughter.* Urbana: University of Illinois Press, 1974.

Detweiler, Robert. *Saul Bellow: A Critical Essay.* Grand Rapids: Eerdmans, 1967.

Dutton, Robert R. *Saul Bellow.* Boston: Twayne Publishers, 1982.

Fuchs, Daniel. *Saul Bellow, Vision and Revision.* Durham: Duke University Press, 1984.

Galloway, David J. *The Absurd Hero in American Fiction: Updike, Styron, Bellow and Salinger.* Austin: University of Texas Press, 1966.

Harris, Mark. *Saul Bellow: Drumlin Woodchuck.* Athens: University of Georgia Press, 1980.

Keegan, Robert. *The Sweeter Welcome: Voices for a Vision of Affirmation, Bellow, Malamud, and Martin Buber.* Needham Heights, Mass.: Humanitas Press, 1976.

Malin, Irving, ed. *Saul Bellow and the Critics.* New York: New York University Press, 1967.

————. *Saul Bellow's Fiction.* Carbondale: Southern Illinois University Press, 1969.

Modern Fiction Studies 25 (Spring 1979). Special issue on Saul Bellow.

Newman, Judie. *Saul Bellow and History.* London: Macmillan, 1984.

Opdahl, Keith Michael. *The Novels of Saul Bellow: An Introduction.* University Park: Pennsylvania State University Press, 1967.

Poirer, Richard. "Bellows to Herzog." *Partisan Review* 32 (Spring, 1965): 264–71.

Porter, Gilbert M. *Whence the Power?: The Artistry and Humanity of Saul Bellow.* Columbia: University of Missouri Press, 1974.

Rodrigues, Eusebio L. *Quest for the Human: an Exploration of Saul Bellow's Fiction.* Lewisburg: Bucknell University Press, 1981.

Rovit, Earl H. *Saul Bellow.* Minneapolis: University of Minnesota Press, 1967.

Scott, Nathan Alexander. *Three American Moralists: Mailer, Bellow, Trilling.* Notre Dame: The University of Notre Dame Press, 1973.

Wisse, Ruth R. *The Schlemiel as Modern Hero.* Chicago: The University of Chicago Press, 1971.

Acknowledgments

"The Man with No Commitments" by Robert Penn Warren from *The New Republic* 13, vol. 129 (October 26, 1953), copyright © 1953 by *The New Republic*. Reprinted by permission.

"The Adventures of Saul Bellow" by Richard Chase from *Commentary* 27 (April 1959), copyright © 1959 by *Commentary*. Reprinted by permission.

"Reality and the Hero" by Daniel Hughes from *Saul Bellow and the Critics*, edited by Irving Malin, copyright © 1967 by New York University Press. Reprinted by permission.

"Odysseus, Flat on His Back" by Irving Howe from *The New Republic* (September 19, 1964), copyright © 1964 by *The New Republic*. Reprinted by permission.

"The Prisoner of Perception" by Tony Tanner from *Saul Bellow* by Tony Tanner, copyright © 1965 by Tony Tanner. Reprinted by permission.

"Alienation and Masochism" by John Jacob Clayton from *Saul Bellow: In Defense of Man* by John Jacob Clayton, copyright © 1968 by Indiana University Press. Reprinted by permission.

"By Way of Mr. Sammler" by John Bayley from *Salmagundi* 30 (Summer 1975), copyright © 1975 by *Salmagundi*. Reprinted by permission.

"*To Jerusalem and Back*" by John Hollander from *Harper's* 20 (Spring 1976), by John Hollander. Reprinted by permission.

"Saul Bellow and the Terms of Our Contract" by Frank McConnell from *Four Postwar American Novelists*, copyright © 1977 by The University of Chicago Press. Reprinted by permission.

"Saul Bellow and the Concept of the Survivor" by Earl Rovit from *Saul Bellow and His Work*, edited by Edmund Schraepen, copyright © 1978 by Centrum Voor Taal—En Literatuurwetenschap. Reprinted by permission.

"Saul Bellow and Changing History" by Malcolm Bradbury from *Saul Bellow and*

His Work, edited by Edmund Schraepen, copyright © 1978 by Centrum Voor Taal—En Literatuurwetenschap. Reprinted by permission.

"The Art of Dr. Tamkin" by Gilead Morahg from *Modern Fiction Studies* 1, vol. 25 (Spring 1979), copyright © 1979 by *Modern Fiction Studies*. Reprinted by permission.

"The Incomplete Dialectic of *Humboldt's Gift*" by David Kerner from *Dalhousie Review* 62 (Spring 1982), copyright © 1982 by *Dalhousie Review*. Reprinted by permission.

"Humboldt's Gift" by Alvin B. Kernan from *The Imaginary Library: An Essay on Literature and Society*, copyright © 1982 by Princeton University Press. Reprinted by permission.

"Reality Instructors" by Jeanne Braham from *A Sort of Columbus: The American Voyages of Saul Bellow's Fiction* by Jeanne Braham, copyright © 1984 by University of Georgia Press. Reprinted by permission.

"Saul Bellow and the Example of Dostoevsky" by Daniel Fuchs from *Saul Bellow: Vision and Revision*, copyright © 1984 by Duke University Press. Reprinted by permission.

"Farcical Combat in a Busy World" by Cynthia Ozick from *The New York Times Book Review* (May 20, 1984), copyright © 1984 by *The New York Review of Books*. Reprinted by permission.

Index